10 $\frac{00}{mo}$ pu

MEMORY CONSOLIDATION

MEMORY

ALBION PUBLISHING COMPANY

CONSOLIDATION

JAMES L. McGAUGH   *Department of Psychobiology,*
University of California, Irvine

MICHAEL J. HERZ   *Laboratory of Psychobiology,*
Langley Porter Neuropsychiatric Institute;
University of California, San Francisco

ALBION PUBLISHING COMPANY
1736 Stockton Street
San Francisco, California 94133

Designer Nancy Clark
Illustrator David A. Strassman

Library of Congress Catalog Card Number 78–167987
ISBN 0–87843–604–9

PREFACE

One of the most obvious features of behavior in man and the other animals is that it is changed by experience. We learn, we remember, and we forget. Since the behavior of most animals, and man in particular, depends so heavily on memory, an understanding of memory has obvious practical, as well as theoretical, consequences. For these reasons research on the neurobiological bases of memory has surged in recent years.

Although we know a great deal about learning and memory from a behavioral perspective, we do not yet understand the *bases* of these processes. We know relatively little about the neurobiological mechanisms that underly our ability to learn, remember, and forget. There are, of course, many theories of memory, as well as a wealth of facts. However, the facts do not yet provide a coherent view of how the molecules, cells, and neural systems of the brain enable us to learn and remember.

The study of the bases of memory is approached in a variety of ways. For example, there is considerable effort to find neurobiological *correlates* of memory. Changes are known to occur in both the electrical and the biochemical activity of neural tissue when animals are trained [see reviews by John, 1967; Glassman, 1967, 1970]. Evidence that these changes or correlates are *involved* in memory processes will, when obtained, be an extremely important contribution to understanding memory.

Another major approach to memory, the one examined in this book, employs the strategy of experimentally modifying the neural processes initiated by a training experience. This approach is guided by the assumption that knowledge of the way in which the development of memory processes can be impaired or enhanced by various treatments that modify neural functioning will provide important clues concerning the neural bases of memory.

Part One of this book examines current facts and theories related to the consolidation hypothesis and some of the major empirical and theoretical issues regarding time-dependent processes in memory storage.

The readings in Part Two are reasonably representative of research in this general area. However, since the published research findings are as extensive as they are controversial, any review is of necessity selective [see reviews by Zeigler, 1957; Glickman, 1961; McGaugh, 1966; John, 1967; Deutsch, 1969; Lewis, 1969; Rosenzweig and Leiman, 1969; Deweer, 1970; Sheer, 1970]. Part Three is an extensive bibliography of works in the field. All citations in both Part One and the readings are cross referenced to this bibliography.

The consolidation hypothesis was originally proposed on the basis of studies of memory in humans. However, because most of the controversies center on findings from experiments with infrahuman subjects, we have not included any analysis of research on memory consolidation in humans. It should be noted that there is renewed interest in the implications of the consolidation theory for human memory [Milner, 1966; Barbizet, 1970; Drachman and Arbit, 1966; Pribram and Broadbent, 1970].

Numerous laboratories are actively involved in investigation of time-dependent processes in memory storage in animals. In our interpretations of contemporary theory we have been strongly influenced by many of our colleagues. In particular we should like to thank Murray Jarvik, Lewis Petrinovich, Harman Peeke, Everett Wyers, Arthur Cherkin, Steven Zornetzer, Gerry Dawson, Paul Gold, and Philip Landfield for their contributions to our thinking about memory-storage processes and for their comments on earlier drafts of Part One.

We thank Brenda Longacre, Dottie Eakin, and the UCLA Brain Information Service for bibliographic assistance, and Karen Dodd for handling all the details involved in preparing the several drafts of the manuscript. We also wish to thank those who have given us permission to reproduce their works.

JAMES L. McGAUGH/MICHAEL J. HERZ

CONTENTS

CURRENT ISSUES IN MEMORY CONSOLIDATION

THE CONSOLIDATION HYPOTHESIS OF MEMORY

The first formal consideration of the possibility that an experience is not permanently recorded in memory until some time after it occurred is credited to Müller and Pilzecker [1900]. They proposed that the neural processes that underlie memory "perseverate" in a labile form after an experience and become "fixed" or "consolidated" later with time. That is, the formation of long-term or permanent memory is based on processes that are time dependent. This *perseveration-consolidation hypothesis*, or simply *consolidation hypothesis*, is supported by evidence from numerous clinical and experimental studies conducted since the turn of the century. However, many of the findings have raised serious questions concerning the adequacy of the hypothesis, and as a consequence it has been surrounded by controversy in recent years.

The consolidation hypothesis was initially proposed as an explanation of *retroactive inhibition* in human memory, the observation that the interpolation of new information interferes with the retention of previous learning. This interference was thought to be caused by interference with neural processes involved in memory consolidation. McDougall [1901] was quick to point out that Müller and Pilzecker's hypothesis provided an explanation of the retroactive amnesia observed with head injuries. As noted by Burnham [1903] and later discussed more extensively by Russell and Nathan [1946], head injuries often produce amnesia for events that occurred shortly before them. In a survey of head-injury cases Russell and Nathan found that approximately 75 percent of the patients had amnesia for events occurring up to half an hour before the trauma. In about 50 percent of the cases the patient was unable to remember only the last few moments before the accident. In many cases, however, there was permanent retrograde amnesia for experiences that had occurred minutes, hours, or even days prior to the injury. These clinical observations of retrograde amnesia are generally consistent with the consolidation hypothesis.

Although the results of both clinical and experimental studies of human memory were interpreted in terms of the consolidation hypothesis, a specific theory of memory consolidation was not put forth until a little over two decades ago, when Hebb [1949] and Gerard [1949, 1955] proposed a *dual-trace hypothesis* of memory storage. According to this view the neural activity initiated by an experience persists for a period of time after the experience, and this reverberating activity in the neural circuits serves as a basis for perseveration by sustaining the memory for a period until "permanent storage" occurs. This shortlasting reverberating trace was assumed not only to provide a basis for short-term memory, but also to produce the neural changes necessary for the consolidation of long-term memory. Thus the hypothesized dual-trace mechanism accounted for the development of permanent or long-term memory and at the same time allowed for an initial "labile" period during which the neural processes underlying memory are subject to interference.

The dual-trace hypothesis was based on neurophysiological and neuroanatomical evidence available at that time. For example, Lashley [1929] investigated the effect of removing portions of the rat's cerebral cortex and found that within given structural regions the degree of interference with memory produced by a lesion depended on the total amount of tissue destroyed. The results of Lashley's early investigations suggested that memory traces may involve large numbers of cells widely spread throughout the cerebral cortex. Lorente de No's discovery [1938] of closed circuits of neurons connected by internuncial fibers suggested the possibility of self-reexciting (that is, reverberating) groups of cells, and these were considered by Hilgard and Marquis [1940] as one possible basis of memory. In later studies Burns [1954, 1958] demonstrated that a single electrical stimulus train can initiate bursts of electrical activity in slabs of isolated cortex which may last 30 min or longer. Whereas such bursts can be interrupted by subsequent massive electrical stimulation, their elicitation becomes easier with repeated stimulation. Verzeano and Negishi [1960] and Verzeano et al. [1970] recorded recurrent patterns of discharge of single cells in the thalamus of monkeys with permanently implanted microelectrodes. Such patterns followed sensory stimulation and appeared to vary with changes in the stimulus. Although it has not yet been shown that such electrophysiological activity has a specific role in memory storage, the recurrent patterns could provide a basis for the neural perseveration postulated by the dual-trace hypothesis.

Thus there appear to be neural processes which *could* serve as a basis for a dual-trace mechanism. The question, however, is whether such a mechanism is needed. Is there clear evidence that recent memory is labile and that the development of long-term memory is time dependent? Let us consider the evidence on this issue.

THE EFFECTS OF ELECTROCONVULSIVE SHOCK ON MEMORY

Although numerous early behavioral and clinical observations suggested that a variety of treatments administered shortly after an experience could disrupt memory of the experience, systematically controlled laboratory investigations of memory mechanisms had to await the development of an experimental tool. In 1938 Cerletti and Bini introduced electroconvulsive shock (ECS) as a treatment for mental illness. Within a few years the results of several studies indicated that ECS produced retrograde amnesia in human patients [Flescher, 1941; Mayer-Gross, 1943; Zubin and Barrera, 1941]. An ECS treatment (or ECT, electroconvulsive shock therapy) consists of passing electric current through the subject's head for a brief period of time. Current of sufficient intensity and duration produces a convulsion unless the subject is first given a drug which prevents the convulsion [for details see McGaugh, 1968*b*].

It remained for Duncan [1949] to take the technique into the animal laboratory, where more adequate control could be exerted. In this now classical study Duncan trained groups of rats to avoid footshock in an active-avoidance task by giving them one training trial followed by ECS every day for 18 days. The ECS was delivered through electrodes attached to the rats' pinnae, with the current of sufficient intensity and duration to elicit convulsions. Animals in different groups were given ECS either 20 sec, 40 sec, 60 sec, 4 min, 15 min, 1 hr, 4 hr, or 14 hr after each of the daily trials. Control subjects were given no ECS. The results indicated that in the groups administered ECS within 15 min after each training trial learning was markedly slower than in the other ECS and nonconvulsed control groups (see Figure 1). The effect was

FIGURE 1 *Mean avoidance responses by rats on 18 daily trials in an active-avoidance task as a function of the trial-ECS interval (expressed in log units). ECS was administered 20 sec, 40 sec, 60 sec, 4 min, 15 min, 1 hr, 4 hr, or 14 hr after each trial. [Duncan, 1949]*

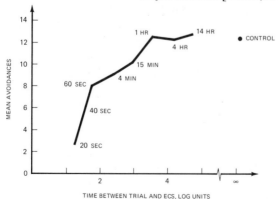

graded: animals given ECS 20 sec after each training trial showed almost no learning, and the longer the interval between training and ECS treatment, the better the learning. Thus ECS appeared to produce a retrograde-amnesia gradient similar to that seen in human patients with head injuries.

Duncan's study was a milestone in the development of the consolidation theory of memory. His investigation marked the transition from reliance on clinical observation to careful laboratory experimentation, and his findings stimulated great interest in the problem of memory consolidation. The appearance in the same year of the first specific hypothesis of consolidation [Hebb, 1949; Gerard, 1949] indicates that the problem was simultaneously under attack on several fronts.

However, Duncan's research was not above reproach. His study raised a number of very important questions, some of which are not yet resolved. The primary question concerns the *basis* of the retrograde amnesia produced by ECS. Are the learning deficits observed in animals administered ECS shortly after each trial the result of retroactive interference with memory processes, or are they caused by the punishing effects of ECS or by some other general effect of the treatment? Are the ECS-produced deficits in learning permanent, or are they merely transient effects? Are they due to the accompanying behavioral convulsion or to interference with neural, electrical, or biochemical activity? Does the graded amnesic effect obtained by Duncan reflect the "true course" of the consolidation process, or were these results specific to the particular conditions of his study? These are only a few of the issues raised by Duncan's findings.

Questions such as these can be answered only by the kind of detailed laboratory research that gradually results in a sizable and reliable body of empirical evidence. It should be emphasized that although most of the research on consolidation has employed ECS as an amnesic agent, many other treatments have been investigated. Of course, many of the controversial issues concerning the amnesia produced by ECS apply to most, if not all, of the other treatments used in experimental studies of memory storage.

During the decade following the publication of Duncan's study, Thompson and his colleagues [Thompson and Dean, 1955; Thompson and Pryer, 1956; Thompson, 1957a, 1957b; Thompson and Pennington, 1957; Thompson et al., 1958] conducted systematic and detailed series of investigations of the generality of the amnesic effects of ECS in rats. Thompson was apparently the first to suggest that multiple convulsions (one after each training trial, as in Duncan's study) might have a cumulative effect on behavior. As an alternative approach he gave animals a single ECS at various intervals after a series of training trials. He then retrained them on the same task and inferred the degree of interference produced by ECS from the savings that were attained during retraining. The results of these experiments provided further evidence that a single posttraining ECS treatment produced retrograde amnesia. Under some conditions interference was obtained even when an hour elapsed between the end of training and the treatment [Thompson and Dean, 1955]. Additional studies indicated that the amnesic effects of ECS were more severe in young rats than in old ones [Thompson, 1957b; Thompson et al., 1958] and that the effectiveness of ECS decreased with increasing degrees of distribution of practice in the original learning [Thompson and Pennington, 1957]. However, with the procedures used in these studies (25 trials, with intervals of 1 min or longer preceding ECS) some consolidation might have occurred prior to the administration of ECS. Thus it is difficult to compare Thompson's results directly with Duncan's.

The results of one study by Thompson [1958a*] show the differential effectiveness of ECS delivered at various intervals after varying amounts of training in tasks of varying degrees of difficulty. Since most of the conclusions concerning ECS-induced retrograde amnesia are based on experiments utilizing avoidance learning of some kind, it is important to note the effect on different types of tasks. In this study Thompson administered ECS to rats after varying amounts of massed training trials on a visual-discrimination task. Contrary to what might be expected if ECS effects were due solely to some gross or general interfering effects on performance, ECS administered very early in training (after only 10 trials) produced amnesia only if it was delivered within 30 sec after the last trial. With additional training (20 trials) interference was produced by ECS administered as long as 30 min after the last trial, but with still further training (30 to 40 trials) it was produced only by ECS delivered within a few minutes after training. That is, the gradient of retrograde amnesia seemed to vary with the degree of training. In a second part of the same study Thompson demonstrated that ECS produced greater degrees of amnesia for complex learning than for simple discrimination tasks. In general his findings have been strongly supported by subsequent research.

ALTERNATIVE INTERPRETATIONS OF RETROGRADE AMNESIA

The findings of Duncan, Thompson, and others in the late 1940s and 1950s provided strong evidence that memory-storage processes are time dependent. However, it was apparent at that time that there might

*The articles included as readings in Part Two are denoted in this discussion by an asterisk.

be other interpretations of the data. The alternative explanations fall into two general categories. One thesis is that the treatments do affect memory processes, but that the graded amnesic effects are not due to effects of the treatment on time-dependent consolidation processes. The other is that the treatments which appear to produce retrograde amnesia do not in fact impair memory; rather, they produce other effects that are mistakenly regarded as evidence of memory impairment. Several hypotheses of this latter type have been proposed in recent years.

DEVELOPMENT OF FEAR

Many investigators [Stainbrook and Lowenbach, 1942; Siegal, 1943; Hayes, 1948; Friedman, 1953] observed signs of fear in rats that were given several ECS treatments. Duncan included controls for the possible punishing effects of ECS in his original study. He reported that learning was not significantly impaired in rats given intense electroshock stimulation of the hindlegs (which did not produce convulsions) shortly after each trial, but the possibility of punishing effects had not been completely ruled out. Coons and Miller [1960] argued that the poor learning observed when ECS treatment closely followed learning trials could also be explained in terms of an ECS-induced fear of the goal, with a resulting conflict that interfered with performance. The active-avoidance task used in Duncan's experiments clearly makes his results susceptible to such an interpretation, and the issue is a critical one. If the effects of ECS are due simply to punishment, they are irrelevant to the problem of memory storage; if punishment can be ruled out as a source of interference, then the findings of ECS studies are relevant for theories of memory consolidation.

The results of Coons and Miller's first experiment confirmed most of Duncan's findings but also indicated that rats given ECS soon after learning trials showed increased fear, as measured by their urination and defecation scores. A second experiment was designed to distinguish between the aversive and the amnesic effects of ECS. The animals were first trained in an active-avoidance task to avoid the shocked side of a grid, and then the conditions were reversed, with shock introduced on the previously "safe" side of the grid. Under these conditions the sooner ECS followed each learning trial, the *faster* was the rate of learning (see Figure 2).

The Coons and Miller study [1960] raised quite explicitly the first of many controversial issues concerning the consolidation theory of

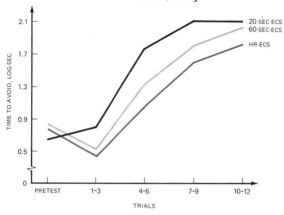

FIGURE 2 *Mean response latencies (log seconds) as a function of trial-ECS interval. Rats were first trained to avoid shock on one side of a grid. They were then shocked for entering the previously safe side. ECS was administered 20 sec, 60 sec, or 1 hr after each daily trial; each point is the average of three trials. Learning of the inhibitory response improved (as indicated by longer avoidance times) with decreasing intervals between each training trial and ECS. [Coons and Miller, 1960]*

memory. In both Duncan's study and this one the animals were given one learning trial and one ECS a day for as many as 17 days. Because of the possibility that ECS might have aversive effects when it is administered repeatedly—a problem that had also been considered by Thompson and his colleagues—investigators began to employ one-trial learning tasks [Pearlman et al., 1959, 1961*] followed by a single ECS to minimize the cumulative effects of multiple convulsions. Many experimenters attempted to distinguish the effect of a single ECS from that of multiple ECS treatments [King, 1965, 1967; Madsen and McGaugh, 1961; McGaugh and Madsen, 1964; Hudspeth et al., 1964; Chorover and Schiller, 1965]. Hudspeth et al. [1964], for example, gave rats repeated trials in a step-down inhibitory-avoidance learning situation (often called passive avoidance). In this task the animals are punished for making a response, and retention is indicated by their reluctance to make the same response on a retention test. The rats received one learning trial and one ECS each day for eight days. As shown in Figure 3, although aversive effects of ECS appeared in later trials regardless of whether the ECS was proceeded by footshock, only amnesic effects resulted from a single convulsion. Chorover and Schiller [1965] obtained similar results. Furthermore, in a study with a discriminated inhibitory-avoidance task McGaugh and Madsen [1964] found only amnesic effects in early trials, whereas with repeated treatments the animals tended to avoid the place in a maze where ECS was administered.

9

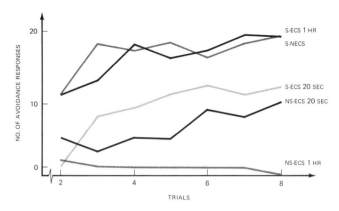

FIGURE 3   *Avoidance responses made by rats on trials 2 to 8 in an inhibitory-avoidance task. The ECS groups were administered ECS either 20 sec or 1 hr after each daily trial. S indicates groups that were given footshock avoidance training. NS indicates no shock avoidance training* [*Hudspeth et al., 1964*]

If ECS modifies behavior simply because its effects are aversive, an ECS treatment given after each extinction trial should facilitate extinction; this is essentially what Coons and Miller [1960] reported. Several studies have shown, however, that ECS interferes with extinction of responses based on both appetitive and aversive learning [Madsen and Luttges, 1963; Gerbrandt and Thomson, 1964; Greenough and Schwitzgebel, 1966]. In an early study Friedman [1953] reported that rats developed no aversion to as many as eight ECS treatments administered twice a day for four days if the behavioral convulsions were prevented by ether anesthesia given prior to the ECS. Thus it appears likely that some correlate of the convulsion, and not simply the passage of current through the brain, is the basis of the aversive quality of ECS. Kesner et al. [1970] recently reported that repeated ECS treatments are not punishing if the current is delivered through cortical electrodes instead of ear-clip electrodes. They suggest that the rats' pinnae may become sensitive following repeated ECS administration via ear clips. This might account for the observation [Dawson and Pryor, 1965; McGaugh and Madsen, 1964] that rats given repeated ECS treatments via ear-clip electrodes avoided the place in a two-compartment box where the ECS was administered.

As these findings show, methods used to investigate a problem may very easily complicate it further. ECS treatments undoubtedly have diverse effects on brain function and behavior. According to the consolidation hypothesis one effect is interference with memory-storage processes. An alternative suggestion is that the amnesic effects do not indicate an actual loss of memory, but are due instead to interference with the *performance* of the learned response. In general, however, the studies of amnesic versus aversive effects of ECS indicate that although aversive effects may appear after several treatments, the impairment of performance produced by a single ECS cannot be attributed to the punishing effects of the treatment. As a result of such findings more recent investigations have, for the most part, utilized a single administration of an amnesic treatment. Also, in most experiments the animals have been given a single training trial followed by a single retention-test trial.

CONDITIONING OF COMPETING RESPONSES

Another interpretation of the results of ECS experiments is the conditioned-inhibition hypothesis proposed by Lewis and Maher [1965]. According to this hypothesis ECS interferes with the performance of a response by causing the subject to be less active in the presence of the experimental situation. (This hypothesis is most relevant, of course, for studies that utilize active-avoidance learning.) More specifically, Lewis and Maher proposed that loss of consciousness is an unconditioned response produced by ECS, and that a weakened version of this loss of consciousness—relaxation and lowered activity level—becomes conditioned to the cues present at the time of ECS administration. They suggest further that the conditioned inhibition is a function of the nearness in time and space of the cues associated with the convulsion. This supposition can account for the graded amnesic effect commonly observed when ECS is administered to different groups of subjects at increasing intervals after the learning trial.

It is possible to invoke a conditioned-inhibition interpretation of the results of many studies, including Duncan's [1949], as well as those of Adams and Lewis [1962a, 1962b]. However, it is extremely difficult to explain the findings of the many one-trial *inhibitory*-avoidance experiments in these terms. Increased inhibition caused by ECS should, according to this hypothesis, facilitate the performance of responses, where retention is indexed by long response latencies. Instead ECS causes retrograde amnesia for both inhibitory- and active-avoidance tasks. Animals given a training trial on an inhibitory-avoidance task followed by ECS exhibit very short response latencies on retention tests given a day or so after the training; they appear to have forgotten that the response was punished. The conditioned-inhibition hypothesis assumes that inhibition is conditioned to the environmental cues present at the time ECS is administered. However, subjects are usually convulsed outside of the experimental apparatus, so that this explanation does not apply in most cases [McGaugh and Petrinovich, 1966]. Furthermore, in direct tests of this hypothesis Leonard and Zavala [1964] and Quartermain et al. [1965*] have shown that in studies in which the animals were given only one ECS treatment the degree of retrograde amnesia obtained with ECS is independent of the place in which the treatment is administered.

Lewis and Maher [1965] also proposed that any procedure that eliminates the behavioral convulsion produced by ECS should prevent the conditioned inhibition. However, retrograde amnesia is readily obtained when convulsions are prevented by light anesthesia with depressant drugs prior to ECS treatment [McGaugh and Alpern, 1966;* Weissman, 1965; McGaugh and Zornetzer, 1970; Zornetzer and McGaugh, in press; McGaugh et al., in press; Zerbolio, 1971]. Similar findings have also been reported in studies of human patients [Ottosson, 1960]. It is also clear that even in unanesthetized animals tonic convulsions are not essential for the production of retrograde amnesia with ECS. In mice, rats, and chicks the current thresholds for retrograde amnesia are lower than those for tonic convulsion [Miller and Spear, 1969; Lee-Teng, 1969; Weissman, 1964; Jarvik and Kopp, 1967b; Dorfman and Jarvik, 1968a, 1968b; Zornetzer and McGaugh, in press; Gold et al., in press].

Finally, since conditioned inhibition should result in a decreased speed of response, ECS subjects would be expected to respond less rapidly than controls regardless of the rewarding or punishing conditions of the learning task. Nevertheless, Herz [1969*] has demonstrated that ECS produces retrograde amnesia for both appetitive and aversive one-trial learning in the same apparatus. That is, the animals showing amnesia respond *more rapidly* than controls in the aversive learning situation and *more slowly* than controls in the appetitive learning situation. Tenen [1965a, 1965b] and Pinel [1969] have also demonstrated retrograde amnesia for one-trial appetitive learning.

Thus, although the conditioned-inhibition hypothesis has stimulated a great deal of research, the overall results do not appear to provide much support for this interpretation.

INCUBATION OF THE CONDITIONED EMOTIONAL RESPONSES

Another interpretation of ECS-produced retention deficits is that the amnesia observed with long training-treatment intervals reflects the effects of ECS, not on memory, but on incubation of the conditioned emotional response (CER) [Pinel and Cooper, 1966; Spevack and Suboski, 1969]. Support for this hypothesis comes from studies such as

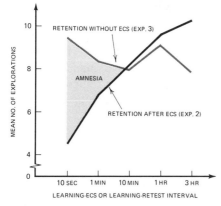

FIGURE 4   *Retention of a one-trial appetitive learning task.*
Retention without ECS was measured by exploration of the
previously rewarded region of the apparatus as a function
of the time between training and retention testing. ECS
groups were treated at various intervals after training and
given retention tests 24 hr later. [*Pinel, 1969*]

that by Chorover and Schiller [1966], who found that ECS given as long
as 6 hr after training attenuated the avoidance response to inescapable
shock. Another group trained with shock punishment that they could
escape retained the avoidance response even when ECS was administered
as soon as 1 min after training. Spevack and Suboski suggested that
such long-term effects of ECS are on the punishment-produced CER
(freezing), and not on memory for a discrete avoidance response; the
short-term ECS effects presumably represent a real effect on memory.
They further maintained that the increase in probability of avoidance
with increasing training-test intervals, as observed on one-trial inhibitory-
avoidance retention tests, reflects *incubation* of the CER.

Although such performance curves do sometimes parallel the
amnesic gradient, this is not always the case. In fact, in most cases the
retention curves and the amnesic gradients are *not* parallel. McGaugh
[1966] found that the retention performance of animals tested within
1 hr after training was higher than that of animals given an ECS within
1 hr after training and tested for retention 24 hr later. Bailey et al.
[1969] found complete retention immediately after one-trial aversive
learning in chicks under the same conditions in which an amnesic
treatment (flurothyl) produced a long gradient of retrograde amnesia
[Cherkin, 1969*]. Pinel [1969] obtained similar results with one-trial
appetitive learning (see Figure 4).

Spevack and Suboski [1969] suggested that the short amnesic
gradients produced when ECS is administered within the first posttraining trial minute are the only ones that represent true amnesia, and
that the longer gradients reflect incubation. However, curves of retro-

grade amnesia do not directly reflect consolidation rates. They reflect the susceptibility of memory processes to the particular amnesic treatment administered, and as such they are extremely sensitive to the different treatments, tasks, and experimental procedures used in various studies [McGaugh and Dawson, 1971; Dawson, 1971; Cherkin, 1969*; Schneider, et al., 1969*]. In particular, the amnesic gradient obtained in any study depends on the intensity and duration of the ECS current. Thus it is clear that some experimental variables that affect retrograde amnesia are, by definition, different from those that influence the retention performance of animals not treated with amnesic agents. Overall, the CER incubation hypothesis is not well supported on either logical or empirical grounds.

It is apparent from the studies cited that the retrograde amnesia produced by ECS might have some explanation other than interference with memory-storage processes. However, on the basis of the evidence thus far, the hypotheses of fear, competing responses, and disruption of CER incubation do not appear tenable. Experiments designed expressly to provide evidence in support of these alternative views have ultimately resulted in further support for the consolidation interpretation of memory formation. Nevertheless, the carefully controlled research stimulated by such alternative theories has led to extremely useful experimental techniques. For example, demonstration of the aversive qualities of multiple ECS treatments has resulted in the use of one-trial learning tasks and a single ECS treatment in investigations of retrograde amnesia. Furthermore, appetitively motivated learning tasks are now used in studies of retrograde amnesia to meet criticisms generated by the conditioned-inhibition hypothesis. Thus, even though the current alternative hypotheses may eventually be ruled out by more conclusive evidence, constant reevaluation of the findings in terms of these explanations, and possibly future ones, can only contribute to our understanding of retrograde amnesia. Moreover, the issues raised in any controversy concerning the basis of ECS-produced amnesia are relevant to all experiments with agents thought to affect memory-storage processes.

THE PERMANENCE OF RETROGRADE AMNESIA

If ECS and other amnesic treatments interfere with memory by disrupting neural processes involved in consolidation, then the amnesia should be permanent. Conversely, if amnesic treatments interfere with other memory processes, such as those involved in retrieval, then the amnesia need not be permanent. It is possible, of course, for treatments to produce temporary amnesias; this is a common occurrence with mild concussions in human patients. However, if *all* retrograde amnesia is only temporary, then it cannot be due to interference with memory-storage processes. Thus the issue of permanence is critical to any interpretation of experimentally induced retrograde amnesia.

Until quite recently very little research explicitly examined this point. Investigators apparently assumed that there was no recovery from experimentally produced retrograde amnesia. Studies such as those by Brady [1951] indicated that the emotional components of CERs attenuated by multiple ECS treatments reappeared spontaneously after a month or so. However, these and similar findings, while of interest, do not appear to be specifically relevant to the problem of memory consolidation [Hunt, 1965]. Repeated ECS treatments may produce many effects [McGaugh, 1968b].

In typical studies the subjects are given a single retention test 24 hr after the initial learning trial and ECS. However, amnesia has been observed after much longer retention intervals. Chevalier [1965], for example, found no evidence of recovery of memory in mice tested either 1, 7, or 30 days after they were given a single training trial on an inhibitory-avoidance task followed by a single ECS treatment. More recently Zinkin and Miller [1967*] reported that when rats were given repeated retention tests 24, 48, and 72 hr after a training trial and ECS treatment, they showed higher response latencies with each test. These results suggested that the amnesia observed on the 24-hr test had diminished with time.

Although Zinkin and Miller suggested that the results of their study cast doubt on the permanence of ECS-produced amnesia, they minimized the possibility that recovery, if and when it occurs, might depend on repeated reexposure to the testing situation. However, as pointed out by Herz and Peeke [1967], in an adequate test for recovery animals that have been tested repeatedly must be compared with animals tested for the first time at the same interval after ECS that the repeatedly tested animals received their last test (72 hr in the Zinkin and Miller study). Since Zinkin and Miller did not include such comparisons, it is not possible to conclude that the amnesia decreased simply with the passage of time. The differential increase in latency could have been due either to habituation or to retrieval of a temporarily suppressed memory as a result of repeated reexposure to the experimental situation in which the original learning had occurred. In subsequent studies with mice Herz and Peeke [1968] found no evidence of recovery from ECS-produced amnesia for one-trial appetitive or inhibitory-avoidance learning on either single or repeated retention tests given 24, 48, and

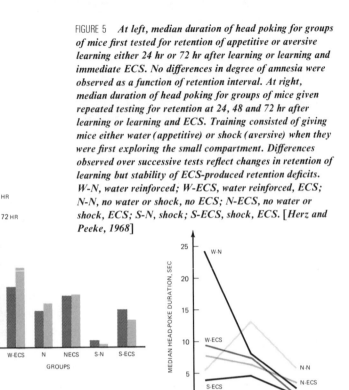

FIGURE 5 *At left, median duration of head poking for groups of mice first tested for retention of appetitive or aversive learning either 24 hr or 72 hr after learning or learning and immediate ECS. No differences in degree of amnesia were observed as a function of retention interval. At right, median duration of head poking for groups of mice given repeated testing for retention at 24, 48 and 72 hr after learning or learning and ECS. Training consisted of giving mice either water (appetitive) or shock (aversive) when they were first exploring the small compartment. Differences observed over successive tests reflect changes in retention of learning but stability of ECS-produced retention deficits. W-N, water reinforced; W-ECS, water reinforced, ECS; N-N, no water or shock, no ECS; N-ECS, no water or shock, ECS; S-N, shock; S-ECS, shock, ECS. [Herz and Peeke, 1968]*

72 hr after training (see Figure 5). Luttges and McGaugh [1967*] gave groups of mice either single or repeated retention tests at several intervals after a single inhibitory-avoidance trial and found no evidence of recovery from amnesia after as much as one month. However, the evidence is conflicting. Kohlenberg and Trabasso [1968] and Koppenaal et al. [1967] demonstrated recovery from amnesia in rats given only single retention tests, whereas Geller and Jarvik [1968a] and Greenough et al. [1968] found no recovery in mice with either individual or repeated tests. King and Glasser [1970] found that ECS produced stable retrograde amnesia in rats over a six-week period. However, when the rats were given repeated testing after initial retention tests 48 hr or one week after training, they evidenced increasing retention on the subsequent tests. In contrast, Hughes et al. [1970a, 1970b] have found that the degree of amnesia in rats may *increase* with time, even with repeated testing.

These conflicting findings have not yet been satisfactorily explained. One interesting point is that most of the studies in which recovery from amnesia was reported were conducted with rats, whereas in most investigations with mice amnesia was found to be permanent with both repeated and single long-term retention tests. It may be that under some conditions ECS produced incomplete interference with memory storage, and that partial storage provides a basis for at least some recovery. This hypothesis is suggested by Pagano et al. [1969], who found that rats given low-intensity ECS (55 mA) recovered from amnesia within 24 hr, whereas those given high-intensity ECS (95 mA) showed no recovery even 48 hr after training and ECS treatment (see Figure 6).

The results of several investigations suggest the possibility that at least part of the memory for a footshock may remain after ECS, and that a variety of manipulations performed hours or days after a learning-ECS sequence may influence the ultimate fate of that memory. Lewis et al. [1968*], for example, trained rats in the usual step-down one-trial inhibitory-avoidance learning paradigm, with groups given footshock alone and footshock followed by ECS, as well as control groups. On tests 20 hr later the footshock-alone group had retained the avoidance response and the ECS group evidenced amnesia. Four hours after testing all groups were administered a "reminder" footshock in another apparatus. On a retest in the step-down apparatus, also 20 hr later, the group that had previously shown amnesia gave evidence of retention. Lewis et al. concluded that the interposed footshock had served as "a reminder for the return of a memory which had been inhibited by ECS." Similar results were obtained in a later experiment with ECS and the protein-synthesis inhibitor cycloheximide as amnesic agents [Quartermain et al., 1970].

FIGURE 6 *Median latencies of rats tested at various retention intervals after inhibitory-avoidance learning. With low-intensity ECS (55 mA) amnesia is observed only on the 1-hr test. FS, footshock only; FS-HECS, footshock, high-intensity ECS (95 mA) 2.5 sec after learning; FS-LECS, footshock, low-intensity ECS (55 mA) 2.5 sec after learning; LECS, low-intensity ECS alone; FS-LECS 30, footshock, low-intensity ECS 30 sec after learning. Numbers in parentheses indicate number of subjects in each group. [Pagano et al., 1969]*

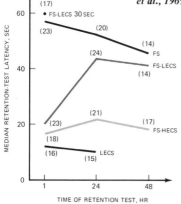

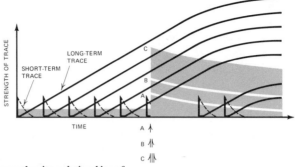

FIGURE 7 *Schematic diagram showing relationships of*
short-term trace (STT), long-term trace (LTT), and noise.
It is assumed that a long-term trace requires a short period
of priming by a short-term trace before it can become viable.
Arrows below the abscissa indicate treatments of three
different degrees of severity (A, B, and C), giving rise to
three increases in noise level, with corresponding differences
in degrees of retrograde and anterograde amnesia.
[*Weiskrantz, 1966*]

These findings are, of course, difficult to reconcile with the hypothesis that retrograde amnesia is due to interference with memory-consolidation processes. It may be that amnesic agents do not completely prevent storage, and that a small or moderate amount of consolidation (whatever the processes involved) is sufficient to provide a basis for restoration of memory through "reminder" procedures. Such a view is consistent with the hypothesis proposed by Cherkin [1969*], who suggested that the use of submaximal amnesic treatments decreases the rate of consolidation but does not stop it. Thus the retention measured 24 hr after learning and amnesic treatment is inflated by posttreatment consolidation which has occurred at a slow rate during the interval between treatment and testing. With maximal amnesic treatments, however, such posttreatment growth of memory will not occur, since consolidation has been stopped. Hence, in terms of this explanation, reminder effects should be eliminated or attenuated by high-intensity ECS or by electrical stimulation of brain structures.

In a very interesting paper Weiskrantz [1966] proposed that ECS-produced amnesia may result from temporary interference with retrieval, as well as storage, of information (see Figure 7). He suggested that the gradient of retrograde amnesia is very brief, and that ECS and other amnesic treatments administered more than a few seconds after training produce their effects by temporarily increasing the noise level in the nervous system, thereby reducing the signal-to-noise ratio. As the interval between ECS treatment and testing increases, the transient noise is assumed to decrease until the signal-to-noise threshold is reached, at which point recovery appears (except in cases where the amnesic agent is given within a few seconds of training). This interpretation might explain the shrinkage of amnesia resulting from head injury in man [Russell and Nathan, 1946], as well as recovery from experimentally induced amnesia.

Nielson [1968] has reported findings that are consistent with Weiskrantz' hypothesis. In an experiment with subcortical brain stimulation as the conditioned stimulus in cats he found that thresholds for eliciting a learned response were highly elevated on tests given 24 hr after an ECS treatment and returned to levels at or near their pre-ECS values on tests given 96 hr after ECS. He also reported that over a period of 96 hr rats recovered from the amnesic effects of an ECS treatment. These findings led him to conclude that ECS produces brain changes which interfere with information retrieval but not with memory-storage processes.

Nevertheless, this explanation is not supported by more recent findings. For example, an ECS treatment affects the performance of a previously learned avoidance response only if the animals are tested within 2 hr after the treatment, and the impairing effects are almost completely eliminated when the convulsions are prevented by light anesthesia with ether prior to the ECS treatment [Zerbolio, 1971; McGaugh and Longacre, 1969]. Moreover, Zornetzer and McGaugh [1969] found that in mice tested 24 hr or 96 hr after training on a one-trial inhibitory-avoidance task retention was not affected by an ECS given 24 hr before the training. The ECS treatment given 24 hr before training should have interfered with retention tested 24 hr after training if ECS had longlasting effects (up to several days) on retrieval processes. Thus, although Weiskrantz' hypothesis might well account for the amnesia observed under some conditions, it does not seem to hold as a general explanation of retrograde amnesia [Cherkin, 1970a; McGaugh and Dawson, 1971].

The conflicting findings in investigations of the permanence of retrograde amnesia indicate that the particular conditions of each experiment may be a factor in the discrepant observations. As with duration of the amnesic gradient, considered below, the effectiveness of the amnesic agent may be the determining factor. It is of interest to note that those studies in which a permanent amnesic effect was reported utilized conditions which, either in the same experiment or in other research from the same laboratory, have been shown to produce relatively complete or total retrograde amnesia, whereas investigations in which recovery was reported did not, as a rule, demonstrate such complete interference. It is likely that recovery, when it occurs, is directly related to the degree of amnesia produced initially, and that recovery is more likely when interference is incomplete [Cherkin, 1969*], particularly under conditions of repeated testing. However, without a direct comparison of repeatedly tested animals with subjects tested for the first time at the same interval after ECS that the repeatedly tested animals received their last test, permanence of interference cannot be distinguished from the effects of repeated exposure to the situation in which the original learning took place [Herz and Peeke, 1967].

It is premature to discard completely any of the theories concerning permanence or recovery with ECS-produced amnesia or to state unequivocally that amnesic effects are due to interference with storage versus retrieval processes. Although it is likely that some instances of recovery can be accounted for in terms of incomplete interference with consolidation processes, we have not yet identified the variables responsible for transience when recovery is obtained. Even so, the numerous studies showing amnesia to be stable over fairly long intervals do indicate that under some, if not most, conditions the memory loss is permanent. This, of course, is all that is required by the most general form of the consolidation hypotheses.

THE NATURE OF THE RETROGRADE-AMNESIA GRADIENT

One of the most controversial areas in memory-consolidation research concerns the length of the gradient of retrograde-amnesia produced by posttraining treatments. Various experimental treatments, procedures, subjects, and amnesic agents employed in different studies might be expected to produce varying results. This is clearly the case. The length of the amnesic gradient—that is, the postexperiential time required for memory to become impervious to impairing treatments—ranges from 10 sec in some studies to days or weeks in others. Although most investigations of the effects of ECS indicate that some degree of interference can be produced by treatments administered up to several minutes after learning, the results of a number of experiments suggest that under some conditions the amnesic gradient may be extremely brief. Chorover and Schiller [1965] and Quartermain et al. [1965*] found amnesia for inhibitory-avoidance learning only in rats treated within a few seconds after training (see Figure 8). Similarly brief amnesic gradients were found with chicks [Lee-Teng and Sherman, 1966] and in other studies with rats [Chorover and Schiller, 1966; Schiller and Chorover, 1967]. At the other extreme Kopp et al. [1966*], utilizing a one-trial inhibitory-avoidance learning paradigm, found significant amounts of retrograde amnesia in mice with ECS delivered 6 hr after the learning trial.

CURRENT ISSUES IN MEMORY CONSOLIDATION

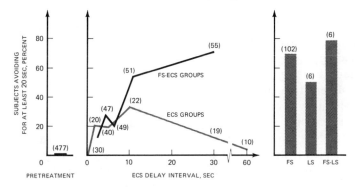

FIGURE 8 *Avoidance performance of rats given footshock and ECS or ECS alone and of control animals in a step-down inhibitory-avoidance task. The curves show performance of FS-ECS and ECS groups as a function of the interval between step-down and ECS on the first three retention trials (one each day). Vertical bars indicate performance of the control groups, which received footshock only (FS), hindleg shock only (LS), or both. Numbers in parentheses indicate the number of subjects in each group. [Chorover and Schiller, 1965]*

Such differences in results are not unusual in the ECS literature [Heriot and Coleman, 1962; Weissman, 1963; Alpern and McGaugh, 1968; Miller, 1968], but there is, as yet, no simple explanation of the discrepancies. Some investigators [Chorover and Schiller, 1966; Spevack and Suboski, 1969] have argued that the true amnesic gradient is quite short, perhaps less than a minute, and that the impairment evidenced with longer training-treatment intervals is due to effects other than interference with memory-consolidation processes. Others [Paolino et al., 1969; Paolino and Levy, 1971] suggest that the variations in the gradient with different treatments are due to effects on separate phases of memory consolidation.

Cherkin [1969*] has proposed that since variations in the amnesic gradient can be produced by varying the intensity and duration of amnesic treatments when the task and training procedures are held constant, the degree of amnesia may vary with the degree of disruption of neural activity produced by the treatment [see also McGaugh and Dawson, 1971]. This hypothesis is strongly supported by evidence from numerous studies that the degree of amnesia produced by ECS varies directly with intensity of the current [Miller, 1968; Dorfman and Jarvik, 1968b; Jarvik and Kopp, 1967b; Hughes et al., 1970a; Lee-Teng, 1967; Zornetzer and McGaugh, in press]. There is evidence that it also varies with duration of the ECS current [Alpern and McGaugh, 1968]. However, the evidence concerning the effect of current duration is conflicting [Paolino et al., 1969; Miller, 1968], and the reason for the discrepancy is not yet clear. Studies of the amnesic effect of the anesthetic flurothyl have shown that amnesia varies with both the dosage and the dwell time used [Cherkin, 1969*].

As Thompson [1958*] had shown, the amnesic gradient is also influenced by the task and training procedures used; whether the gradient is short or long depends on the amount of training prior to ECS treatment. The findings reported by Schneider et al. [1969*] indicate that the gradient obtained in any study may also depend on the criterion used as evidence of retention. Rats were given a simple training trial on a step-down inhibitory-avoidance task, followed by an ECS treatment and a single retention test. When they were permitted a maximum of 30 sec to respond on the retention test, the gradient was short; that is, many animals given ECS appeared to remember the punished response and did not step down. However, when the maximum latency permitted was 600 sec, amnesia was seen even in rats given ECS 6 hr after training; that is, many of the animals responded after 30 sec but within 600 sec. This result helps to explain the variations in amnesic gradient. Studies using short maximum response latencies on the retention test have typically shown short gradients [Chorover and Schiller, 1965], whereas studies in which long gradients were obtained have typically employed long maximum response latencies on the retention tests [Kopp et al., 1966*].

Other recent data suggest that evidence of amnesia following ECS may depend on the response used as an index of retention. For example, if changes in heart rate are used as an index of learning, ECS may produce no amnesia [Mendoza and Adams, 1969], even when the same animals give responses indicating amnesia for inhibitory avoidance [Hine and Paolino, 1970*]. ECS produced amnesia for a punished response, whereas changes in heart rate indicated that the animals had learned to fear the apparatus. It may be that the consolidation rate is faster for fear than it is for association of the fear with specific cues. Or it may be that with the procedures used (transpinneal ECS) the ECS was less effective in disrupting activity in structures involved in retention of nonspecific fear than in the structures involved in controlling the overt inhibitory-avoidance response. Such an argument implies, of course, that different aspects of learning may be mediated by different neural structures. This appears to be a reasonable hypothesis. Whether it proves to be an adequate explanation of the findings of Hine and Paolino remains to be seen.

The amnesic gradient is also known to vary with the intensity of

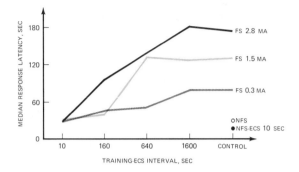

FIGURE 9 *Effect of footshock intensity (0, 0.3, 1.5, or 2.8 mA) and training-ECS interval (10, 160, 640, or 1600 sec) on retention of an inhibitory-avoidance response by 60-day-old mice. Results indicate that degree of amnesia is a function of the interaction between these two factors. [Ray and Bivens, 1968]*

the footshock used in training [Ray and Bivens, 1968] (see Figure 9), and with the degree of water deprivation in an appetitively motivated learning task [Peeke et al., 1969]. Under some conditions the gradient for appetitively motivated tasks is shorter than that for aversively motivated learning [Herz, 1969*]. Several studies indicate that the amnesic gradient is influenced by the subject's familiarity with the training apparatus prior to the training and amnesic treatment. In several instances prior habituation was found to shorten the gradient [Lewis et al., 1968a, 1969; Miller and Misanin, 1969]. Other research [Dawson and McGaugh, 1969b, 1970; Galosy and Thompson, 1971] indicates that under some conditions familiarization may have no effect or may even *lengthen* the amnesic gradient. It could be, of course, that the effect of prior familiarization varies with the task, procedures, and species used in the study. At present, however, we have no clear understanding of the effects of familiarization.

Retrograde amnesia may also vary with the experimental subjects used. The gradient differs for different strains of mice [McGaugh et al., unpublished] and rats [Heinze, 1970], as well as with the biological state of the animal at the time of treatment. ECS administered to mice at night, during the peak hours of activity and metabolic rate, produces greater amnesia than treatments given during the day [Stephens et al., 1967; Stephens and McGaugh, 1968].

There is abundant evidence that the effects of ECS and other amnesic agents depend on the length of the interval between training and amnesic treatment. These findings are generally interpreted as supporting the major assumption of the consolidation hypothesis–that the processes involved in memory storage are time dependent. However, the issue of time dependence is somewhat more complex than it might appear. Numerous recent findings show that the effectiveness of an amnesic agent depends on the events or conditions during the interval between training and treatment. In mice and in fish the amnesic gradient is lengthened if the animals are retained in the experimental apparatus after training [Davis and Agranoff, 1966; Davis, 1968; Robustelli and Jarvik, 1968]. These results suggest that the onset of consolidation is "triggered" by some critical change in stimulation. Another possible interpretation is that the detention increases the animals' susceptibility to the amnesic treatment. That is, the effect might be comparable to that of increasing the intensity and duration of the amnesic treatment or of decreasing the time interval between training and ECS.

A number of studies have also shown that consolidation may be influenced by deprivation of sleep, particularly the sleep stage termed rapid-eye-movement (REM) or paradoxical (because the EEG activity is somewhat like that of the waking state). Fishbein [1970] and LeConte and Bloch [1971] have found that in rats and mice retention is impaired if the animals are deprived of REM sleep in the interval between training and the retention test. Fishbein et al. [1971] also found that ECS given two days after training produced amnesia in mice if they were deprived of REM sleep during this interval, and if the ECS was given shortly after they were removed from the conditions that produced REM sleep deprivation. No effect was found if ECS was delayed for an hour. Thus deprivation of REM sleep appears to act in some way to maintain the susceptibility to ECS-induced amnesia. The basis of this effect is unknown.

There is some evidence suggesting that the effectiveness of ECS in producing retrograde amnesia depends on the stimulation given just prior to treatment. For example, the footshock given in inhibitory-avoidance tasks may have some effect on the amnesic qualities of ECS. Schneider and Sherman [1968] pointed out that variations in the effectiveness of ECS with length of the training-treatment interval might be due to the effect of the interval between footshock and ECS. They found that ECS given 6 hr after training produced amnesia, but only if it was administered 30 sec after a second footshock. However, these findings have not yet been confirmed in other investigations [Banker et al., 1969; Jamieson and Albert, 1970; Gold and King, unpublished; McGaugh et al., unpublished]. In fact there is some evidence from these studies that footshock given prior to ECS may *decrease* its amnesic effects. In a study with goldfish Davis and Klinger [1969] obtained amnesia with treatments of KCl and protein-synthesis inhibitors given 24 hr after training when the animals were placed in the training apparatus just prior to treatment, but they found ECS ineffective.

In an earlier study Misanin et al. [1968] had reported that an ECS administered 24 hr after training produced amnesia for a CER if the cue previously paired with punishment was presented just prior to the

ECS treatment. These results suggest that ECS affects recently *retrieved* memory as well as recently *acquired* memory. Here, too, however, the findings are conflicting. In a more extensive subsequent study Dawson and McGaugh [1969a] failed to replicate these results. Understanding of the reasons for these conflicting findings will require additional research.

Although most of the research discussed so far has focused on the effects of ECS on overt behavior, and by inference on memory processes, the underlying assumption has been that ECS produces its amnesic effects through alterations in neural function. There have been several attempts to account for the variation in results in terms of modification of different aspects of neural activity. Chorover and DeLuca [1969], for example, found that the pattern of brain seizures recorded from the cortex of rats is markedly influenced by a footshock administered prior to ECS treatment (see Figure 10). Three types of electrocorticographic (ECoG) records were obtained: a normal, type *N* seizure pattern followed by postictal depression; a type *A* pattern, characterized by delayed onset, variable frequency, and prolonged postictal depression; and a type *B* pattern, in which there was no detectable seizure activity.

FIGURE 10   *Frequency (percent of group of rats) of different varieties of electrocorticographic (ECoG) responses (normal, type A, or type B) to ECS (35 to 50 mA, delivered through ear snaps) as a function of the footshock-ECS intervals. Note the difference in relative incidence of type A and type B abnormalities of ECoG, particularly at the three shortest intervals. The normal ECoG response to ECS consisted of hypersynchronous bilaterally symmetrical epileptiform activity of the grand-mal type. Type A activity consisted of asynchronous and bilaterally asymmetrical ECoG seizure activity, typically of delayed onset, variable frequency, and reduced amplitude. The type B pattern showed no detectable seizure activity and little departure from pre-ECS amplitude and frequency. [Chorover and DeLuca, 1969]*

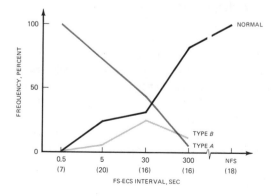

With a footshock-ECS interval of 0.5 sec all ECoGs were of type A. As the interval was increased, the frequency of type N patterns increased and that of type A decreased. With a 5-min footshock-ECS interval most of the seizure patterns were normal. Chorover and DeLuca suggested that the modification in seizure pattern was due to the arousal produced by the footshock, and that it is "possible that the numerous apparent differences in the temporal characteristics of ECS-induced RA might actually reflect differences in the state of arousal at equivalent FS-ECS intervals in different experiments" [Chorover and DeLuca, 1969, p. 148].

More recently Carew [1970] has suggested that the ECS parameters used by Chorover and DeLuca (current intensity and duration) were near the threshold for producing brain seizures. At the threshold a footshock does attenuate seizures. However, as the ECS current level is increased the attenuating effect of footshock decreases, and at higher ECS intensities only normal ECoG seizure records are obtained. Thus the conclusions of Chorover and DeLuca may apply only to studies using ECS current that is near the brain-seizure threshold and in which ECS follows the footshock by a few seconds.

Other studies have shown that the threshold for ECS-induced brain seizures is approximately the same as that for retrograde amnesia [Lee-Teng and Giaquinto, 1969; Zornetzer and McGaugh, in press]. In day-old chicks given transcranial ECS seizure spikes were obtained only when the current was above the value needed to produce amnesia (see Figure 11). Furthermore, in mice ether anesthesia administered prior to ECS stimulation elevates the thresholds for brain seizures and retrograde amnesia [McGaugh and Zornetzer, 1970; Zornetzer and McGaugh, in press]. Thus it is becoming increasingly evident that the passage of current through the brain is not in itself a sufficient condition for producing amnesia. Electroshock stimulation of sufficient intensity to produce brain seizures is also sufficient to produce amnesia, but it is not yet known whether the seizures are merely signs of neural disturbance or whether they play a role in causing retrograde amnesia.

It is also becoming evident that even at ECS current levels above the seizure threshold the degree of amnesia varies with current intensity [Zornetzer and McGaugh, in press]. Thus the occurrence of a seizure is not a sufficient condition for producing maximum amnesia. Several studies have shown that the pattern of electrical activity produced by ECS varies with current intensity. For example, Zornetzer and McGaugh

FIGURE 11 *Sample bipolar EEG records from day-old chicks following transcranial ECS (5 to 15 mA). Type I responses were obtained primarily from current levels which produced no retrograde amnesia (5 mA). The other types of responses, all of which included some degree of spike activity, were obtained from chicks which were stimulated with higher current intensities (10 or 15 mA) and which produced amnesia. A indicates background EEG before stimulation; B, C, and D were recorded immediately, 20 sec, and 5 min, respectively, after stimulation. [Lee-Teng and Giaquinto, 1969]*

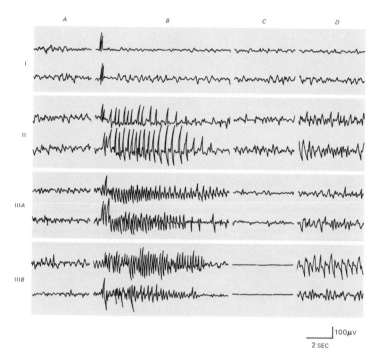

100μV
2 SEC

[1970] found that when seizures were induced in rats by frontal cortex stimulation, the average frequency of spikes in the primary after-discharge, the duration of primary afterdischarge, and the probability of a secondary afterdischarge varied systematically with current intensity (see Figure 12). In a similar study of the effects of flurothyl on brain seizures in two-day-old chicks Herz et al. [1970] found that the number of EEG seizure spikes varied directly with the dose (partial pressure and dwell time of the flurothyl) within the dosage ranges that produce dose-dependent degrees of retrograde amnesia (see Figure 13). Moreover, the increases in activity recorded from multiple units in the reticular formation during convulsions was higher with doses known to produce amnesia than with doses below the amnesia threshold.

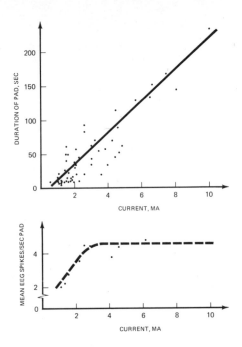

FIGURE 12   *At top, relationship between duration of primary afterdischarge (PAD) and intensity of direct frontal cortex stimulation in rats. Throughout the intensity range used this relationship was linear. Below, the mean number of EEG spikes during the primary-afterdischarge period as a function of current intensity. The relationship was linear up to about 3.0 mA, but then spike frequency reached an asymptotic level.* [*Zornetzer and McGaugh, 1970*]

Other evidence indicates that the postictal depression typically observed after ECS is not essential for producing amnesia. In mice anesthetized with ether prior to ECS treatment postictal depression is rarely seen. However, at ECS current intensities which produce seizures the degree of amnesia obtained is equal to, and sometimes greater than, that produced by ECS in unanesthetized animals [McGaugh and Alpern, 1966; Zornetzer and McGaugh, in press; McGaugh et al., in press]. The degree of amnesia produced by ECS may also depend on the period required for return of a normal EEG pattern after treatment. In particular, Landfield et al. [unpublished] found that the degree of amnesia produced by ECS was greater in rats in which ECoG theta activity was absent for an extended period following the treatment. Little or no amnesia was found in animals in which the theta activity was present shortly after ECS treatment.

Thus the preliminary evidence provided by these studies strongly suggests that variations in the effectiveness of amnesic treatments are closely correlated with electrographic signs of neural disturbance.

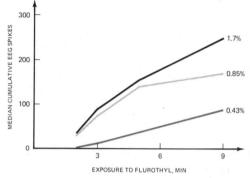

FIGURE 13 *Median cumulative number of striatal EEG spikes exceeding 200 μV, recorded from two-day-old chicks (five in each group), as a function of duration of exposure (2, 3, 5, and 9 min) to different concentrations of flurothyl vapor (0.43, 0.85, or 1.7% v/v in three groups of chicks). No retrograde amnesia was obtained with 0.43 percent regardless of exposure duration, whereas graded amounts of amnesia resulted from increasing durations of the higher doses.* [*Herz et al., 1970*]

This is, of course, completely consistent with even the earliest form of the consolidation hypothesis. It seems quite clear that further research on the problem of memory consolidation should be directed to discovering more about how the nervous system is actually affected by treatments that produce retrograde amnesia.

The evidence reviewed here clearly indicates that there is no single gradient of retrograde amnesia. However, the view that there is one "true" gradient representing the time necessary for memory processes to become impervious to external interference cannot yet be dismissed. It is possible that the various gradients obtained in different experiments are due to the influences of performance factors which mask or distort such a true gradient. Although this appears unlikely, until more data are available concerning the temporal parameters of the physiological substrates involved in memory-storage processes, this view cannot be ruled out. It seems most likely that the efficiency of memory-storage processes varies with biological factors such as strain, sex, and age, as well as with the experimental procedures used, and that such variations will give rise to differences in sensitivity to amnesic treatments applied at different times after training. The effectiveness of any treatment administered at a particular time after training will depend on the degree of "fixation" of the trace and the effectiveness of the treatment in disrupting neural processes. The retrograde-amnesia curves are interference curves. At best they provide only indirect measures of memory-storage processes.

It might seem from the discussion thus far that the controversies surrounding memory consolidation are largely due to the use of ECS as an amnesic agent. However, much of the data supporting the time-dependent nature of memory processes has been obtained with a variety of other treatments that affect brain function—anoxia [Thompson, 1957*a*], heat narcosis [Otis and Cerf, 1958], audiogenic seizures [Essman and Hamburg, 1962], and hypothermia [Beitel and Porter, 1968; Riccio et al., 1968*a*, 1968*b*; Jacobs and Sorenson, 1969]. Whether the amnesia induced by these various techniques results from common modes of action in the central nervous system is as yet unknown.

The diversity of manipulations which have been observed to produce interference is striking. Many anesthetics, for example, produce amnesia [McGaugh and Petrinovich, 1965; Weissman, 1967; Jarvik, 1968]. In one of the early investigations of one-trial learning and drugs Pearlman et al. [1961*] found that the administration of ether to rats within 5 (but not as long as 10) min after a single inhibitory-avoidance learning trial produced significantly more impairment than in unanesthetized controls. More recent studies [Herz, 1969*; Peeke et al., 1969] show significant amnesia with ether administered to mice within 5 (but not as long as 15) min after a single appetitive learning trial. As in the case of ECS, the maximum interval between training and ether treatment at which significant amnesia can be produced is variable. Abt et al. [1961] found significant ether-induced amnesia in mice up to 24 min after a single inhibitory-avoidance trial, and Pearlman [1966] found significant interference up to 10 min after a similar learning trial with rats. In addition, Essman and Jarvik [1961] and Herz et al. [1966], both using mice and aversive learning, and Gutekunst and Youniss [1963], with chicks and imprinting as the learning task, found significant amnesia with ether administered immediately after training.

Jarvik [1964] has pointed out that the ambient temperature appears to be a critical variable in the production of amnesia with ether. He found no significant amnesic effects when the room temperature was below 27°C. In addition, Alpern and Kimble [1967] were unable to obtain any amnesia with ether administered at 24°C to mice after an inhibitory-avoidance trial, but they found significant degrees of amnesia at 38°C even when the ether was administered 24 hr after learning. The duration of exposure to the ether is also an important variable. Herz et al. [1966] found no amnesia when mice were retained in the ether chamber (at 31°C) for only 40 sec after training, whereas complete amnesia was obtained with 70 sec of treatment. Other experimenters [Alpern and McGaugh, 1968; McGaugh and Zornetzer, 1970; Zornetzer and McGaugh, in press] have also found no amnesic effects with ether administered for 40 sec or less after training.

Cherkin [1968] has suggested that these results, which are quite consistent with the findings concerning the effects of different ECS currents and durations, are due to the effect of ambient temperature on the concentration or partial pressure of the anesthetic. Although the temperature conditions utilized by Alpern and Kimble [1967], which did not affect memory, produced an ether concentration of approximately 65% v/v, the effective doses used by them and by Herz et al. [1966] range from 90 to 100% v/v.

Pearlman et al. [1961] also found that the barbiturate sodium pentobarbital (30 mg/kg) produced significant amounts of retrograde amnesia in rats when it was administered as long as 10 (but not 20) min after a single inhibitory-avoidance learning trial. These results extended the findings of Leukel [1957], who had found significant interference with 14-unit multiple-T-maze learning acquisition when pentobarbital (44 mg/kg) was administered to rats 1 min after each daily trial, but no effect was found with a training-treatment interval of 30 min. However, Weissman [1967] found no amnesia in rats given pentobarbital (40 mg/kg) within 5 min after a single inhibitory-avoidance learning trial. Additional evidence indicates that amnesia is obtained if secobarbital is administered to rats within 2 min of massed visual-discrimination learning trials [Paré, 1961]. Nitrous oxide anesthesia produced amnesia in mice if it was administered immediately (but not 15 min) after massed active-avoidance learning trials [Bovet et al., 1966]. Halothane produced amnesia in day-old chicks when it was administered immediately (but not 1.5 hr) after a single inhibitory-avoidance learning trial [Cherkin and Lee-Teng, 1965].

Carbon dioxide anesthesia has also been found to produce amnesia in rats, with the interval between training and anesthesia a critical variable. Leukel and Quinton [1964] demonstrated amnesia with CO_2 administered within 5 (but not 30) min after each daily one-way active-avoidance learning trial. However, their results also indicate that the CO_2 treatment produced punishing effects as well. Taber and Banuazizi [1966] demonstrated amnesia in mice treated with CO_2 as long as 30 (but not 60) min after training. Hypoxia seems to be ruled out as a major factor, since nitrogen alone produced no interference with performance. Dose dependency of the CO_2-produced amnesic effect was also demonstrated by Paolino et al. [1966]. They found that 25 sec of exposure to CO_2 produced amnesia in rats with training-treatment intervals as long as 4 min, whereas a 15-sec exposure was effective only if it was administered within 1 min after the learning trial. Amnesic effects of CO_2 have also been obtained with cockroaches in a one-trial inhibitory-avoidance situation [Freckleton and Wahlsten, 1968].

Various convulsant drugs have also been found to produce marked amnesia [Weissman, 1967], although the evidence concerning the amnesic effects of subconvulsive ECS indicates that the occurrence of a behavioral convulsion is not a necessary condition for production of retrograde amnesia. The results of Pearlman et al. [1961*] suggest that under some conditions pentylenetetrazol is a more effective amnesic agent than ECS. Almost complete impairment of inhibitory-avoidance learning was obtained in rats given pentylenetetrazol (20 mg/kg) 8 hr after learning, and significant amnesia was found even when the drug was given four days after the single trial. However, subsequent findings, such as those of Palfai and Chillag [in press] and Weissman [1967], indicate that in higher doses (up to 58 mg/kg) pentylenetetrazol may have less amnesic effect than ECS. The basis of the discrepancy in these findings is as yet undetermined.

Experiments with flurothyl, a convulsant form of ether, further substantiate the effectiveness of ether as an amnesic agent. Alpern and Kimble [1967] found that flurothyl (at a concentration of 1.66% v/v) produced significant amnesia for a passive-avoidance response in mice with training-treatment intervals as long as 4 hr. Bohdanecký et al. [1968], using the same concentration of flurothyl, observed relatively complete amnesia for an inhibitory-avoidance response with training-treatment intervals as long as 1 hr and significant interference with flurothyl anesthesia induced 6 hr after an avoidance trial. With both drugs the amnesic effects were more pronounced than those produced with ECS under the same experimental conditions. Research by Cherkin [1969*] with inhibitory-avoidance learning in day-old chicks further substantiates the dose-dependent amnesic effects of flurothyl. Using three different doses (0.43, 0.85, and 1.7% v/v) and four durations of anesthesia, Cherkin found that the degree of amnesia increased with the dose and duration. With the largest dose and duration significant amnesia was obtained with treatment as long as 24 hr after learning.

The additional results of research with anesthetics and convulsants further clarify the effect of dosage on the degree of amnesia produced. Flurothyl (1.7% v/v) and >100% v/v ether can produce interference as long as 24 hr after learning, and possibly longer, whereas the maximum effective interval thus far observed with ECS is 6 hr [Kopp et al., 1966*]. However, it is not yet known whether the various treatments observed to produce amnesia exert their effects through common processes or at the same central nervous system locus. As is the case with ECS, little is known about how many of these drugs affect the function of neural processes involved in learning and memory. However, the results of experiments with chicks suggest that two different amnesic agents, ECS and flurothyl, produce similar effects on electrical activity in the brain [Lee-Teng and Giaquinto, 1969; Herz et al., 1970].

THE EFFECTS OF SPREADING DEPRESSION ON MEMORY

Cortical spreading depression (SD) has been used extensively in investigating memory storage. Dusser de Barenne and McCulloch [1941] observed that stimuli applied directly to the surface of the cortex may produce a decrease in local electrical activity which tends to spread from the locus of stimulation, eventually involving the entire cortex. In more thorough investigations Leão [1944, 1947] subsequently determined that strong electrical stimulation, certain chemical substances (such as KCl), and even mechanical stimulation produced this gradually spreading change in surface negative potential. The shift in potential was later attributed to massive extracellular chloride shifts [Van Harreveld and Schade, 1959]. Bureš and Burešová [1960a, 1960b], who have reviewed much of the research on spreading depression, have shown that in rats the application of 25 percent KCl to the exposed surface of both hemispheres up to 2 hr after an inhibitory-avoidance learning trial produced significant retrograde amnesia. This is the same result found with ECS administered at comparable posttrial intervals under the same conditions [Bureš and Burešová, 1963]. Chorover and Schiller [1966] suggested that these results may have been produced by an effect on motor activity rather than memory; that is, the particular training procedures employed in the Bureš and Burešová study could have reduced exploratory activity, which was used as the index of passive avoidance, so that ECS and SD treatments may have merely caused an increase in motor activity. Nevertheless, a number of studies have provided clear evidence of amnesia with posttrial SD in a variety of training tasks. For example, in an investigation utilizing inhibitory-avoidance training without confinement, Pearlman [1966] found that SD was as effective as ether anesthesia in producing memory interference when it was administered 10 (but not 15) min after the learning trial.

Although it has generally been assumed that the amnesic effects of SD are due to its effect on cortical activity, there is evidence that depression can spread subcortically to the amygdala [Fifkova and Syka, 1964]. This is important in view of the evidence that electrical stimulation of the amygdala can interfere with avoidance learning [Goddard, 1964; McIntyre, 1970]. Kupfermann [1966] investigated the effects of bilateral slits in the temporal cortex, which can prevent the subcortical spread of depression, on SD-produced interference with inhibitory-avoidance learning. His results indicate that significant interference is produced independently of the presence of slits. Findings reported by Carlson

[1967], however, suggest that the various components of appetitive and aversive learning may be differentially stored in the cortex and subcortex. Carlson concluded from her studies that the appropriate complex motor responses involved in active- and inhibitory-avoidance learning are stored in the cortex and the emotional and cue components of such learning are stored in the subcortex. In appetitive learning, however, none of these components appears to be stored subcortically. This highly interesting thesis warrants further investigation. If it proves valid, it has important implications for research in memory processes.

The fact that the two hemispheres of the brain can be depressed independently (the wave of negativity apparently does not invade the commissures that connect them) has also made it possible to train animals with one hemisphere functional and the other one depressed and then examine the conditions necessary for transferring information from the trained to the naïve hemisphere. Russell and Ochs [1963] and Ray and Emley [1964] reported that rats required at least one learning trial with both hemispheres functional after learning trials with one side depressed in order to show evidence of retention on a subsequent test in which the hemisphere originally trained was depressed and the hemisphere originally depressed was functional. (However, see Bureš and Burešová, [1970] and Schneider [1967] for critical analyses of studies using SD.)

Ray and Emley [1964] also reported that for transfer to occur there must be an interval of at least 10 min, during which both hemispheres are functional, between a single learning trial and depression of the trained side. When SD was begun 15 sec after the single trial, no transfer was observed. Thus, according to these findings, both the transmitting and the fixation processes are time dependent.

In a subsequent extensive series of experiments Albert [1966a, 1966b] studied in considerable detail the influence of both SD and polarizing current on memory. He trained rats in an active-avoidance task (shuttle box) while one hemisphere was depressed with KCl. By depressing the trained side at various intervals after a subsequent transfer trial (given when both sides were functioning normally) he found that transfer of information from the transmitting side to the untrained, or receiving, side required approximately 3 min. He also found that consolidation of the information in the receiving hemisphere could be disrupted if either SD or pulsating cathodal current was applied to the receiving side within 2 hr after the transfer trial, and that short periods (2 min) of SD followed by longer ones increased the effective interval for the second SD treatment. These findings suggest that the short periods of SD slowed, but did not stop, consolidation.

Albert [1966b] also reported that SD which normally produced amnesia 2 hr after transfer was ineffective 30 min after transfer when it was preceded by 16 min of pulsating anodal cortical stimulation. This suggests that surface positive current accelerates consolidation processes, with the magnitude of the effect apparently dependent on the duration of polarization. Additional experiments showed that it was possible to impair consolidation with cathodal polarization and then restart it with anodal current administered up to 11 hr later. These indications that consolidation is not completely blocked by cathodal polarization and SD suggest that the mechanism for holding information during the consolidation period is resistant to treatments which block consolidation itself. Thus there may be two separate processes that mediate the holding and consolidation of information. Finally Albert found that animals given a transfer trial followed 5 min later by 10 min of cathodal polarization retained the transferred information for several hours, whereas those given 4 min of SD 5 min after transfer did not.

On the basis of these results Albert concluded that there may be several processes underlying the consolidation of information. The first is a short transfer period, during which there is patterned neural firing which may represent learning [Hebb, 1949]. The reverberatory activity initiated during this period may also give rise to two holding mechanisms, the first of which perhaps serves as the basis of recall during the consolidation process, without providing a basis for consolidation. This mechanism has a lifetime of only a few hours and can be disrupted by SD but not by cathodal polarization. The second holding mechanism is inadequate for recall but is a template for consolidation. According to Albert's data, this mechanism has a lifetime of over 11 hr and is subject to disruption by both SD and surface negative current. The completion of consolidation is probably dependent on this second holding mechanism. Similar findings have been obtained by McGaugh [1968c] and by Barondes and Cohen [1968b*] in studies conducted with experimental procedures quite different from those used by Albert.

The results of investigations with SD provide further support for the general hypothesis that treatments which interfere with or depress local electrical activity will interfere with memory consolidation. Although Albert's work [1966a] indicates that the medial cortex must be intact for transfer to occur, and that protection from the effects of SD can be obtained only with anodal polarization of this area, the role of depression of subcortical structures cannot be ignored. The observation that at least some components of avoidance learning may be subcortically stored [Carlson, 1967] suggests the need for further research on the effects of cortical and subcortical depression on various learning tasks.

Perhaps the most interesting findings on the effects of SD concern the multiprocess nature of memory consolidation. Although several studies [Agranoff, 1968; Barondes, 1968; McGaugh, 1968a] have produced

results that support a multitrace view of memory-storage processes, Albert's work [1966a, 1966b] provides the most extensive evidence. Even though Albert's findings have not yet been replicated in other laboratories, their internal consistency argues for their future usefulness. Because we have at least some information about the effects of SD on electrophysiological responses in many parts of the brain, it seems likely that this technique will be useful in future research on memory processes. Much will depend, of course, on the replicability of Albert's findings. It may well be that they will generate still another controversy in memory-consolidation research. It should be noted that under some conditions SD produces longlasting, but reversible, impairment of neural activity [Avis and Carlton, 1968; Burešová and Bureš, 1969]. Thus any interpretation of its effects must take into account the possibility of effects on retrieval processes, even with posttrial applications.

THE ROLE OF RNA AND PROTEIN-SYNTHESIS INHIBITORS IN MEMORY

In the past decade much consideration has been given to the role of macromolecules in the various stages of memory storage. Although there have been some attempts to examine possible modifications in RNA after behavioral training [Hyden and Egyhazi, 1962; Hyden et al., 1969; Zemp et al., 1966], most of the evidence bearing on this question concerns the effects on retention of drugs that impair RNA and protein synthesis [see reviews by Booth, 1967; Gurowitz, 1969; Rosenzweig and Leiman, 1968; Agranoff, 1968; Barondes, 1968; Glassman, 1969.]

After the initial suggestions that memory storage might involve the synthesis of macromolecules, a number of investigators reported that the learning of various kinds of tasks was impaired by drugs that affect RNA synthesis [Dingman and Sporn, 1961; Chamberlain et al., 1963; Corning and John, 1961]. These studies did not, however, provide any evidence that the drugs acted by influencing time-dependent memory processes. In fact, these early studies did not provide particularly convincing evidence that the drugs acted by selectively impairing the neurochemical processes involved in learning [McGaugh and Petrinovich, 1965].

The most extensive research in this area has utilized drugs that interfere with protein synthesis. Flexner et al. [1963*] reported that retrograde amnesia could be produced by treating mice with intracerebral injections of the protein-synthesis inhibitor puromycin. The effects depended on the locus of the injections, as well as the time of the injection. Specifically, they found that retention of a learned position response in a Y-maze was impaired in mice if puromycin was injected bilaterally into the temporal cortices within one to three days after training. During this interval injections into either the ventricles or the frontal cortex were ineffective. Eleven to 43 days after training puromycin injected into any one of these structures produced no deficit, but combined frontal, ventricular, and temporal injections were capable of producing memory destruction. Publication of these findings was followed by numerous attempts to replicate and extend them, and many new controversies were generated as a consequence.

Several studies showed that learning was unimpaired by doses of actinomycin-D, which produced up to 95 percent inhibition of RNA synthesis [Barondes and Jarvik, 1964; Cohen and Barondes, 1966]. However, the drug appears to block long-term memory, since retention is seen for only a day or so after acquisition [Appel, 1964; Agranoff et al., 1967]. That is, the amnesia occurs even though acquisition is unaffected. Similar effects have been observed with a number of amnesic agents, including ECS.

Of particular interest is the further evidence that the processes underlying performance during or shortly after training are different from those involved in the formation of more permanent memory. Barondes and Cohen [1966], for example, found that mice trained under the influence of puromycin (bitemporal injections given 5 hr prior to training) did not differ from saline-injected controls in learning a task. On a test given 15 min after training there was still no difference between the puromycin-treated and saline controls, but retention gradually declined in groups tested at successively longer intervals until, 3 hr after training, the drugged animals showed only 7 percent savings, in comparison to 91 percent for controls. These results suggest that the initial stage of memory storage may not require protein synthesis.

In an extensive and careful series of experiments Agranoff and his colleagues investigated the effects of puromycin and other antibiotics on shuttle-box shock-avoidance learning in goldfish [Agranoff, 1968; Agranoff et al., 1966*]. In general their findings are similar to those obtained by Barondes and Cohen [1968*]. Goldfish injected within 30 min after training displayed retrograde amnesia on a test given several days later. As appears to be the case with mice, goldfish injected prior to training learned normally but showed little or no retention on tests given several days later. However, Swanson et al. [1969] found that short-term memory in mice was not completely spared by intracranial injections of acetoxycycloheximide. Injections given 5 hr before training severely impaired, but did not completely prevent, short-term memory, but short-term retention was unimpaired in mice treated 2 hr before or immediately after training. In general, however, antibiotics appear to block the formation of long-term memory without completely preventing short-term memory.

Similar results have been obtained with ECS. Geller and Jarvik [1968b], McGaugh and Landfield [1970], and Zerbolio [1971] found that mice given an ECS shortly after training evidenced retention several hours after treatment. That is, ECS appears to prevent consolidation without destroying short-term memory processes [McGaugh and Dawson, 1971]. Evidence of "short-term decay," as the phenomenon has been termed, was also found in rats treated with cathodal polarization of the brain cortex after training [Albert, 1966b].

Many studies of the amnesic effects of antibiotics indicate that the degree of amnesia decreases as training prior to drug treatment is increased. Overtraining can attenuate or completely prevent amnesia [Barondes, 1968; McGaugh et al., unpublished]. Since protein synthesis is probably never completely inhibited (usually 80 to 95 percent inhibition is reported), it may be that with overtraining the small amount of protein-synthesizing ability remaining is sufficient for consolidation. It is also possible, of course, that consolidation does not require protein synthesis, and that the amnesia produced with protein-synthesis inhibitors is caused by other effects of the drugs. However, the evidence from studies of protein-synthesis inhibitors is generally taken as an indication that memory consolidation involves protein synthesis. This conclusion is based on the assumption that the drug effects are specific–that is, that the impairment of memory is due specifically to interference with protein synthesis. Several reports, however, suggest that the amnesic effects produced with some antibiotics may not be due solely to inhibition of macromolecular synthesis. Cohen et al. [1966] noted that electrical recordings taken from the brains of mice 5 hr after intracerebral injections of puromycin showed markedly diminished and irregular activity; cycloheximide-treated mice, however, did not evidence such abnormalities. These results suggest that the effects of puromycin on memory may have been due to electrical rather than biochemical changes. Puromycin has also been observed to increase seizure susceptibility in mice and goldfish given subconvulsive doses of pentylenetetrazol [Cohen and Barondes, 1967; Agranoff, 1968]. Cycloheximide antagonized both the puromycin-induced amnesia and the puromycin effect on susceptibility to seizures [Cohen et al., 1966].

In experimental studies with rats Nakajima [1968] has found that injecting actinomycin-D into the hippocampus causes abnormal electrophysiological activity. He suggested that the learning deficiencies which were observed are due to the abnormal discharges rather than to inhibition of macromolecular synthesis. However, we do not yet know why amnesia is correlated with abnormal electrical activity in the brain. The seizure activity might be produced by the same conditions that cause retrograde amnesia but play no causal role in the amnesia. Recent findings indicate that ECS current sufficient to produce amnesia and brain seizures also produces a brief but significant inhibition of brain protein synthesis [Cotman et al., 1971]

There are several problems that must be considered in interpreting the results of studies using intracerebral injections. Bohdanecka et al. [1967], for example, found that needle punctures of the hippocampus similar to those produced by intracerebral injections produced retrograde amnesia for inhibitory-avoidance learning if they were inflicted 1 hr before, immediately after, or 1 hr after training. Hudspeth [personal communication] found that such needle punctures produce extensive brain-seizure activity. In addition, Avis and Carlton [1968] found that hippocampal SD produced marked depression of the hippocampal electrical record shortly after induction and also led to deficits in retention of conditioned suppression learned 24 hr earlier. However, memory for the response apparently returns over a period of weeks [Hughes, 1969].

Finally, Flexner and Flexner [1967] reported that the memory deficits produced by injections of puromycin one or more days after training, which were stable for at least three months, could be restored by a single intracerebral injection of saline either 30 hr or 60 days after puromycin treatment. Restoration of memory was not found with these procedures when cycloheximide was used as the protein-synthesis inhibitor [Rosenbaum et al., 1968]. Flexner and Flexner [1968] also observed restoration of memory in mice with puromycin administered before or immediately after training and tested with saline injections five days later, although the savings scores were lower than those reported in their earlier study. They concluded from these results that puromycin affects the "expression of memory," but not the basic underlying memory substrate. However, at least some of the memory loss appears to be due to interference with memory storage, since complete recovery was not observed when injections were given shortly after the training. For reasons which are not yet clear, puromycin appears to have no effect on memory in adrenalectomized animals [Flexner and Flexner, 1970].

In other research with protein-synthesis inhibitors Barondes and Cohen [1968b*] found, like Albert [1966b] and McGaugh [1968b], that under some conditions it was possible to restart consolidation processes that had been stopped by treatment with an amnesic agent. In replication of earlier work, they found that learning in mice was unimpaired, but amnesia appeared within 6 hr after training under 95 percent protein-synthesis inhibition produced by cycloheximide. The amnesic effect was prevented if the mice were stimulated 3 hr after training with one of several treatments, such as amphetamine, corticosteroid, or even footshock. No such results were obtained with stimulation 6 hr after the training. Barondes and Cohen suggested that the treatments restart consolidation processes impaired by the protein-synthesis inhibitors, and that the effectiveness of the treatments is based on the arousal state induced. According to this view an appropriate state of arousal is essential for consolidation. It is too early to evaluate this interesting hypothesis. It is not clear that the treatments which restart memory storage do so because they induce arousal. Little is known about the effective range of restarting treatments. Perhaps a change in stimulation, either depressing or arousing, is all that is necessary. Such questions can be answered only by further research. There is little doubt that these and similar findings have already stimulated strong interest. They are also likely to generate further controversy.

The present data on the effects of protein-synthesis inhibitors on memory reflects to a great extent the fact that this approach to the study of memory is relatively new. Since earlier investigations implicated RNA and protein synthesis in the formation of memory, it was reasoned that inhibitors of such synthesis should interfere with memory consolidation. Although the early reports suggested simply that inhibitors such as puromycin were capable of impairing memory when they were administered days or weeks after training, more recent data indicate that there are effects other than biochemical ones which may be responsible for the observed memory deficits. In addition, the discrepant findings in various investigations of the same inhibitor suggest that many of the variables involved in memory interference by protein-synthesis inhibitors are unknown. As has been observed with other amnesic agents, differences in task, species, and physiological condition may play important roles. Although there appears to be evidence implicating protein synthesis in consolidation processes, this point is at present highly controversial. Some questions have been answered, but since each study appears to raise at least as many new questions as it answers, this area of research should continue to be active, as well as controversial.

THE EFFECTS OF RESTRICTED BRAIN STIMULATION ON MEMORY

ECS and other amnesic agents are generally assumed to impair memory formation by disrupting or modifying neural functioning in some way. However, it has also been argued that with the severity of many such treatments, the observed retention deficits might actually result from physiological effects other than neural ones. For this reason a number of investigators have examined the effects of treatments thought to have a more direct effect on relatively restricted regions of the central nervous system. The experimental question was whether it is possible to produce effects on memory similar to those found with ECS and other agents by stimulation restricted to specific regions of the brain. The answer is a complicated and qualified yes. Mahut [1962, 1964], for example, found significant interference with acquisition of maze learning in rats and discrimination learning in cats when electrical stimulation was applied to the thalamic portion of the reticular formation (intralaminar and midline nuclei) immediately (but not several minutes) after each response. Similar stimulation administered to the midbrain tegmentum was ineffective. Higher-intensity tegmental stimulation, however, appeared to interfere with learning in rats when it was delivered immediately after a single inhibitory-avoidance trial [Glickman, 1958] or before or during each response in a reversal-learning situation with cats [Thompson, 1958b]. Burns and Mogenson [1958] and Stamm [1961] reported that electrical stimulation of various areas of the cortex interfered with learning of bar-pressing tasks with rats and alternation tasks with cats, respectively.

Deficits resulting from electrical stimulation of two specific areas, the basal ganglia (principally the caudate nucleus) and the limbic system (hippocampus and amygdala), have been more systematically investigated. Rosvold and Delgado [1956] observed that electrical stimulation of the head of the caudate nucleus through permanently implanted electrodes resulted in a significant performance deficit in monkeys when it was administered during acquisition trials on a delayed-alternation problem, but the same stimulation delivered during visual-discrimination trials was ineffective. Thompson [1958b] found that significant deficits in reversal learning were produced by bilateral caudate stimulation (10 Hz) administered for 8 sec immediately or 17 sec after each response. The deficit increased with increases in voltage, frequency, pulse duration, and stimulus-train duration. Unilateral stimulation produced no effect.

Similar results were obtained by Buchwald et al. [1961b] with bilateral caudate stimulation in cats. Stimulation with 5 pulses/sec, which exceeds the threshold for production of caudate-initiated spindles, impaired visual-discrimination performance when it was administered during the presentation of a signal, just before the response, but only in the early stages of training, prior to the attainment of 100 percent performance. Similar stimulation administered during the delay in a delayed-response situation prevented the attainment of high accuracy. In a more detailed investigation of the effects of 60-Hz amygdaloid stimulation in rats, Goddard [1964] reported that continuous stimulation during the entire time the subject was in the apparatus produced inability to learn an active-avoidance response, but it had no effect on food-motivated maze learning or on inhibitory-avoidance learning. However, such stimulation did produce retroactive impairment of CER

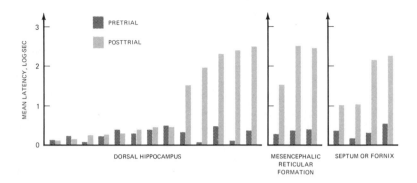

FIGURE 14 *Effects of afterdischarges elicited by stimulation of the dorsal hippocampus, the mesencephalic reticular formation, or the septum or fornix on retention of an inhibitory-avoidance task in cats. Each pair of bars represents the mean latency required by each animal to enter a cubicle before and after receiving mouthshock and stimulation delivered through bipolar subcortical electrodes —1.0 to 2.0 mA, 0.3 to 1.0-msec pulses of 30 to 100 Hz for 5 sec. Amnesia was observed only in the first eight animals in the dorsal hippocampus group.* [*Kesner and Doty, 1968*]

learning when it was presented immediately after a punishing shock and continued for 5 min.

In a later study Kesner and Doty [1968] obtained significant interference with inhibitory-avoidance learning in cats with dorsal-hippocampal and amygdaloid stimulation (5-sec trains of 30- to 100-Hz square-wave pulses, 0.3 to 1.0 msec in duration) delivered 4 sec after punishing shock (see Figure 14). Their results also appear to indicate that to be effective such stimulation must produce afterdischarges in the amygdala; stimulation of the septum, fornix, or ventral hippocampus, which did not produce such afterdischarges, produced no interference. Similar results with rats were obtained by Brunner et al. [1970] with unilateral dorsal-hippocampal stimulation administered immediately after footshock in a step-down task (1.5-sec train of 60-Hz ac shock, 25 to 50 μA), although amnesia was also obtained with comparable stimulation of the cortex overlying the hippocampus, as well as the septal area.

Barcik [1969] administered ECS (via cortical screws) or local bilateral dorsal-hippocampal stimulation (300 to 900 msec of 40-Hz 1-msec biphasic pulses at 3.0 to 3.6 volts, sufficient to produce hippo-campal afterdischarges) 3 or 30 sec after footshock in an inhibitory-avoidance task. The results indicate that hippocampal stimulation initiated as long as 30 sec after footshock was as effective as ECS in producing amnesia. Also, Lidsky and Slotnick [1970] found that in mice bilateral stimulation of the dorsal hippocampus (8 sec, 3 V, 100 Hz, 1-msec pulses) given 40 sec after inhibitory-avoidance training produced retrograde amnesia comparable to that obtained with transcorneal ECS (18 mA, 200 msec). No amnesic effects were obtained with comparable stimulation of the cortex. The hippocampal stimulation produced no convulsions, but since no electrophysiological records were taken, the extent of the brain-seizure activity produced is not known. On the basis of Barcik's study [1969], it appears likely that seizure discharges were produced [see also Hirano, 1965, 1966].

McIntyre [1970] recently found that amnesia could be produced in rats by unilateral electrical stimulation of the amygdala. The rats were first given repeated amygdaloid stimulation (40 μA, 60 Hz, 60 sec duration) once every 12 hr until bilateral convulsion was elicited (this process is referred to as "kindling" of a seizure). Convulsions were then elicited by amygdaloid stimulation after each session in a CER task. The amygdaloid stimulation prevented development of the CER to the tone, and the amnesia was stable over six weeks. No amnesia was found with kindled convulsions elicited by stimulation of the anterior limbic field.

However, there is clear evidence that in rats stimulation of the frontal cortex of sufficient intensity to produce brain seizures produces amnesia. Zornetzer and McGaugh [1970] found that in an inhibitory-avoidance task 3-mA stimulation of the frontal cortex produced amnesia comparable to that obtained with 50-mA ECS administered transpineally. The amnesic effect was found even in amygdalectomized rats. It appears that the amygdala is not a critical structure for producing retrograde amnesia with seizure-inducing stimulation.

A number of studies have shown that when comparable ECS current is delivered to different animals, the degree of amnesia obtained depends on the method of administration. For example, the amnesic effect of ECS delivered transcorneally is greater than that produced by transpineal ECS [Schneider et al., 1969; Dorfmann and Jarvik, 1968a]. It may be simply that a greater proportion of the current reaches the brain with transcorneal stimulation. It might also be that different brain structures are affected by the two types of stimulation. Gold et al. [in press] found that when electroshock current was delivered directly, amnesia was obtained at lower intensities with anterior than with posterior cortical stimulation. Rats were trained on an inhibitory-avoidance task and given 0.5 sec of electrical stimulation 5 sec later. With anterior cortex stimulation, amnesia was found with 5 mA. This level is subconvulsive, but it is probably above the brain-seizure threshold [Zornetzer and McGaugh, 1970]. With posterior cortex stimulation no amnesia was found with current levels below 10 mA. Stimulation at 20 mA produced complete amnesia with both anterior and posterior cortical stimulation.

Vardaris and Gehres [1970] also studied the effect of electrical stimulation delivered to the posterior cortex of rats and found that current of 10 mA produced cortical seizures and amnesia in most of the animals. Since not all animals had seizures, it appears that with posterior cortical stimulation 10 mA is just above the seizure threshold. Although these findings are consistent with those of Gold et al., it is not yet clear why greater amnesia is obtained with anterior cortical stimulation. Apparently the brain-seizure threshold is lower in the anterior cortex, and it may be that this region is critically involved in memory storage or readily elicits seizures in other structures involved in consolidation.

Although findings such as these suggest that interference with memory consolidation can be produced by electrical stimulation of various parts of the brain, criticism has been leveled against the techniques utilized in many of the experiments. In some cases stimulation was administered during or immediately after the event on which the subject would have to rely in order to show improvement on subsequent trials. Therefore any experimental manipulation that could interfere with registration of the sensory experience—reward, attention, set, or postural orientation—might produce deficits that would be interpreted as amnesia. Even in the experiments which interposed delays of several seconds between an experience and interfering stimulation the current intensities and durations were often of sufficient magnitude to produce current spread, making it extremely difficult to determine whether the target structure or some other nearby site had been involved in production of the deficit. An extreme example of this is the study by Kesner and Doty [1968], in which afterdischarges in the amygdala were necessary for the production of interference after dorsal-hippocampal stimulation.

A technique of proven usefulness in ECS studies is examination of the effectiveness of treatment at successively longer intervals after a learning trial. As we have seen in repeated instances thus far, this approach has generally yielded evidence that the effectiveness of the amnesic agent diminishes as the time between learning and treatment increases, until a point is reached at which interference is no longer obtained. With ECS and other agents this interval, usually considered to be the consolidation interval, has been in the range of minutes or hours. With such long consolidation periods, it appears unlikely that the observed deficits are the result of interference with sensory registration, reward, or postural orientation.

Several investigations have also employed this technique with electrical stimulation and lesions of the brain. For example, Wyers et al. [1968*] delivered a single bilateral pulse (0.2 to 0.9 mA, 0.3 to 1.0 msec, square wave) to the caudate-putamen of rats 0.1, 1.0, 5.0, or 30.0 sec after strong footshock from a lever in an inhibitory-avoidance situation. Complete interference with retention was obtained at all intervals, indicating that such low-intensity stimulation was an extremely effective amnesic agent. No amnesia was found with comparable stimulation of adjacent sites (overlying cortex and corpus callosum, internal capsule). This control appears to rule out the possibility that the effects are due to current spread. Wyers and Deadwyler [1971] recently obtained complete interference with footshock–caudate-stimulation intervals as long as 5 min but found that the same treatment was ineffective 10 min after footshock. Complete interference was also obtained with a single bilateral pulse delivered to the ventral hippocampus 0.1 sec after footshock [Wyers et al., 1968*].

In attempts to broaden the generality of such amnesic effects Peeke and Herz [1971] found this type of stimulation sufficient to produce significant learning deficits when it was administered during appetitively motivated Lashley III learning trials. Different groups of animals received single bilateral caudate pulses either after each choice point or after completion of a 30-sec reward period following each trial. A third group received the same number of stimulations as the choice-point group, but massed at the end of the 30-sec reward period following each trial. The results indicate that although learning was impaired with all groups, as compared with implanted and nonimplanted control animals, the two groups that receive multiple stimulations showed the greatest deficit, with some of the animals never attaining the learning criterion. Single bilateral caudate pulses were also observed to impair the development of extinction in a water-motivated appetitive learning situation, with pulses delivered once every 12 sec being significantly more effective than pulses administered once every 4 sec [Herz and Peeke, in press].

These results indicate that this technique for producing retrograde amnesia is not restricted to one type of learning. Low-level stimulation of the caudate nucleus is sufficient to produce severe disruption of several different learning paradigms. Whether these effects will ultimately be shown to be due primarily to direct modification of activity in the basal ganglia or to indirect effects exerted at remote sites will be determined only by additional research.

In an intriguing study Hudspeth and Wilsoncroft [1969*] obtained a graded amnesic effect in inhibitory-avoidance learning in mice with electrically produced lesions (0.10 mA dc, electrode-anode, skull-screw cathode) administered bilaterally to the dorsal frontal cortex (cingulate field) immediately, 10 min, and 45 min after footshock in a step-through avoidance apparatus. Immediate stimulation produced complete inter-ference, 10-min treatment affected only partial deficits, and 45-min current was ineffective. Lesions of cortical areas immediately adjacent to but outside of the cingulate field were also ineffective. It is of interest to note that this area projects heavily to both the caudate nucleus and the hippocampus.

A number of studies have also shown that it is possible to facilitate learning with electrical stimulation of the hippocampus [Patel, 1968; Stein and Chorover, 1968; Erickson and Patel, 1969] and the reticular formation [Denti, 1965; Bloch et al., 1966; Denti et al. 1970]. Erickson and Patel [1969] gave rats unilateral dorsal-hippocampal stimulation (30 μA ac, 30 μA dc, or 200 μA ac at 60 Hz for 3 sec) 10 sec after each trial in a discriminated-avoidance lever-pressing task. Animals given the 30-μA ac or dc stimulation learned an avoidance response signifi-cantly faster than unstimulated controls (see Figure 15). Since many trials were given during the sessions, it is possible that the effects were due to pretrial stimulation—the direct effects of posttrial stimulation on subsequent trials in the same session. The fact that hippocampal stimulation enhanced performance and cortical stimulation did not warrants further examination. Also, the fact that the performance of the operated control animals was inferior to that of unoperated controls suggests that such stimulation may have more than com-pensated for the tissue damage resulting from the implantation of electrodes. This effect has also been observed by Denti et al. [1970] and Landfield et al. [1971].

Somewhat similar results were obtained by Stein and Chorover [1968]. Rats were given a single bilateral stimulation (7.0 to 12.0 μA, 100 Hz, 3 sec) to the dorsal hippocampus after a series of trials. Facilita-tion of open-field maze learning with spaced trials was observed on retention tests given several hours after training and posttrial stimulation, but impairment was observed when several trials and stimulations were given in rapid succession.

In several experiments by Denti and her colleagues [Denti, 1965; Bloch et al., 1966; Denti et al., 1970] facilitation of active-avoidance learning in rats was obtained with immediate posttrial stimulation of the mesencephalic reticular formation (100 to 200 μA, 300 Hz, 10 sequences of 6-sec stimulation at 3-sec intervals for a total of 90 sec). Since the electrode implantation impaired performance in operated but un-stimulated controls, it is not clear whether these results represent facilitation of learning or compensation for a lesion effect. Other findings [Deweer, 1970; Bloch, 1970] suggest that facilitation of learning

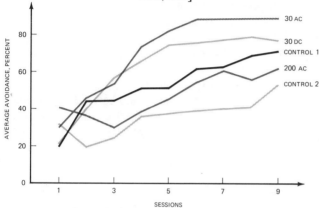

FIGURE 15 *Average percentage of discriminated-avoidance performance over 5-hr sessions as a function of unilateral dorsal hippocampus stimulation and control conditions. The task consisted of pressing a lever during a 5-sec conditioned stimulus to avoid footshock. 30 AC, 30 μA ac; 30 DC, 30 μA dc; 200 AC, 200 μA ac; control 1, unoperated animals; control 2, animals implanted with hippocampal electrodes but not stimulated. Stimulation consisted of a 3-sec brain stimulus (60 Hz) 10 sec after each avoidance or escape response. Both low-intensity groups (30 AC and 30 DC) learned significantly faster than controls. [Erickson and Patel, 1969]*

can be obtained where the electrode-produced lesion has no impairing effect.

Using procedures comparable to those in the Denti studies, Landfield et al. [unpublished] have demonstrated facilitating effects with posttrial bilateral stimulation of the ventral hippocampus (30 μA, 100 Hz, 180 sec duration). Facilitation was found with both active-avoidance and discriminated-avoidance tasks (selective avoidance of one goal box of a T-maze, where punishing shock was given). No facilitation was found with stimulation given 5 min after training. Thus the effect was retrograde. The stimulation provided almost complete compensation for the electrode-produced lesion.

The evidence that selective brain stimulation affects memory-storage processes when it is applied immediately after learning trials, with effects diminishing with longer intervals, suggests that minimal treatment of critical brain structures is as effective as massive stimulation of the entire brain. Although the technique of ECS and systemic drug treatment have helped greatly to characterize the phenomenon of memory consolidation, such results in no way clarify the role of various brain structures and systems in the formation of memory. It is possible that many such questions will be resolved by specific investigation of the degree of involvement of various brain structures in the different phases of memory formation through techniques such as posttrial electrical stimulation, lesions, and subcortical SD.

Much of the early research on brain stimulation is difficult to interpret in terms of memory effects because in many of the studies such effects were only a peripheral concern. As with much of the early drug research on memory, treatments were administered variously before, during, and after learning, making it difficult to distinguish performance effects from memory effects. The more recent studies, however, which have specifically investigated effects on memory, indicate that much can be learned about the various mechanisms involved in memory processes when attention is focused on specific portions of the nervous system. It is likely that further research with these techniques will provide more information about the brain sites involved in consolidation and the manner in which they are affected by ECS and various drugs. It is of interest that interference of one sort or another has been obtained with experimental manipulation of a wide variety of brain areas. Although it appears unlikely, the possibility that interference with memory formation results from disturbances of normal activity in any part of the brain cannot yet be ruled out. However, the evidence to date suggests that manipulation of the reticular formation, limbic system, and basal ganglia most readily affect consolidation processes.

DRUG FACILITATION OF MEMORY CONSOLIDATION

Although most of the present conclusions concerning memory consolidation are based on evidence of memory impairment, there is also evidence that memory storage can be *enhanced* by pharmacological agents that affect the central nervous system, as well as by electrical stimulation of the brain. However, the most extensive research in this area has been with drugs [see reviews by McGaugh and Petrinovich, 1965; McGaugh, 1966, 1968a; Weissman, 1967; Dawson and McGaugh, in press].

The earliest such study appears to be that by Lashley [1917], who reported that low doses of strychnine given to rats before daily training trials increased the rate of maze learning. There were apparently no further studies of this effect until 50 years later, when McGaugh and Petrinovich [1959] replicated and extended Lashley's findings and suggested that strychnine might influence learning by facilitating the neurobiological processes involved in memory consolidation. Of course, many other interpretations of these results are possible [Thiessen et al., 1961; Whishaw and Cooper, 1970]. Since the experimental animals were drugged while training was taking place, the drug might appear to improve learning by affecting attention, motivation, arousal, retrieval, activity level, or other processes that influence performance rather than retention. That is, the procedures used in these studies did not provide any clear way of distinguishing the drug's effects on memory-storage processes from other influences on performance. Subsequent attempts to clarify the basis of the facilitating effects observed with strychnine and other drugs have focused on the viability and generality of the effect and on differentiation of the drugs' effects on consolidation from their effects on performance. Again, in the course of this research controversial issues have arisen.

The first approach to these questions concerned the generality of the effects of pretrial injections of strychnine and other analeptic agents on learning of different types of tasks. The underlying assumption was that if drugs enhance performance by affecting the basic neural mechanisms of learning, then facilitation should be found with a wide variety of tasks. Evidence of such generality has been obtained. Pretrial injections of strychnine sulfate and other analeptics have been found to facilitate maze learning, discrimination learning [McGaugh and Thomson, 1962; Petrinovich, 1963; Hunt and Krivanek, 1966], and avoidance learning [Kelemen and Bovet, 1961] in rats and classical conditioning in rabbits and cats [Cholewiak et al., 1968; Benevento and Kandel, 1967].

These findings have, however raised additional questions. For example, it is not at all clear that the facilitating effects of strychnine on classical conditioning are due to effects on neural processes underlying learning. Cholewiak et al. found that strychnine (0.30 mg/kg) enhanced performance of the conditioned response (nictating membrane in rabbits) during extinction as well as acquisition. In fact, rabbits trained without strychnine and extinguished under strychnine responded more to the conditioned stimulus during extinction than they did during acquisition. Thus it appears that strychnine can influence performance by acting on processes, perhaps sensitization in this case, which are not directly involved in memory. In this respect such studies have clarified the basis of drug effects on acquisition. In addition, Whishaw and Cooper [1970] reported that strychnine depressed exploratory activity in rats. This effect could cause them to make fewer entrances into blind alleys, and hence fewer errors in maze-learning tasks. However, this explanation does not readily apply to facilitation found with other types of learning.

The second approach has been to administer the drug *after*, rather than before, the training session. Evidence of learning facilitation with posttrial injections provides more convincing support for the interpretation that analeptics influence memory processes rather than performance, since animals are never under the influence of drugs when they are tested.

Numerous studies have shown that several analeptics facilitate learning when they are injected after training. Facilitation has been observed with such diverse tasks as maze learning [McGaugh et al., 1962a, 1962b; Garg and Holland, 1968], discrimination learning [Krivanek and Hunt, 1967; Krivanek and McGaugh, 1968; Luttges and McGaugh, 1970], oddity learning [Hudspeth, 1964], delayed alternation [Petrinovich et al., 1965], avoidance learning [Bovet et al., 1966; Zerbolio, 1967; Krivanek, 1968], and latent learning [Westbrook and McGaugh, 1964*]. The analeptics investigated to date include strychnine, diazadamantanol, picrotoxin, pentylenetetrazol, bemegride, caffeine, and amphetamine. These drugs affect brain activity within a few minutes after administration and are metabolized fairly rapidly. Thus with posttrial injections they can influence posttraining neural processes without directly influencing subsequent performance. The degree of facilitation found in different studies has varied with the experimental conditions— the particular drug, dose, time of injection, strain of animals, task, and training conditions.

In many, if not most, of the experiments in this area the animals are given drug injections after each daily training session. However, it is possible to obtain facilitation with only a single injection. For example, Olivero [1968] trained mice to avoid a shock (two-way shuttle) by responding to a tone within 5 sec. At the end of four days of training (100 trials per day), when the mice had attained a performance level of approximately 75 percent (correct responses), they were given an additional 25 trials in which a light was presented along with the tone. Injections of strychnine or nicotine were given either shortly before or immediately after this session. Then, 24 hr later, the mice were given 100 trials with only the light signal (no tone) to test whether they had learned to respond to the light during the 25-trial transfer session. On this retention test saline-injected controls performed at approximately a 30 percent level, whereas mice injected with strychnine or nicotine either before or immediately after the transfer session performed at approximately a 70 percent level. The performance of mice injected with strychnine 1 hr after the session was similar to that of controls.

Single posttrial injections have also been found to facilitate inhibitory-avoidance learning. Franchina and Moore [1968*] injected rats with strychnine (0.0125 to 0.200 mg/kg) or saline within 15 min after a single training trial on an inhibitory-avoidance task and found that the degree of facilitation measured on retention tests given over the next several days varied directly with the dose. In a later study Franchina and Grandolfo [1970] found even greater facilitating effects when footshock was associated with a particular conditioned stimulus. The strychnine injections appeared to facilitate the storage of specific information presented beforehand.

Although posttrial injections of analeptics appear to facilitate learning over a wide range of experimental conditions, there are several reports of failure to obtain such facilitation [Louttit, 1965; Prien et al., 1963; Schaeffer, 1968; Stein and Kimble, 1966]. Despite the fact that the facilitating effects have been replicated by many investigators, these negative reports cannot be disregarded. The questions are, what are the limits of the generality of the effect, and what conditions produce either no facilitation or impairment? Although these questions cannot as yet be answered with complete satisfaction, some suggestions have been provided by recent findings. For example, the environmental conditions during rearing of the experimental animals appear to be an important factor in susceptibility to drug facilitation. In a very interesting study Shandro and Schaeffer [1969] investigated the effects of strychnine on learning in rats reared in restricted and enriched environments. They found that in general posttrial injections facilitated maze performance in enriched animals and impaired it in the restricted animals. In a related study LeBoeuf and Peeke [1969] found that rats reared in an enriched environment and injected daily from 21 to 52 days of age with strychnine (1.0 mg/kg), learned a maze as adults more rapidly than strychnine-injected animals reared in a restricted environment. Since similar results were obtained when these treatments were administered from 51 to 70 days of age [Peeke et al., 1971*], the effects were apparently not limited to specific developmental periods. It seems that strychnine somehow augments the effect of rearing conditions, since no environmental differentiation was observed in saline- or water-injected controls.

Calhoun [1966] found that the degree of stimulation provided by the posttraining environment was also a crucial factor. In mice given posttraining strychnine injections, discrimination learning was facilitated if the environment was quiet but was impaired if the mice were highly stimulated during the interval after treatment. Several studies have shown that the effects of a given drug and dosage vary with the strain of animal [McGaugh et al., 1961; Breen and McGaugh, 1961; Garg and Holland, 1968; Petrinovich, 1967; Krivanek and McGaugh, 1968]. Petrinovich [1967] reported that doses of strychnine that facilitated learning in some strains of rats produced impairment in other strains. McGaugh and Krivanek [1970] also found facilitation of learning in mice with posttrial injections of strychnine in low doses (0.025 to 0.100 mg/kg) and high doses (1.00 to 1.25 mg/kg), but not intermediate doses (see Figure 16).

As in the studies of memory impairment discussed above, other important factors are the age of the experimental animals [Doty and Doty, 1966] and the complexity of the training task [Hall, 1969; Coker and Abbott, 1967]; the degree of facilitation apparently increases with age and with complexity of the task. Variables such as these are undoubtedly factors in some of the studies which report no facilitation of learning with posttrial administration of analeptics. It remains to be seen whether the incidence of such negative reports will decrease as the significance of strain, dosage, task, and environmental stimulation is taken into consideration.

If analeptics do facilitate learning by influencing memory-consolidation processes, as most of the evidence seems to indicate, the effects of the posttrial injections should be time dependent; that is, the degree of facilitation should decrease as the interval between training and drug administration is increased. In a series of experiments McGaugh and Krivanek [Krivanek and McGaugh, 1968, 1969; McGaugh and Krivanek, 1970; McGaugh, 1968a] studied the effect of injection time of analeptics on discrimination learning in mice. For each drug examined (strychnine, pentylenetetrazol, and amphetamine), dose-response effects were first systematically investigated. The mice were injected each day immediately after three massed trials on a visual-discrimination task. Doses that produced significant facilitation were then investigated in terms of the relationship between injection time and effect on learning. As shown in Figure 16, the most effective dose of pentylenetetrazol (15 mg/kg) was found to facilitate learning with a posttrial injection interval of 15 min, but not with intervals of 30 min or longer. Strychnine (0.100 or 1.00 mg/kg) facilitated learning with injections given up to 1 hr (but not 2 hr) posttrial. Amphetamine (0.5 or 2.0 mg/kg) facilitated learning with immediate posttrial injections, but not with a 15-min posttrial interval.

These findings clearly indicate that memory-storage processes are susceptible to facilitating influences for a relatively long time (at least 1 hr) after training. There is, however, no single gradient of retrograde facilitation; it varies with the drug used in the various experiments. This is consistent with the findings discussed earlier concerning memory-storage impairment with ECS and other amnesic agents. It seems likely that some conditions will be found under which treatments several hours after training will effect facilitation. With all drugs investigated, however, the posttrial injection effect has been time dependent, in accordance with the consolidation hypothesis.

The overall viability and generality of these drug effects strongly support the hypothesis that drugs can facilitate memory consolidation. However, we do not yet know the neurobiological bases of such effects.

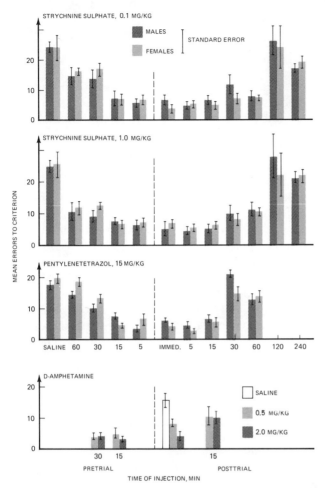

FIGURE 16 *Facilitating effects of various drugs on number of errors to criterion of discrimination learning in mice as a function of injection 60, 30, 15, or 5 min before or immediately, 5, 15, 30, 60, 120, or 240 min after each daily training trial. [Data for strychnine sulphate, Krivanek and McGaugh, 1968; data for pentylenetetrazol, Krivanek and McGaugh, 1969; data for d-amphetamine, McGaugh and Krivanek, 1970]*

Studies of drug facilitation of learning have so far provided few leads concerning the way or ways that drugs act on the nervous system to improve retention. The fact that facilitation is produced by drugs that have quite different mechanisms of action points to some general effect on neural structures. It might be that the drugs act by stimulating structures involved in arousal or activation. For example, Alpern [1968] found that learning in rats was facilitated by implanting strychnine crystals in the mesencephalic reticular formation. In addition, Grossman

[1969] found that discrimination learning in rats was facilitated by either pretrial or posttrial injections of small quantities (5 to 10 μg) of pentylene-tetrazol directly into the hippocampus. Rats were given six trials a day on a T-maze brightness-discrimination problem, with food used as a reward. The learning performance of animals implanted with cannulae was inferior to that of unoperated controls. The performance of animals treated 5 min before training was superior to that of operated controls but comparable to that of unoperated controls. The performance of rats given the drug after each session was superior to that of all other groups. The drug injections were found to facilitate discrimination-reversal learning as well as simple discrimination learning.

The results of drug stimulation of the hippocampus and reticular formation are highly similar to those of electrical stimulation of these areas. There is little information, however, about the effects on learning with stimulation of other neural structures. At the biochemical level there is some evidence that analeptics facilitate RNA synthesis [Carlini and Carlini, 1965; Talwar et al., 1966; Pevzner, 1966; Nasello and Izquierdo, 1969]. Such evidence is interesting in view of the currently popular theory that consolidation involves RNA and/or protein synthesis. However, it is not yet clear whether such effects result directly from alteration of biosynthesis or indirectly from modifications of neural activity. Clearly, it is too early to regard these data as conclusive evidence that learning is related to RNA synthesis. This problem should be pursued, however, and undoubtedly it will be.

Essman [1966] reported that the amnesic effects of ECS were attenuated in mice treated with tricyanoaminopropene (TCAP) prior to training. These findings are of interest because of evidence suggesting TCAP enhances RNA synthesis. This compound has also been reported to enhance learning in various types of learning tasks [Chamberlain et al., 1963]. However, it is not at all clear that the learning effects are due specifically to the biochemical effects of the drug.

Strychnine has also been found to attenuate ECS-induced amnesia. Bivens and Ray [1966] injected mice with low doses of strychnine 10 min prior to training in an inhibitory-avoidance task and administered ECS either 15 sec or 30 sec after the trial. On a retention test given 24 hr later the retention deficit of the strychnine-injected mice was significantly less than that of saline-injected controls. These findings were interpreted as indicating that strychnine increases the rate of consolidation. However, Riccio et al. [1968a] found that strychnine potentiated the amnesic effects of hypothermia. Interpretations of these results must, of course, take into account the impairment produced by strychnine in highly stimulated animals, as reported by Calhoun [1966].

In a later study McGaugh [1968c] found that ECS effects on memory could be attenuated with drug injections given after training. Thus it does not appear that strychnine acts simply by increasing the rate of consolidation, as suggested by the findings of Bivens and Ray. The degree of attenuation of amnesia decreased as the interval between ECS and drug injection was increased. Significant attenuation was obtained with a 3-hr interval, but not with a 6-hr interval. These results are highly similar to those for anodal and cathodal cortex stimulation [Albert, 1966b] and with cycloheximide and amphetamine [Barondes and Cohen, 1968b*]. In all these studies stimulation applied within a few hours after treatment with an amnesic agent appeared to restart or accelerate impaired consolidation processes.

It seems increasingly likely that the effects of analeptics on memory storage may be due to general effects on neural excitability rather than to some specific effect at a cellular level. It would be interesting to know whether ECS-induced amnesia is attenuated by posttrial stimulation of specific neural structures, such as the reticular formation. Denti [1965] found that the amnesic effects of the anesthetic pentothal were attenuated by posttrial stimulation of the reticular formation. However, some of these effects, arresting and restarting consolidation, have not yet been replicated in other research [Hunt and Duncan, in press]. If they prove reliable, these procedures will be extremely useful in the dissection of memory processes.

Although the basis or bases of facilitation phenomena, like the basis (or bases) of amnesic agents, is still a mystery, future investigations of the neurophysiological, anatomical, and biochemical substrates of such behavioral modifications should bring us closer to a solution.

CONCLUSIONS

It is clear from studies of drug facilitation of memory storage and studies of memory-storage impairment that longlasting representation of an experience does not become fixed or consolidated at the time the experience occurs. Although many of the processes involved have been incompletely investigated, and consequently are not well understood, the fact that a variety of treatments can enhance or impair memory when they are administered hours and even days after the event provides extremely strong evidence that memory storage involves time-dependent processes. A number of controversies have arisen concerning the adequacy of the consolidation hypothesis as an explanation of the various phenomena observed in different studies. We have discussed some of the evidence bearing on these issues, but many of the discrepancies in the literature are not yet understood.

Several alternative hypotheses have been offered to explain retrograde interference with memory that is produced by ECS and other amnesic agents. However, none of these alternatives adequately accounts for the diverse findings in experiments with a wide variety of learning paradigms, experimental organisms, and interference treatments. Retrograde amnesia has been observed in humans, cats, rats, mice, birds, and insects. It has been seen with massed and spaced presentation of trials, and with single and multiple learning trials involving inhibitory and active avoidance, appetitive learning, maze learning, discrimination learning, reversal learning, lever pressing, and nonsense syllables. It has been produced with ECS, drugs, SD, protein-synthesis inhibition, anoxia, audiogenic seizures, brain lesions, and brain stimulation.

Although it is possible under some special circumstances involving various combinations of experimental conditions to apply one or another of the alternative explanations to given sets of results, it is difficult to account for the diverse observations in terms of any one of them. The conditioned-inhibition hypothesis or conditioned-fear explanation, for example, seemed to explain the findings with active-avoidance learning paradigms and multiple ECS treatments. However, these explanations proved inadequate in experiments involving one-trial inhibitory-avoidance learning and single applications of ECS. In fact, they were probably responsible for the design of studies which indicated that aversive effects were obtained only with multiple ECS treatments. Thus far the chief value of these theories has been the stimulation of careful well-controlled experiments which have resulted in additional evidence of the time dependence of memory processes.

Questions concerning the manner in which amnesic agents such as ECS produce interference, and whether the amnesic effects produced by treatments as diverse as brain stimulation and protein-synthesis inhibitors result from disturbance of the same mechanism, are not as easily resolved. We know relatively little about the neural consequences of a learning trial. In fact, if we knew more about them, it would not be necessary to investigate memory storage indirectly with retroactive-interference techniques. Although it was initially speculated that memory begins as electrical activity reverberating through circuits of cortical neurons, cortical electrical activity, as reflected in the EEG, can be almost eliminated without producing complete amnesia. It may be that ECS and other agents cause amnesia as a consequence of their disruptive effect on neural electrical activity. However, studies such as Albert's [1966b], showing that pulsating polarizing currents either facilitated or interfered with memory, depending on the polarity, suggest that disruption of electrical activity is too simple an explanation to account for retrograde amnesia. Until we know more about the role of various brain structures in learning, and the manner in which biochemical and electrical activity in them is affected by experience, such questions must remain unanswered.

One conclusion that emerges from the data thus far is that the nature of the amnesic gradient is probably a function of the effectiveness of the treatment employed. It is apparent from the conflicting results of research with ECS, CO_2, and flurothyl that in studies of retrograde amnesia, as in investigations of the pharmacological effect of drugs, data indicating an amnesic effect do not provide sufficient information without an accompanying dose-response curve. Judging from the wide range of amnesic gradients observed in various studies—from no amnesia with learning-trial–ECS intervals of 30 sec to significant interference with ECS administered as long as 6 hr after learning—it is quite likely that in the first instance the amnesic treatment itself was submaximal and failed to produce complete amnesia. Of course, until more is known about the mechanisms involved in the production of amnesia we cannot accept this as a full explanation of these extremely discrepant amnesic gradients. It seems likely that controversies concerning the permanence of retrograde amnesia also stem from inadequate dose information. In experiments in which recovery has been observed it often appears that there was also relatively incomplete interference, since only partial deficits resulted in animals treated shortly after learning. Thus, although it is unlikely that this is the only factor in recovery, the degree of amnesia originally obtained appears to have some bearing on the occurrence or nonoccurrence of recovery.

The occurrence of a behavioral convulsion, however, is apparently unrelated to the production of retrograde amnesia with ECS. The fact that significant degrees of interference follow ECS administered to animals treated with anesthetic and anticonvulsant drugs, and also follow subconvulsive shock, suggests that the amnesic effects are related more to the flow of current through the brain (or through specific structures) and possible interference with EEG activity, slow potentials, or biochemical activity than to the motor aspects of the convulsion. However, since ECS and other amnesic agents produce changes in cortical and subcortical electrical activity, shifts in dc potentials, and changes in brain amine levels, it is difficult to determine whether one or all of these factors play a causal role in producing amnesia. Without further data concerning the necessary conditions for such interference, there is no way to determine which consequences of ECS, or any other amnesic agent, are actually responsible for the amnesia.

Perhaps the most interesting and potentially important area of research related to memory consolidation is that concerned with the impairment and facilitation of memory through direct manipulation of specific brain areas. It is possible in retrospect to interpret a number of studies involving electrical stimulation of the brain in terms of direct effects on memory. However, it has been only recently that investigations were designed explicitly to test the hypothesis that the stimulation of structures thought to be involved in various aspects of memory storage at increasing intervals after learning will produce graded amnesia. Most studies of retrograde amnesia have employed ECS, perhaps on the assumption that widespread disturbances in brain function were needed to produce amnesia. However, studies of single-pulse stimulation of the caudate nucleus and small lesions of the dorsal frontal cortex applied at varying intervals after learning indicate that it is possible to obtain typical gradients of retrograde amnesia through involvement of circumscribed areas of the brain. It is not known whether such effects are restricted to the basal ganglia, the reticular formation, and the limbic system, although the results of earlier studies suggest that memory interference may be obtained with manipulation of other areas as well. Because of the consistency of these results with the findings from studies utilizing ECS and other amnesic agents, it seems likely that further research with restricted brain stimulation will add greatly to our knowledge concerning the substrates of memory processes.

The results of research with protein-synthesis inhibitors are less easily understood. A number of antibiotics have been found to interfere with retention in a variety of organisms and experimental situations. However, because of the lack of consistency in experimental conditions, as well as the number of inherent variables, the role of protein synthesis in memory-storage processes is not at all clear. Studies with puromycin indicate that although learning is acquired normally under conditions of massive inhibition of protein synthesis, severe retention deficits are evidenced hours to days afterward. These results suggest that the initial stage of memory storage may not require protein synthesis, but that later phases are dependent on this biochemical substrate. There is much evidence that RNA and protein synthesis are somehow implicated in various stages of memory storage, but many of the discrepancies must be clarified before such a relationship can be accepted unequivocally.

Evidence of the time dependency of memory processes has also come from investigations of learning facilitation with posttrial applications of a variety of drugs. This line of research has been at least as controversial as that concerning the production of retrograde amnesia. However, it is clear from these studies that the administration of such substances not only reduces the number of trials required for animals to reach a given criterion of learning, but also decreases the number of errors made during acquisition. The fact that these effects are produced by treatment *after* learning makes it extremely difficult to attribute the results to drug effects on performance. As with memory interference, we know little about the mechanism of action of such substances, but the wide range of experimental conditions and organisms with which facilitation has been demonstrated argues for its generality. The more recent findings of an interaction of facilitating and interfering effects appear to substantiate the contention that both techniques affect the labile representation of experience during a period when memory storage is extremely susceptible to external manipulation.

The experimental findings reviewed suggest that there are at least two distinct stages in memory storage. The first stage involves the formation of a template of some sort that may provide a basis for the changes involved in the permanent storage of information. It is this stage of memory that is somehow susceptible to interference produced by ECS and other amnesic agents. Evidently the facilitation resulting from posttrial administration of various drugs also operates on this stage of memory, since facilitating drugs such as strychnine can attenuate the interfering effects of treatments such as ECS [McGaugh and Dawson, 1971]. Although we still know relatively little about the mechanisms affected by these treatments, recent data concerning the direct application of the facilitating drugs and stimulation to circumscribed neural structures suggests that this information is within reach. Clearly, most of the important problems in this area of research remain to be solved. It is hoped that the facts, theories, and critical analyses presented here will stimulate further investigation into the manner in which the neural representation of experience becomes firmly established.

PART TWO

READINGS IN
MEMORY CONSOLIDATION

THE EFFECTS OF DEGREE OF LEARNING AND PROBLEM DIFFICULTY ON PERSEVERATION

ROBERT THOMPSON

This study aimed to determine the relative effects of the level of learning and the difficulty of the problem on perseveration time in rats. The results of Exp. I suggest that PT increases early in practice and is then followed by a decrease with further practice. In Exp. II, PT was found to increase with the difficulty of the problem.

It has been repeatedly demonstrated that the interpolation of such treatments as ECS or anoxia selectively disrupts memories of newly acquired habits [Duncan, 1949; Ransmeier and Gerard, 1954; Thompson and Dean, 1955; Thompson and Preyer, 1956]. These data provide strong evidence for the Muller and Pilzecker [1900] perseveration theory which states that the complete establishment of the memory trace occurs at some time following training through the persistence of certain neural events. The period through which these hypothetical events act (perseveration time) may be approximated by determining the maximal interval after training at which the interpolation of an ECS still produces a significant deficit in memory [Thompson, 1957a].

It might be expected that perseveration time (PT) will be a function of a number of variables. The results obtained by Thompson and Pennington [1957], for example, suggest that PT decreases with increasing degrees of distributed practice in the original learning of the habit. In the present study, the relative effects upon PT of both the level of learning and the difficulty of the problem were investigated. Due to the character of these variables, two separate experiments were performed. Experiment I examines the effects of four levels of learning, while the effects of three problems differing in difficulty are reported in Exp. II.

I METHOD

The Ss were 160 male albino rats of the Harlan strain. At the beginning of experimental training, Ss ranged in age from 75 to 160 days. All Ss were kept in individual cages containing a constant supply of food and water. Handling was practiced three days prior to the onset of preliminary training.

A two-choice discrimination box was employed which utilized the motive of avoidance of electric shock. A detailed description of the apparatus has been presented elsewhere [Thompson and Bryant, 1955].

The cerebral shock unit was the same as that used in a previous study [Thompson and Dean, 1955]. A current strength of approximately 50 ma. lasting for .5 sec. was administered through alligator clips mounted on Ss' ears.

Preliminary training which was carried out over a period of five days was the same as that previously described [Thompson and Pryer, 1956].

The test problem involved the discrimination between horizontal and vertical stripes, the vertical striped card constituting the positive stimulus for all Ss. The thickness of the alternating black and white striations was $\frac{1}{2}$ in. A response to the positive card admitted S to the goal box, whereas a response to the locked negative card was punished. Punishment consisted of receipt of an electric shock from the grid section located below the negative stimulus card. The correction technique was used.

Four main groups of rats, each containing 40 Ss, were given 10, 20, 30, and 40 trials, respectively, on the test problem. The intertrial interval was 45 sec. The positive card was switched from the right to the left window in a prearranged random order. The specific training procedure was as follows. The S was placed into the start box and the door raised. Failure to leave the start box within 5 sec. was followed by a brief shock from the grid floor. No further shock was given unless S made an error. An error was defined as an approach response to the negative card which brought Ss' forefeet in contact with the charged grid section. Throughout this study, only initial errors were recorded.

Each main group was divided at random into four subgroups of 10 Ss each. One subgroup from each main group received a convulsive shock 30 sec. after the completion of the last training trial. The second and third subgroups from each main group were given an ECS 3 min. and 30 min., respectively, after completing the last training trial. The

TABLE 1 *Mean errors on 30 postshock trials for all subgroups*

	Trials			
Shock cond.	10	20	30	40
30 sec.	11.0	9.5	7.4	4.5
3 min.	9.3	8.3	6.6	2.9
30 min.	7.6	7.7	5.5	3.2
Control	8.0	5.6	4.3	3.2

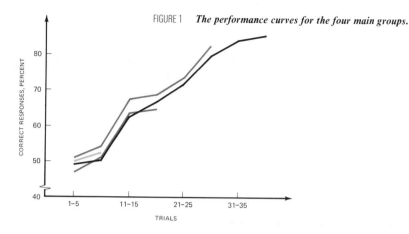

FIGURE 1 *The performance curves for the four main groups.*

CORRECT RESPONSES, PERCENT

TRIALS

TABLE 2 *Analyses of variance of postshock error scores for each level of learning*

Source of variation	df	10 trials		20 trials		30 trials		40 trials	
		MS	F	MS	F	MS	F	MS	F
Between groups	3	23.53	3.26*	26.60	4.83†	16.25	3.37*	5.15	1.37
Within groups	36	7.21		5.50		4.82		3.76	
Total	39								

*$P = .05.$ †$P = .01.$

remaining subgroup from each main group constituted the controls to which no ECS was given.

Twenty-four hours later, all Ss were given 30 trials on the same discrimination problem (45-sec. intertrial interval). The training procedure was identical to that involved in initial training. The number of errors made during this postshock period was utilized as the index of retention.

| RESULTS

Figure 1 presents the separate performance curves derived from the four main groups on the initial training trials. In terms of performance on the last 10 trials, the level of learning attained by the 10-trial group was at chance, while the 20-, 30- and 40-trial groups were approximately at the 60%, 75%, and 80% levels, respectively.

The mean error scores for all subgroups on the postshock training trials are summarized in Table 1. The convulsed Ss tended to be inferior to the controls for all levels of learning, this trend being particularly appreciable in the 20-trial group. However, the information in Table 2 shows that ECS produced significant retroactive effects when administered either after 10, 20, or 30 trials, but failed to cause any significant interference when administered after 40 trials.

For the purpose of estimating the duration of perseveration for each level of learning, the differences between the experimental and corresponding control subgroups were subjected to a t test. With respect to the 10-trial group, the Ss given an ECS 30 sec. after training made more errors than the controls ($P = .02$). The two other shock conditions, however, failed to cause any significant memory deficits. For the 20-trial group, all subgroups receiving an ECS were significantly inferior to the controls on the postshock trials ($P < .05$). Only the 30-sec. and 3-min. shock conditions produced significant deficits for the 30-trial group ($P = .01$ and $.05$, respectively). Concerning the 40-trial group, none of the differences between the experimentals and the controls approached statistical significance.

To summarize, these data suggest that, during the early phase of learning, PT increases with increasing amounts of practice. This was shown by the fact that Ss given 10 trials revealed a PT of about 30 sec., whereas Ss given 20 trials revealed a PT of at least 30 min. With additional training, however, it appears that there is a decrease in PT. Thus, 30 trials yielded a PT of about 3 min., while a PT of less than 30 sec. was produced by 40 trials.

II METHOD

The Ss were 90 experimentally naive albino rats of the Harlan strain, of which 60 were females. Their ages at the beginning of preliminary training ranged from 50 to 110 days.

On Days 1 and 2, each S was allowed to explore the goal box for periods of 15 min. Cards placed against the windows prevented S from entering the choice chamber.

On Day 3, S was trained to run from the start box through the choice chamber and into the goal box in order to avoid shock, while medium gray cards were placed against the windows through which each S was trained to run on Day 4.

On Day 5, Ss were randomly divided into three main groups of 30 Ss each. One group was trained on a position habit (Problem P), while the other two groups received training on one of two visual discrimination habits (Problems D_1 and D_2). With respect to Problem P, Ss were trained positively to the nonpreferred side. Black cards were placed against both windows for half of the Ss, while white cards were used for the remaining half. The card on the preferred side (negative) was locked throughout training. Problem D_1 was a brightness discrimination involving a white card (positive) and a black card (negative). Problem D_2 was the same as Problem D_1, save for the negative card which consisted of alternating black and white vertical stripes, the thickness of the striations being $\frac{1}{2}$ in. The positive card was randomly switched from left to right during training for both visual discrimination problems.

For all problems, a response to the positive stimulus (card or position) admitted S to the goal box, whereas a response to the locked negative stimulus (card or position) was punished. Punishment involved receipt of an electric shock from the grid section located below the negative stimulus. The specific training procedure was the same as in Exp. I. Using an intertrial interval of 45 sec., training on Day 5 was terminated when S reached the criterion of five consecutive errorless trials.

Each main group was divided into three equal subgroups of 10 Ss. Two subgroups from each main group were given an ECS 20 sec. and 15 min., respectively, following the completion of the last criterion trial. The remaining subgroup from each main group constituted the controls to which no ECS was given.

On Day 6, all Ss were given additional trials (45-sec. intertrial interval) on the same problem that was mastered on the previous day. The training procedure was identical to that involved in original learning. The Ss having Problem P received 10 trials, while Ss having either Problem D_1 or Problem D_2 received 20 trials. The number of errors committed on Day 6 was used as the index of retention.

II RESULTS

Table 3 presents the original learning scores for all subgroups. It is apparent that the three problems were of unequal difficulty. Use of the t test showed that Problem P was significantly easier than Problem D_1 ($P < .01$ for trials to criterion and errors to criterion). Similarly, Problem D_2 was more difficult than Problem D_1 ($P < .01$). To determine whether there were any significant differences in initial learning speed among the subgroups trained on the same problem, an analysis of variance was applied to both criterion measures. All Ss were far from statistical significance.

TABLE 3 *Mean trials and mean errors to criterion for all subgroups*

Shock cond.	Problem P		Problem D_1		Problem D_2	
	Trials	Errors	Trials	Errors	Trials	Errors
20 sec.	2.8	2.4	15.5	7.6	40.2	18.8
15 min.	2.8	2.0	16.8	7.3	34.4	15.2
Control	2.4	2.0	16.4	8.1	33.2	15.6

Shock cond.	Problem P			Problem D_1			Problem D_2		
	M	Diff.	t	M	Diff.	t	M	Diff.	t
20 sec.	1.3	.8	1.54	3.4	1.7	2.68*	7.7	3.5	3.30†
15 min.	.5			1.9	.2	<1.00	6.6	2.4	1.91
Control	.5			1.7			4.2		

*$P = .02$.   †$P = .01$.

TABLE 4   *Mean errors on retention trials for all subgroups*

The error scores for all subgroups on the relearning trials can be seen in Table 4. With respect to the 20-sec. shock condition, *t*s for the differences between the experimental *S*s and the corresponding controls revealed that ECS resulted in significant retroactive inhibition on Problems D_1 and D_2, but failed to cause any interference on Problem *P*. Furthermore, it is to be noted that while the 15-min. shock condition produced no apparent memory deficit on Problem D_1, it did cause a marginally significant deficit on Problem D_2 ($P = .10$). Thus, PT seems to increase with problem difficulty, varying from less than 20 sec. for Problem *P* to about 15 min. for Problem D_2.

DISCUSSION

The essential findings of these experiments are that the level of learning as well as the difficulty of the problem varies the degree to which ECS disrupts memory. This has been shown by consideration of perseveration time which represents a measure of retroactive inhibition derived from the classical Muller and Pilzecker theory. Other factors which have been found to influence the duration of perseveration are the length of the intertrial interval [Thompson and Pennington, 1957] and the age of *S* [Thompson, 1957*b*].

As previously discussed [Thompson and Pennington, 1957; Thompson and Pryer, 1956], the effects of these variables on PT may perhaps best be explained in terms of the differential accrual of perseverative activity from trial to trial. It is apparent, however, that such an explanation is only post hoc, and that adequate predictions based upon the theory must await formal statements concerning the organic nature of perseveration. Conceivably, insight into the perseverative process may come with the investigation of PT as affected by physiological variables. That such variables exist has already been shown by Pennington [1957], who recently found that PT is longer in brain-damaged rats than in normals.

This study was conducted at Louisiana State University and supported, in part, by a grant-in-aid from the Graduate Research Council. Reprinted from the *Journal of Experimental Psychology*, 1958, **55**, 496–500, by permission of the American Psychological Association.

A BRIEF TEMPORAL GRADIENT OF RETROGRADE AMNESIA INDEPENDENT OF SITUATIONAL CHANGE

DAVID QUARTERMAIN/RONALD M. PAOLINO/NEAL E. MILLER

Rats were given a single electroconvulsive shock at varying intervals after receiving a punishing shock to the feet immediately after stepping into a compartment. Significant amounts of retrograde amnesia for the memory of the punishment were shown when electroconvulsive shock was administered up to and including 30 seconds after the punishment but not at 60 seconds. This brief temporal gradient cannot be explained in terms of changed stimulus cues or learned interference analogous to retroactive inhibition.

Previous studies have shown that electroconvulsive shock (ECS) given shortly after a learning experience can interfere with the learning. This interference typically has been interpreted as a disruption of a consolidation of the memory trace [Glickman, 1961]. Two other interpretations, however, are possible: (1) that ECS reduces the amount of learning by removing the subject from the stimulus situation, and thus preventing him from adequately noticing it, and possibly from rehearsing in it, after the reinforcement has indicated its biological significance, or (2) that ECS conditions many random brain impulses to the cues involved in the immediately preceding learning and hence produces a learned interference analogous to retroactive inhibition. The purpose of this study was to secure additional information on the effects of the interval between the learning experience and ECS, and to test hypothesis 1 by substituting sudden removal for ECS, and hypothesis 2 by administering ECS after subject had been removed from the situation, a procedure which should reduce the chances for retroactive inhibition.

METHOD

Subjects were 310 male rats of the Holtzman strain, 90 to 150 days old, housed in individual wire-mesh cages and having free access to food and water. An equal number of rats from each shipment was assigned to the various groups to cancel out shipment effects. The apparatus, a modification of that described by Jarvik and Essman [1960], was a compartment 38 by 38 by 44 cm, with a vertical slot cut into one end, into which fitted

69

a start box (19 by 15 by 15 cm) which could be raised and lowered by means of a lever. A guillotine door separated the two compartments. The entire apparatus was constructed of $\frac{1}{4}$-inch (0.6-cm) Plexiglas, except for the floors, which were made of stainless steel rods $\frac{3}{32}$ inch (0.24 cm) in diameter, spaced 1.25 cm on centers. The interior was illuminated from above by a 100-watt bulb. A 60-cy a-c grid shock (GS) of 1.0-ma intensity was delivered for 2.0 seconds to the grid floor of the large compartment through a 820,000-ohm resistor connected in series with the rat. An ECS (100 ma for 0.3 sec) was delivered through small padded alligator clips, soaked in saline, attached to the animal's ears before the animal was placed in the start box. Subjects that did not exhibit tonic flexion or tonic extension in response to ECS were discarded. Durations of GS and ECS, as well as time intervals between GS and ECS, were automatically triggered and timed by a system of relays and timers. Actual intensities of GS and ECS were monitored on milliammeters.

A rat was placed in the start box and was lowered until level with the large compartment. The guillotine door was opened, activating a timer which was stopped when all four of the rat's paws were in the large compartment. The door was immediately closed and GS was delivered. Closing the door prevented retracing, which could have occurred in previous studies and confused the interpretation by making any aversive effects of ECS summate with any amnesic ones, as demonstrated by Coons and Miller [1960].

The effects of the GS-ECS interval were studied with eight experimental groups ($N = 30$, for each group) with 0.1, 1.0, 2.0, 5.0, 7.5, 15.0, 30.0, and 60.0 seconds separating presentation of GS and ECS. In all of these groups ECS was administered in the large compartment. Three control groups were also run: a "no-GS, no-ECS" group ($N = 10$), a "GS, no-ECS" group ($N = 20$), and an "ECS, no-GS" group ($N = 10$). In the "ECS, no-GS" control group, four animals were convulsed immediately after stepping into the large compartment; three, after 15 seconds; and three, after 60 seconds. (As there were no no differences among these ten animals, results for the three subgroups were combined into one group.) All animals were removed from the large compartment immediately after they had convulsed.

To test hypotheses 1 and 2, two further groups were treated as follows. In one group (black bag, no-ECS), 20 subjects were removed by hand from the large compartment and were dropped into a black cloth bag within 2 seconds of the termination of the GS. Subjects not in the bag at the end of an automatically timed 2 sec were discarded. Mean

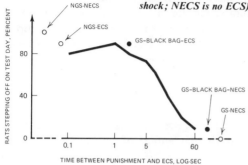

FIGURE 1 *Effects of electroconvulsive shock (ECS) as a function of GS-ECS interval and situation. The punishment was a grid shock (GS). It was administered to both "black bag" groups, one of which received ECS (NGS is no grid shock; NECS is no ECS). The time scale is logarithmic.*

time for removal from the compartment to the bag was 1.5 seconds. Subjects were left in the bag for 60 seconds. Rats of the second group (black bag, ECS 2.0 seconds) were lifted by hand from the large compartment and dropped into the bag, in which they were convulsed 2 seconds after the termination of the GS. This procedure produced a more drastic stimulus change than could be accomplished by leaving the animal in the compartment and, for example, turning off a light and a tone.

Retention was tested 24 hours later, with the same procedure as in initial training, except that no GS or ECS was administered. Retention of the avoidance response was indicated when subjects failed to step out into the large compartment within 180 seconds.

RESULTS

The percentage of subjects in each group which stepped out within the criterion time was considered a more appropriate measure than response latencies, since none of the control group receiving GS but no ECS stepped off on the test day. These data, plotted logarithmically, are shown in Fig. 1. An overall analysis of the experimental groups (the GS-ECS interval differing from one to another) indicates that the percentage of subjects failing to avoid the large compartment on the test day is inversely related to the GS-ECS interval ($\chi^2 = 75.46$, $p < .001$). Comparisons between the "GS, no-ECS" control group and the ECS groups (Fisher's exact probability test) showed: (1) significant retention deficits occurred when ECS was administered up to and including 30.0 seconds after termination of GS ($p < .05$ at 30.0 seconds), but not after 60.0 seconds ($p = .2$); (2) no significant difference between the "ECS, no-GS" and the "no-ECS, no-GS" control groups ($p = .5$), indicating that the single ECS did not have aversive properties. The "black bag, no ECS" group was similar to the 60-sec group and not reliably different from the one receiving no ECS. The "black bag, ECS 2.0 seconds" group was significantly different ($p = .01$) from the control group with no ECS, and not significantly different ($p = .2$) from the group given ECS at the same interval in the apparatus itself.

When the data are plotted in terms of latencies, the curve is essentially the same, except for the fact that the "0.1 sec" group is slightly above, instead of below, the "1.0 second" group. The mean number of bolluses excreted by each group also yielded a curve similar to that in Fig. 1, except that it was inverted. This would be expected, since memory for the shock should produce fear, and hence increase the number of feces.

These results demonstrate that as the GS-ECS interval is increased there is a significant increase in the percentage of subjects avoiding the large compartment, and that a delay of 30.0 seconds is the maximum interval at which significant amnesic effects are produced under the present conditions. The absence of any impairment of retention in the "black bag, no ECS" group indicates that the rapid change of stimulus cues used in this experiment cannot account for the impaired avoidance learning. Although it is possible that ECS produces a still more drastic change of stimulus cues than removal to the black bag, if stimulus change is an important determinant of the retention deficits, then the present drastic procedure should have produced at least some effects.

It is also clear from the results of the "black bag, ECS 2.0 second" group that the effects of ECS are independent of location of the rat at the time of administration of ECS. These results, utilizing a drastic change of stimulus cues, confirm those which Leonard and Zavala [1964] found with a less drastic one. It would appear, therefore, that the retention deficits produced by ECS in this study cannot be accounted for in terms of a learned interference analogous to retroactive inhibition, and are the result of a true amnesia, probably brought about by physiological changes.

The brief GS-ECS interval necessary for amnesia in this study shows excellent agreement with the temporal curve recently observed by Chorover and Schiller [1965]. However, since other studies have shown significant retention deficits with much longer ECS delays, this leaves a puzzle. It is possible that these differences may be in part the result of different task and procedural variables employed in one-trial situations. For example, studies which have shown significant ECS effects with long GS-ECS intervals have generally used learning tasks in which the subjects have received considerable training under deprivation of food or water before the punishment shock is administered [Weissman, 1963; Heriot and Coleman, 1962]. It is possible that the greater response strength before punishment in these studies is a factor determining the effective ECS interval. On the other hand, it is possible that different stages of the consolidation process are disrupted by different intensities of ECS or by different types of treatment. Further information on the foregoing possibilities should give clues to the physical basis for the memory process.

Supported by grant MH02949 to Neal E. Miller from the National Institute of Mental Health. Reprinted from *Science*, 1965, **149**, 1116–1118, by permission of the American Association for the Advancement of Science.

EFFECTS OF ELECTROSHOCK ON MEMORY: AMNESIA WITHOUT CONVULSIONS

JAMES L. McGAUGH/HERBERT P. ALPERN

Mice received a single training trial on an inhibitory avoidance task and a retention trial 24 hours later. Electroshock stimulation, administered 25 seconds after the training trial, produced amnesia even if the convulsion was prevented by ether anesthesia. The amnesia produced by such shock is apparently due to the electric current and not to the convulsion.

Investigators of time-dependent processes in memory storage have made extensive use of electroconvulsive shock (ECS) as a technique for producing retrograde amnesia. A single such ECS produces amnesia for events that occur shortly before the treatment [Leonard and Zavala, 1964; Madsen and McGaugh, 1961; Weissman, 1963; Quartermain et al. 1965]. The general interpretation of this finding has been that electroshock current interferes with relatively long-lasting processes underlying memory storage. Overall, the evidence is highly consistent with this interpretation [McGaugh and Petrinovich, 1966]. Other interpretations have stressed the possibility that the behavioral effects are due to the convulsions rather than to the current [Lewis and Adams, 1963; Lewis and Maher, 1965]. The effects produced by a *series* of shock treatments (for example, attenuation of a conditioned emotional response; aversive and disruptive effects) do, in fact, seem to be due to the convulsions. The disrupting effects of a series of shocks are not obtained if the shocks are administered while the animals are under ether anesthesia [Friedman, 1953; Hunt, 1965; Stone and Walker, 1949]; the anesthesia prevents both the convulsions and the behavioral effects.

We have now investigated the amnesic effects of single electro-shocks administered to mice under ether anesthesia. Our findings indicate that elicitation of a convulsion is not a necessary condition for the production of amnesia. Our evidence strengthens the idea that electroconvulsive shock produces retrograde amnesia by direct interference with processes of memory storage.

METHOD

Two hundred Swiss-Webster mice (60 to 70 days old) were used as subjects. All animals were given two trials, separated by 24 hours, on an inhibitory, avoidance-learning task [Essman and Alpern, 1964]. On each trial a mouse was placed on a small (2.25 by 6.25 cm) metal platform extending from the outside wall of a box and directly in front of a hole (3.75 cm in diameter) leading to the darkened interior of the box. A 40-watt bulb was located 19 cm above the platform. The apparatus was placed on the edge of a table so that the platform was approximately 1 m from the floor of the room. All mice were given one "training" trial and one retention test trial 24 hours later. On each trial the time the mouse spent on the platform before it stepped into the box was recorded.

The mice were divided into ten groups, each with ten males and ten females. The treatments given the different groups are shown in Fig. 1. Mice in six groups (left bar of each pair) received a foot shock of approximately 3 ma as they stepped from the small platform into the box. The controls received no other treatment.

The "ether" animals were placed in a desiccator that contained cotton saturated with approximately 10 ml of diethyl ether immediately after the trial and were removed 25 seconds later. The anesthesia was sufficient to cause loss of consciousness (as indicated by complete ataxia) for approximately 1 minute. Two groups were given electroshocks 1 hour after the trial. Mice in one of these groups were anesthetized prior to stimulation and were completely anesthetized at the time shock was administered. Two other groups were given electroshock 25 seconds after the training trial; one of these groups was anesthetized with ether before stimulation. The electroshock consisted of a current of approximately 20 ma, delivered for 200 msec, by way of corneal electrodes. During electroshock stimulation the mouse was held in the experimenter's hand. The shock elicited tonic convulsions, with full leg extension, in all unanesthetized mice. The current elicited only a slight and brief twitch in the anesthetized mice.

Four groups (right-hand bar in each pair shown) did *not* receive foot shock as they stepped into the box on the first trial. The controls received no treatment. One group was anesthetized for 25 seconds. Another group was anesthetized for 25 seconds and then given electroshock. The fourth group was given electroshock 25 seconds after the

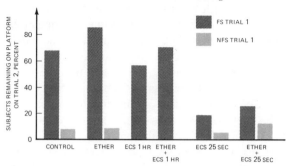

FIGURE 1   *Effects of electroconvulsive shock on one-trial avoidance learning.*

trial. These four groups served as controls for possible effects of ether and shock when administered without prior foot shock.[1]

RESULTS

On the first trial the median step-through latency was 2 seconds. Ninety-six percent of the mice entered the box in less than 10 seconds. Figure 1 shows the percentage of mice in each group remaining on the platform for 10 seconds or longer on the 24-hour retention test. This criterion was attained by over 50 percent of the mice in four of the groups given foot shock on the first trial: controls (foot shock only), ether, ECS at 1 hour, and ether and ECS at 1 hour. The differences among the four groups did not approach statistical significance ($H = 2.42$, $df = 3$, $p > .05$; Kruskal-Wallis test). Thus, no amnesia was found with ether, delayed ECS, or delayed ECS administered during ether anesthesia.[2] The results shown on the right in Fig. 1 indicate that the ether and ECS treatments did not affect the second trial latencies of mice which were not given foot shock on the first trial.

The results obtained for the two groups of mice given electroshock 25 seconds after the foot shock indicate that electroshock produced amnesia even when it was administered while the animals were anesthetized. The latencies of the two groups were similar; for both groups they differed significantly from those of all the other four foot-shocked groups ($p < .01$), but they did not differ significantly from those of the four groups which were not given foot shock on the first trial ($H = 8.03$, $df = 5$, $p > .05$).

These results indicate quite clearly that the retrograde amnesia produced by electroshock is due to the current and does not depend

[1]Thirteen mice succumbed following the ether or shock treatments. The losses were distributed throughout the groups.

[2]Previous research [e.g., Pearlman et al., 1961] has shown that under some conditions ether anesthesia can produce retrograde amnesia. The anesthesia procedures of the present study would not, however, be expected to produce amnesia.

upon the elicitation of a behavioral convulsion. The findings are, of course, completely inconsistent with the suggestion that the retrograde effect of electroconvulsive shock is due to conditioning of competing responses which are elicited by the shock [Lewis and Adams, 1963; Lewis and Maker, 1965]. The findings of this study are consistent with other evidence [Ottosson, 1960; Weissman, 1965] that prevention of tonic convulsions does not attenuate retrograde amnesia induced by electroconvulsive shock. Subsequent attempts to understand the basis of the amnesic effect of such shocks should focus on the neurophysiological and biochemical effects of electroshock stimulation.

Supported by NIH research grants MH 07015 and MH 10261. Reprinted from *Science*, 1966, **152**, 665–666, by permission of the American Association for the Advancement of Science.

INTERFERENCE WITH ONE-TRIAL APPETITIVE AND AVERSIVE LEARNING BY ETHER AND ECS

MICHAEL J. HERZ

Studies were undertaken to explore the effects of two amnesic agents on appetitive and aversive learning in the same apparatus. Ss given electroconvulsive shock (ECS) within 80 sec or 15 min of punishing shock and Ss administered ECS or ether 20 sec after the end of a 60-sec water-reinforcement period evidenced significant deficits on retention tests. The footshock-ECS Ss showed significantly shorter latencies and greater activity than Ss given footshock alone. Conversely, Ss given water reinforcement and ECS had longer latencies and less activity than Ss given only water reinforcement. The results support the contention that postrial ECS and ether disrupt perseverative neural processes representing appetitive as well as aversive learning and suggest the possibility that memory consolidation takes place at different rates for the two types of tasks.

The results of studies demonstrating interference with learning by means of electroconvulsive shock (ECS) and other agents have, for the most part, been interpreted as demonstrating interference with memory [McGaugh, 1966; John, 1967]. Typically such investigations indicate that these experimental treatments, when administered after a learning trial, attenuate or abolish evidence of retention on later test trials. Although various alternative interpretations have been offered to explain the results of experiments showing retroactive interference with learning, they have been based primarily on the effects of ECS and other treatments on aversive learning. Coons and Miller [1960], for example, argued that the observed interference of ECS with acquisition of active-avoidance learning was the result of the aversive qualities of the treatment, since its administration following extinction trials had a facilitating rather than disruptive effect. Lewis and Maher [1965], in their "conditioned-inhibition" interpretation of retrograde amnesia, hypothesized that the unconsciousness resulting from ECS is an unconditioned response, and that a weakened version of loss of consciousness—i.e., relaxation and/or lowered activity level—becomes conditioned to the cues present at the time ECS is administered. This explanation was also intended primarily to account for the results of ECS on active-avoidance learning, where lowered activity and slower running were the behavioral effects interpreted as interference.

Although there have been several studies demonstrating retrograde amnesia in appetitive learning situations, the degree of interference observed with ECS given at specific intervals following such learning has differed from study to study. Tenen [1965a, 1965b] found that ECS given as long as 60 min after a one-trial water-reinforced learning trial produced interference with retention. Schiller and Chorover [1967], however, found retention deficits only if ECS was administered within 1.5 sec, but not longer than 90 sec, after food-reinforced maze-learning trials.

Because of the inconsistencies in the results of investigations utilizing different experimental paradigms as well as a variety of interference techniques, it was felt that a comparison of the effect of several amnesic agents on different types of learning would add much to our knowledge concerning the consolidation of memory. Consequently, the present research was undertaken to compare the degree of interference produced by ether and ECS administered at various intervals after single appetitive and aversive learning trials in the same experimental apparatus.

METHOD

Sixty-day-old male Swiss-Webster albino mice (12 to 14 per cage) were maintained on a 23-hr water-deprivation schedule for at least five days prior to the beginning of experimentation. The Ss had access to dry food pellets at all times and were given water bottles for 1 hr each day.

The apparatus consisted of a 10.8 × 10.8 chamber 6.1 cm high, with a 2.7 × 2.2 cul-de-sac 4.5 cm deep centered on one wall 1 cm above the floor. A metal drinking cup was recessed into the floor of the cul-de-sac. A start box 11.1 cm long and 2.2 cm wide, with a guillotine door, was attached to the chamber on the wall opposite the cul-de-sac. A more detailed description of the apparatus is given by Herz and Peeke [1968].

Ether anesthesia was induced in a 1,000-ml glass container into which Ss were placed until they had reached respiratory arrest. The chamber rested in a water bath, which was maintained at 30 to 35°C.

Electroconvulsive shock was produced by passing 770 volts (60-Hz sine wave, 18.5 ma) through the animal via earclips (covered with electrode paste) for 800 msec. All ether and ECS Ss were artificially respirated until breathing appeared stable. Mortality rates were 18 percent with ECS and 35 percent with ether in each of the following experiments.

Experiment 1   The first experiment dealt with the effects of the two agents on passive-avoidance learning. The Ss were introduced into the start box on the experimental day, and the latency to the first head poke (interrupting a photocell beam in the cul-de-sac) and cup touch (recorded with a drinkometer) were recorded. Experimental Ss received a 2-ma dc shock (between the cup and the metal floor) when the empty cup was touched, and after a 60-sec interval they were removed from the chamber. Control Ss received no shock but were removed 60 sec after the first cup touch and were either returned to their home cages (N-N) or administered ether (N-E) or ECS (N-ECS) within 25 sec after removal. Experimental-group Ss were either returned to their cages (S-N) or administered ether or ECS within 25 sec (S-E_1 and S-ECS_1) or 15 min (S-E_{15} and S-ECS_{15}). On the test day, 24 hr later, the Ss were reintroduced into the start box, and the same latencies, as well as frequencies and durations, of head pokes and cup-touch sessions and the frequencies of discrete cup touches (licks), were recorded during the 3-min test period.

Nonparametric analyses of variance (Kruskal-Wallis) performed on the experimental-day latency scores of all eight groups (22 Ss per group) revealed no significant differences among the groups. However, additional analyses of variance of each of the seven dependent measures recorded on the test were significant ($p < .001$ in all cases). Significant learning was demonstrated on all the measures; that is, latencies were greater and frequencies and duration were lower for shocked controls S-N than for nonshocked controls N-N, N-E, and N-ECS (Mann-Whitney U test; $p < .001$ in all cases). Since similar results were obtained with all the measures, only the data for head-poke latency, the most

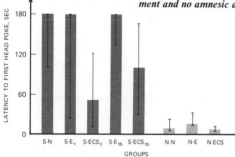

FIGURE 1   *Medians and interquartile ranges of latencies to the first head poke on the test day. The first letter of the abbreviated group designation represents the reinforcement condition (W, water; S, shock; and N, no reinforcement), and the second letter or set of letters represents the amnesic agent (E, ether; ECS, electroconvulsive shock; and N, no amnesic agent). The subscript indicates the time between the initiation of reinforcement and the amnesic treatment (to the closest minute). Thus S-E$_1$ indicates shock + ether administered within 80 sec of the first shock, W-ECS$_1$ indicates water + ECS administered within 80 sec of the initiation of drinking (in experiment 2), and N-N denotes no reinforcement and no amnesic agent.*

sensitive indicator, are presented here (see Figure 1). ECS administered within 25 sec of removal from the apparatus (85 sec after 2-ma shock) resulted in significantly shorter latencies for shocked ECS Ss than for the shock-alone controls S-N ($p < .003$ in all cases), an indication that ECS had effectively attenuated retention of the previously punished response. However, latencies of the animals given ECS 85 sec after shock (S-ECS$_1$) differed significantly from those of nonshocked controls, N-N, N-E, and N-ECS ($p < .001$ in all cases), indicating partial retention of the passive-avoidance experience. There were no significant differences between the nonshocked controls N-N and nonshocked ECS controls N-ECS on any of the measures, indicating that a single ECS had no aversive effect on performance.

ECS administered within 15 min of the shock-avoidance trial (S-ECS$_{15}$) resulted in significantly briefer head-poke latencies than those observed in shocked controls SN ($p < .03$), indicating partial attenuation of the aversive experience. However, for all these measures the group given ECS after 85 sec (S-ECS$_1$) evidenced significantly greater attenuation ($p < .025$). No interference was produced with ether at either interval.

Experiment 2   The second experiment paralleled the first, except that appetitive learning was investigated. The Ss were run as in the initial study, but water was available in the drinking cup for the experimental groups. All Ss were allowed access to the full cup for 60 sec (during

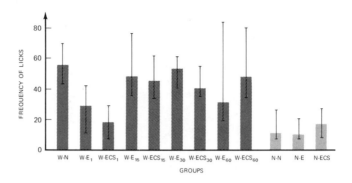

FIGURE 2 *Medians and interquartile ranges of lick frequencies on the test session.*

which they spent 35 to 40 sec drinking and consumed approximately $\frac{3}{4}$ cc of water) and were then removed from the apparatus. The Ss in the water-only group W-N received no further treatment. Additional water-reinforced groups were administered ether or ECS within 25 sec (W-E$_1$ and W-ECS$_1$), 15 min (W-E$_{15}$ and W-ECS$_{15}$), 30 min (W-E$_{30}$ and W-ECS$_{30}$), or 60 min (W-E$_{60}$ and W-ECS$_{60}$). Nonreinforced control groups (N-N, N-E, and N-ECS) were the same as in the first experiment. Twenty-four hours later a 3-min test was conducted (with no water present), and latency and frequency data were recorded as before.

As in the first experiment, overall analysis of variance of latency scores indicated no significant difference among the 12 groups (22 Ss per group) on the experimental day. Analyses of variance of the various measures on the test day resulted in values significant beyond .01 level. In addition, comparisons of the water-reinforced group W-N with the nonreinforced groups N-N, N-E, and N-ECS revealed significantly briefer latencies ($p < .03$) and greater frequencies and durations ($p < .001$) for the reinforced group, indicating that the brief drinking experience was sufficient to differentiate among the originally comparable groups.

Since similar results were obtained with all the measures, only the data for licks are presented here (see Figure 2). ECS administered within 25 sec of removal from the apparatus 85 sec after the start of drinking resulted in significant interference with retention of the drinking experience; the W-ECS$_1$ group evidenced significantly fewer licks than the W-N group ($p < .001$). In addition, there were no significant differences between the W-ECS$_1$ group and the nonreinforced control groups N-N, N-E, and N-ECS, indicating no retention of the drinking experience. Although the difference between groups W-N and W-ECS$_{15}$ approached significance, ECS administered 15 min after the

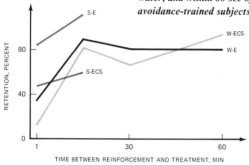

FIGURE 3 *Percent of retention as a function of the time intervening between reinforcement and administration of amnesic agent. The points graphed at 1 min represent treatment administered within 80 sec of the initiation of drinking, the beginning of the 60-sec period of access to water, and within 80 sec of the first shock in the case of avoidance-trained subjects.*

drinking trial had no significant effect; slight but significant attenuation was observed with the 30-min ECS group on frequency of discrete cup touches and duration of cup-touch sessions, suggesting partial interference.

The group administered ether within 25 sec (W-E$_1$) differed significantly from the W-N group ($p < .04$), indicating that some attenuation of the drinking experience had been obtained. However, in all these measures the W-E$_1$ group differed significantly from the nonreinforced groups N-N and N-E ($p < .01$), indicating less interference with ether than ECS administered at the same interval (W-ECS$_1$). There were no significant differences between the water-reinforced group W-N and any of the remaining ether groups on any of the measures.

A graphic comparison of the effectiveness of the two agents in the present appetitive and aversive learning situation suggests that in spite of the failure to obtain reliable interference at some of the learning-trial–amnesic-agent intervals, strong evidence for a graded effect was obtained. Figure 3 represents the amnesic effect obtained with the most sensitive measure in each of the two experiments. In the appetitive situation the frequency-of-licks measure yielded the greatest degree of retrograde amnesia, while latency to head poke on the test day reflected the maximal attenuation in the inhibitory-avoidance paradigm. The percent of retention graphed here is the ratio of the level of performance achieved by each experimental group to that obtained by the baseline water- or shock-reinforced group for the appropriate study and was derived as follows:

$$\text{Percent retention} = 100 \, \frac{X_{\text{W-ECS}_1} - X_{\text{N-N}}}{X_{\text{W-N}} - X_{\text{N-N}}}$$

where $X_{\text{W-ECS}_1}$ = the mean of group W-ECS$_1$ or any experimental group, $X_{\text{N-N}}$ = the mean of group N-N, and $X_{\text{W-N}}$ = the mean of group W-N for experiment 2 or group S-N for experiment 1.

Although the gradients appear to differ for the two types of learning, it is not certain that this represents a true difference in the rate of consolidation between appetitive and aversive learning. Shocked animals in the shortest learning-to-ECS group had an interval of approximately 80 sec between shock and ECS, while comparable water-reinforced subjects could have had as little as 20 sec between termination of drinking (by removal from the apparatus) and ECS. Hence it is possible that the difference in the gradients is only a reflection of differences in the reinforcement-ECS interval. However, the difference obtained between the two learning situations appears to be greater than could be accounted for by this small 60-sec difference.

DISCUSSION

The results of these experiments indicate that it is possible to obtain retrograde amnesia in situations utilizing both appetitive and aversive motivation. In addition, they demonstrate that when the experimental conditions for the two types of reinforcement are equated as closely as possible, the degree of amnesia produced at various intervals after learning appears to depend on the type of motivation, as well as on the type of amnesic agent. Although neither of these findings is new, the observation that the rate of consolidation apparently differs for the two types of learning in the same experimental situation suggests a possible explanation for the variable gradients which have been obtained in various investigations of retrograde amnesia. For example, the maximum interval following learning at which it has been possible to produce retrograde amnesia with ECS ranges from 30 sec or less with rats [Chorover and Schiller, 1965; Quartermain, et al., 1965] to 6 hr with mice [Kopp et al., 1966]. It is possible that the observed discrepancies reflect species differences, but the results of the present investigation also raise the possibility that task variables such as the type and magnitude of reinforcement, such as footshock intensity, may be equally important. The relevance of differences between tasks was indicated some time ago by Thompson [1958a], who observed that ECS administered immediately after learning produced greater interference after complex learning than after simple discrimination learning.

Although ether effectively interfered with retention for appetitive learning when it was administered within 80 sec after initiation of drinking, it produced no attenuation of inhibitory-avoidance learning. This result is difficult to interpret in view of observations that interference with inhibitory-avoidance learning can be obtained with ether administered 5 to 10 min after the learning trial [Pearlman et al., 1961; Pearlman, 1966], and that ether administered immediately after a single inhibitory-avoidance learning trial can abolish evidence of retention as completely as ECS [Herz et al., 1966]. It has been demonstrated that the ambient temperature at which ether is administered is an important variable in ether-induced retrograde amnesia [Herz et al., 1966; Alpern and Kimble, 1967], and in the present investigation relatively high temperatures were employed (30 to 35°C)[1] to maximize such effects. The observed interference with appetitive learning produced by ether under the conditions of this investigation, however, suggests that the difference between the two tasks may have contributed to the difference in the effectiveness of ether as an amnesic agent.

The differential effectiveness of the two amnesic agents on the two tasks is consistent with earlier observations that under optimal conditions ECS may produce retrograde amnesia when it is administered hours after learning, whereas ether appears to be relatively ineffective when it is administered more than 10 min after learning. Recent data suggest that the different amnesia gradients observed in various studies may reflect the dose dependence of retrograde amnesia. Alpern and McGaugh [1968] have demonstrated that the degree of amnesia produced by ECS is a function of the duration of the ECS, with longer durations producing greater degrees of interference. In addition, Miller [1968] observed that higher ECS intensities produced amnesia at much longer learning-ECS intervals than did lower intensities. These results, together with those of the present investigation, suggest that the degree of retrograde amnesia produced under any given set of experimental conditions—the specific task, the amnesic-agent dosage, and the species—is dependent on an interaction between the rate of consolidation for the task and the degree of interference with that task by the amnesic agent.

It is difficult to interpret these findings in terms of the hypothesis of ECS-produced fear [Coons and Miller, 1960] or conditioned inhibition [Lewis and Maher, 1965]. Both these hypotheses would predict that administration of amnesic agents would have similar effects with both approach and avoidance learning. The conditioned-inhibition hypothesis, for example, maintains that the interference produced by amnesic agents, especially ECS, is the result of relaxation conditioned to the

[1]Temperatures such as these closely approximate the boiling point of ether (34.6°C) and raise the possibility that the ether concentration was at or near 100 percent. While non-treated ether control animals (N-E) did not appear debilitated, it is quite probable that they were somewhat hypoxic. Further studies, in addition to stating concentration or partial-pressure data, should investigate the possibility that the observed amnesic effects of this drug are independent of the consequent hypoxia.

cues of the experimental apparatus. Although amnesic treatments were administered outside the apparatus in the present studies, making it difficult to establish conditioned relaxation, we would anticipate from this theory that whether the reinforcement conditions are appetitive or aversive, the amnesic agents should effect the dependent measures in the same way. However, the results actually produced were in opposite directions. Whereas the agents administered after water reinforcement increased latencies and decreased frequency and duration-measure scores, their application after shock decreased latencies and increased scores obtained on the other variables.

In summary, the results of the present investigation indicate that retrograde amnesia can be obtained as much as 80 sec or longer after both appetitive and aversive learning trials, considerably longer than the brief intervals observed by Chorover and Schiller [1965] and Quartermain et al. [1965]. In addition, these observations suggest that the rate of memory consolidation varies as a function of the type of learning task and that the degree of amnesia obtained depends on an interaction between the consolidation rate for the specific task and the effective dosage of the amnesic agent for that task. Finally, the differences in the degree of amnesia observed in the two types of learning situations are not explained by the aversive qualities of the amnesic agents or by the conditioned-inhibition hypothesis; rather, such differences appear to support the contention that these amnesic agents produce interference through modification of the time-dependent processes involved in memory formation.

An earlier version of this article appeared in the *Journal of Neurobiology*, 1969, **1**, 111–122. Reprinted by permission of John Wiley & Sons, Inc.

KINETICS OF MEMORY CONSOLIDATION: ROLE OF AMNESIC TREATMENT PARAMETERS

ARTHUR CHERKIN

The consolidation theory states that with the passage of time the engram of a recent learning experience grows increasingly resistant to disruption by amnesic treatment. The time required to reach complete resistance ("consolidation time") is a controversial issue; current estimates range from 10^1 to 10^5 sec. The present study suggests a parsimonious interpretation of the divergence, namely, that weak amnesic treatments fail to block memory consolidation but do slow its rate, so that post-treatment consolidation inflates the retention scores measured 24 hr later and leads to variably shortened "consolidation times."

This study utilizes 2880 neonate chicks trained in a one-trial avoidance paradigm. Retrograde amnesia was induced by treatment with flurothyl ($CF_3CH_2OCH_2CF_3$) vapor. Apparent "consolidation times" determined by conventional data analysis varied widely as a function of flurothyl concentration and exposure time, ranging from 4 min under weak amnesic conditions (0.85 percent flurothyl; 1-min exposure) to 24 hr under strong conditions (1.7 percent flurothyl; 8-min exposure). With 1.7 percent flurothyl, the consolidation half-time was found to be 9.8 hr.

The brain takes time to consolidate information input into a durable memory trace. How much time has yet to be settled; estimates based on clinical data and retrograde amnesia experiments range from seconds to days [Booth, 1967; Rosenzweig and Leiman, 1968]. Weiskrantz [1966] has pointed out that "it is extremely difficult to discover any consistent factor which would account for the differences in maximum interval over which retrograde amnesia extends" and has suggested that the explanation is to be found in impairment of memory retrieval rather than of consolidation. I propose the alternative interpretation that the responsible factor is a methodological factor, namely, the use of in-complete amnesic treatments that decrease the rate of consolidation but do not stop it, so that retention measured 24 hr later is inflated by post-treatment consolidation and misinterpreted as reflecting a steep consolidation gradient.

Glickman [1961] postulated that "the interval following a learning trial, during which time interference with retention can be produced, is a direct function of the degree of physiological severity of the interpolated procedure (amnesic treatment)." The severity of ECS (electroconvulsive shock) treatment is a function of current and duration. There are reports that the critical factor is duration but not current [Alpern and McGaugh, 1968], or current but not duration [Miller, 1968], and that at a constant duration amnesia is current-dependent [Weissman, 1963, 1964, 1965; Miller, 1968; Jarvik and Kopp, 1967b; Dorfman and Jarvik, 1968b; Pagano et al., 1969; Lee-Teng, 1969; Ray and Barrett, 1969a] or current-independent [Paolino et al., 1966; Lee-Teng, 1967]. Dose-dependence has been reported with convulsant drugs [Weissman, 1967], and concentration-dependence [Quinton, 1966; Alpern and Kimble, 1967] and duration-dependence [Paolino et al., 1966; Quinton, 1966] have been reported with anesthetic agents. This report describes the concentration-dependence and duration-dependence of retrograde amnesia induced in chicks by inhalation of flurothyl, a chemoconvulsant known to be amnesic in mice [Alpern and Kimble, 1967; Bohdanecky et al., 1968]. The results confirm that interference can be produced 24 hr after a learning experience [Alpern and Kimble, 1967; Nieschulz, 1967] and suggest a quantitative interpretation of variable consolidation gradients within the framework of consolidation theory.

METHOD

Neonate chicks are advantageous for quantitative memory studies; they peck a suitable target but learn in one trial to avoid that target if it is coated with an aversive liquid when first pecked [Cherkin and Lee-Teng, 1965; Lee-Teng and Sherman, 1966]. We used 2880 two-day-old White Leghorn cockerels (Kimber K155), individually housed in cartons 8.5 cm diameter by 16.5 cm deep. The target was a 3×5-mm microminiature lamp (5 v rating, operated at 2.6 v) cemented to the tip of a 3.5×200-mm plastic tube and coated with liquid methyl anthranilate $(NH_2C_6H_4COOCH_3, Givaudan)$.[1] Flurothyl $(CF_3CH_2OCH_2CF_3$; b.p. $63.9°C)$ was obtained from Ohio Medical Products.

Environmental conditions The carton temperature was 32.5 to 34.5°C, the relative humidity was 40 to 46 percent, the illumination was 23 footcandles, and the masking white noise level was 76 db. Chicks were acclimated to the carton for 2 hr before the training trial. Each chick remained in its carton throughout the experiment and was not fed, watered, or touched.

Experimental and control groups Three parameters were varied: (1) interval between training trial and flurothyl treatment, termed the *training-treatment interval* (4 to 2880 min), (2) *concentration of flurothyl vapor* (0.43 to 3.0% v/v), and (3) duration of exposure to the vapor, termed the *exposure time* (1 to 16 min).[2] For each experiment on a batch of 240 chicks, the training-treatment interval and the flurothyl concentration were constant, while the exposure time was varied. Five experimental groups ($N = 40$) from a single shipment had exposure

[1]Dr. Morely R. Kare kindly suggested this repellant.

[2]The operational interval between training and addition of liquid flurothyl was increased by 1 min to allow for uptake and distribution of flurothyl, as estimated from the latency of opisthotonos. The operational exposure time was decreased by 1 min for the same reason. The stated concentrations are nominal; actual concentrations were reduced by diffusion through the carton and uptake in chick tissues. Monitoring by vapor phase chromatography and infrared spectrophotometry indicated a loss of approximately 2.5%/min. The relative partial pressures at the site of action remain the same as the nominal concentrations, standing in the ratios 3.0:1.7:0.85:0.43. The mean induction times ($\pm$ s.d.) for tonic extension were: 59.2 ± 12.0 sec in 0.85% flurothyl, 39.6 ± 8.0 sec in 1.7% flurothyl, and 24.6 ± 5.1 sec in 3.0% flurothyl. The CD_{50} (concentration convulsing 50% of chicks within 10 min, and 95% confidence limits) was 0.40% (0.33 to 0.49) in cartons and 0.49% (0.44 to 0.54) in glass; the lethal concentration (LD_{50}) was 10.3% (8.6 to 12.5) in cartons and 10.1% (9.2 to 11.2) in glass.

times of 1, 2, 4, 8, or 16 min; a sixth group ($N = 40$) received no flurothyl treatment and served as a nontreated control.

Training trial The training was one-trial avoidance conditioning. A transparent plastic cover with a 3-cm circular aperture was centered over the chick carton. The microminiature lamp was dipped into methyl anthranilate, passed through the aperture, and hand-held approximately 1 cm in front of the beak. A timer was started when the chick oriented to the lamp, typically within 0.5 sec. Ten sec later the lamp was withdrawn. The latency of the first peck was recorded to the nearest 0.1 sec; the range of median latencies in 70 groups was 0.8 to 1.9 sec. Six per cent of chicks failed to peck in 10 sec; they were replaced to maintain 40 trained chicks per group.

Amnesic treatment Liquid flurothyl was dispensed into each carton and a tight lid was applied. The volume of 21, 42, 84, or 150 μl was calculated to produce a vapor containing 0.43, 0.85, 1.7, or 3.0% v/v flurothyl, respectively. Full tonic convulsions with opisthotonos occurred in all chicks treated with 42 to 150 μl of flurothyl. After 1, 2, 4, 8, or 16 min (all plus 1 min for uptake and distribution) the flurothyl vapor was replaced by room air.

Test trial Conditions for the memory retention test, applied 20 to 24 hr after flurothyl treatment, were identical with training conditions except that the lamp was dry. All testing was "blind"; each carton was coded with a random number, the cartons were mixed, and the code was not broken until the results were recorded.

The criterion of amnesia was a peck at the lamp within 10 sec. The "experimental score" is the percentage of a group of flurothyl-treated chicks that met this criterion. The "control score" is the corresponding percentage of a parallel group of nontreated control chicks. The control score varied from day to day (Table 1). An "induced peck score" was defined to represent amnesia assignable to the flurothyl treatment, as follows: induced peck score = 100 (experimental score − control score/100 − control score).

RESULTS
Learned avoidance response The anthranilate-induced inhibition of pecking was established within the 10-sec training trial; the median number of pecks at the anthranilate-coated lamp was two, compared with seven at a water-coated lamp [Bailey et al., 1969]. The learned avoidance persisted at least nine days [Cherkin, 1970a].

Flurothyl concentration, % v/v	Training-treatment interval, min	Proportion pecking at test trial*				p†	Induced peck score‡
		Experimental		Control			
		N	%	N	%		
0.43	4	120	38.4	40	27.5	0.3	14.9
	64	120	23.3	40	22.5	>0.9	1.0
0.85	4	120	92.5	40	20.0	0.001	90.6
	64	120	58.3	40	15.0	0.001	50.9
	256	120	58.3	40	37.5	0.03	33.3
	1440	118	39.8	40	22.5	0.08	22.3
1.7	4	114	97.4	40	30.0	0.001	96.2
	64	119	86.5	40	22.5	0.001	82.6
	256	115	69.5	40	35.0	0.001	53.2
	1440	113	56.6	40	27.5	0.002	40.2
	2880	110	24.5	38	26.3	>0.9	−2.4
3.0	256	96§	59.4	40	20.0	0.001	49.3§

*Experimental groups were treated with flurothyl vapor for 4, 8, or 16 min; control groups were not treated.

†Significance level of the difference between experimental and control groups (χ^2 test with Yates' correction).

‡Equals 100 (experimental % − control %) ÷ (100 − control %). The pooled score is the mean of the scores at 4, 8, and 16 min, weighted for number of chicks (N).

§Only 28 chicks were available for the 3.0 percent 16-min group; of these, nine did not survive this severe flurothyl treatment. The unweighted mean is 52.3 percent.

A dissimilar target (a 3-mm stainless steel ball fixed to a 1-mm wire) elicited prompt pecking in chicks trained to avoid the anthranilate lamp, proving that peck performance was unimpaired by methyl anthranilate and that the learned avoidance was not a generalized avoidance response [Cherkin, 1970b]. The possibility that flurothyl interfered with peck performance rather than with memory was ruled out in separate experiments; for example, of 89 anthranilate-trained flurothyl-treated chicks that avoided the lamp, 88 pecked the ball.

Retrograde amnesia It is conventional to consider that retrograde amnesia is exhibited when the raw experimental response differs significantly from the raw control response in the predicted direction [Alpern and McGaugh, 1968; Miller, 1968; Paolino et al., 1966; Alpern and Kimble, 1967; Bohdanecky et al., 1968; Lee-Teng and Sherman, 1966; Quartermain et al., 1965]. When this conventional analysis is applied to the chick data, flurothyl appears to produce amnesia when administered 4 min to 24 hr after training. The longest intervals at which significant differences were observed (χ^2 test; $p < 0.05$) depended upon the flurothyl treatment parameters. For a 1-min exposure to either 0.85 per cent or 1.7 per cent flurothyl, the interval was 4 min. For exposures of 2, 4, 8 or 16 min to 0.85 per cent flurothyl, it was 64 min; for the

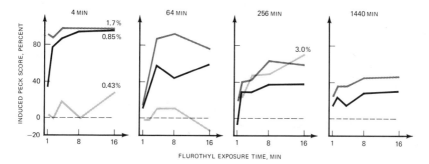

FIGURE 1 *Dependence of induced peck score upon flurothyl exposure time and concentration for four training-treatment intervals. Each point represents 33 to 40 experimental chicks, except for 3.0% flurothyl, 16-min exposure (28 chicks), which is uncertain because of excessive mortality (32%).*

FIGURE 2 *Dependence of induced peck score upon flurothyl concentration. Each point represents pooled data for flurothyl exposure times of 4, 8, and 16 min (N = 110 to 120 except for 3.0% flurothyl, where N = 96). The broken lines are extrapolations.*

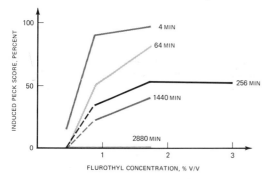

same exposures to 1.7 per cent flurothyl, the interval was 1440 min. The divergence from 4 to 1440 min occurred solely as a result of manipulating the amnesic-treatment parameters rather than reflecting the progress of memory consolidation. Thus, the conventional analysis does not seem to be justified.

Dependence of amnesia upon exposure time and concentration of flurothyl The induced peck scores at exposure times of 4, 8, and 16 min differed only slightly (Fig. 1); they were pooled for determining the concentration dependence (Table 1; Fig. 2). The sensitivity of the concentration-response relationship was found to be a function of the consolidation interval (Fig. 1). The 64-min interval was optimal for discriminating between 0.43, 0.85, and 1.7 per cent flurothyl; 0.85 per cent flurothyl produced significantly less amnesia than 1.7 per cent flurothyl ($\chi^2 = 22.2$; $p < 0.001$) and was therefore incompletely amnesic. At the 256-min interval, the amnesia produced by 3.0 per cent flurothyl did not significantly exceed that produced by 1.7 per cent flurothyl.

DISCUSSION

The chick results confirm numerous experiments with rats and mice that demonstrate increased amnesia with increased intensity of various amnesic treatments [Alpern and McGaugh, 1968; Miller, 1968; Weissman, 1963, 1964, 1965, 1967; Jarvik and Kopp, 1967b; Dorfman and Jarvik, 1968b; Pagano et al., 1969; Ray and Barrett, 1969a; Quinton, 1966; Alpern and Kimble, 1967]. It remains to develop a parsimonious interpretation of this reliable effect, as follows.

Retrograde amnesia experiments have (1) a training trial to convey new information to an animal, (2) an amnesic treatment to block consolidation of that information input, and (3) a test trial to estimate the engram present *at the moment just following the amnesic treatment.* The test, however, is delayed for 24 hr to avoid the confounding effects of residual short-term memory, proactive performance deficits, and circadian variations. An amnesic treatment must meet three criteria: no destruction of consolidated engram, complete block of ongoing consolidation (so that no additional engram is formed before the test trial), and no effects upon performance or memory retrieval at the test trial.

In this experiment, the evidence for the first criterion is that the effect of flurothyl decreased as the training-treatment interval increased, whereas engram destruction would cause the same amount of amnesia after every interval.

Evidence for complete block of consolidation has not been provided in any retrograde amnesia experiment. The conventional assumption that tonic convulsion is an acceptable criterion [Alpern and McGaugh, 1968; Miller, 1968; Weissman, 1963, 1964, 1965; Alpern and Kimble, 1967; Quartermain et al., 1965] is clouded by observations of a poor correlation between seizure pattern and retrograde amnesia in rodents [Miller, 1968; Weissman, 1963, 1964, 1965; Jarvik and Kopp, 1967b, Dorfman and Jarvik, 1968a, 1968b; Ray and Barrett, 1969a; McGaugh and Alpern, 1966; Kesner and Doty, 1968] and chicks [Lee-Teng, 1969], and by our results; chicks could experience little amnesia despite full tonic convulsion (Fig. 1, TTI = 64 min, 1-min, exposure to 0.85 and 1.7 per cent flurothyl). The amnesic effect of flurothyl appears to approach a maximum in this experiment at a

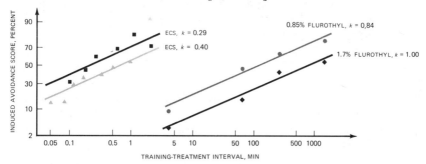

FIGURE 3 *"Consolidation" gradients with various amnesic treatments in chicks. The ordinate is on the probit scale, the abscissa on the logarithmic scale. The values of k represent the relative amnesic effectiveness compared with that of 1.7% flurothyl. The regression lines represent y = 1.27 + 0.82 log t + 0.82(1 − k) log t', as explained in the text. The points represent experimental data (for 1.7% flurothyl a value of 102.3% at 2880 min is not shown, and for ECS, k = 0.29, five plateau values after 2.1 min, of 67 to 83%, are not shown). ECS data for k = 0.29 are from Lee-Teng and Sherman [1966], and ECS data for k = 0.40 are from Magnus et al. [unpublished].*

concentration of 1.7 per cent to 3.0 per cent flurothyl with an exposure time of 8 to 16 min (Fig. 1, TTI = 256 min).

Evidence for the absence of performance or retrieval effects is provided by separate experiments [Cherkin, 1970a] in which (1) the marked performance deficit observed after 1 hr largely disappeared after 24 hr and (2) the amnesic effect persisted for nine days, the maximum tested.

Interpretation of concentration-dependence The interpretation of the smaller retrograde amnesia found with 0.85 per cent flurothyl compared to 1.7 per cent flurothyl (Fig. 3) is that the lower concentration slowed but did not block memory consolidation, so that additional engram formed during the 20 to 24 hr before the test trial.

To quantitate the concentration-dependence it is convenient to shift attention from amnesia to memory retention, as indicated by avoidance of the lamp during the test trial. The induced avoidance score is equal to 100 − induced peck score. Memory retention is a function of the interval between the training trial and the flurothyl treatment. The probit of the avoidance score, y, appears to be linearly related to the logarithm of this interval, t, over a considerable range [Cherkin, 1966a, 1966b]. Assuming complete block by the amnesic treatment, the empirical linear relation is $y = \alpha + \beta \log t$, where α is the intercept at $\log t = 0$ and β is the slope constant. I have suggested that α may be an empirical measure of "learning strength" and that β is an empirical measure of the rate of consolidation. The linear relationship

91

does not imply a unitary process because the transfer function between the engram and the measured behavioral response is unknown.

To account for post-treatment consolidation we require a third term, $\Delta y = (1 - k) \beta \log t'$, where k is a factor (0 to 1) that describes the effectiveness of an incomplete amnesic treatment and t' is the time between that treatment and the test trial. Two arbitrary assumptions are required: (1) no consolidation occurs during the acute phase of the convulsion and (2) post-treatment consolidation commences at the end of the acute phase. From the experimental data for 1.7 per cent flurothyl (Fig. 3), with $k = 1.00$ and t in seconds, I have calculated α as 1.27 probits and β as 0.82 probits per log second. The value of k for 0.85 per cent flurothyl is 0.84, calculated as $y = 1.27 + 0.82 \log t + 0.82$ $(1 - k) \log t'$. The linear regressions are plotted in Fig. 3, compared with regressions using ECS data in chicks [Lee-Teng and Sherman, 1966; Magnus et al., unpublished].

It is clear that the less effective the amnesic treatment, the shorter the observed "consolidation time." The consolidation half-time (CT_{50}) [Cherkin, 1966a, 1966b] calculated for $k = 1.00$ by setting $y = 5.00 = 1.27 + 0.82 \log CT_{50}$, equals 35,400 sec or 9.8 hr. The apparent CT_{50} calculated for $k = 0.84$ (obtained with 0.85 per cent flurothyl) equals 1.6 hr. Variability of amnesic effectiveness occurs with dissimilar agents as well as with quantitative differences in other treatment conditions, e.g., in the ECS current *at the brain sites critical to consolidation* [Miller, 1968; Pagano et al., 1969; Ray and Barrett, 1969a; Dorfman and Jarvik, 1968a; Kesner and Doty, 1968] or in the partial pressure of inspired ether vapor [Cherkin, 1968].

The interpretation that divergent consolidation gradients arise from variable amnesic treatments is parsimonious and plausible, but it must be qualified because of the uncertainty of interpreting retrograde amnesia experiments. Deutsch [1969] has made a critical analysis of this uncertainty. Weiskrantz [1966], for example, has suggested a quite different interpretation, namely, that consolidation is vulnerable to disruption for less than 30 sec after information input [Paolino et al., 1966; Lee-Teng and Sherman, 1966; Quartermain et al., 1965; Magnus et al., unpublished; Chorover and Schiller, 1965] and that the "amnesia" observed after longer intervals reflects impaired retrieval. The critical prediction that such "amnesia" must disappear with time [Weiskrantz, 1966] has been supported [Zinkin and Miller, 1967; Kohlenberg and Trabasso, 1968; Lewis et al., 1968b; Nielson, 1968] and denied [Chevalier, 1965; Luttges and McGaugh, 1967; Herz and Peeke, 1967, 1968; Geller and Jarvik, 1968a; Riddell, 1969] in recent reports. The amnesia induced by flurothyl in chicks persisted for nine days, the maximum studied [Cherkin, 1970a]. Conceivably, amnesic treatments impair both retrieval and consolidation [Riddell, 1969]. More detailed studies of retention as a function of the time after amnesic treatment should permit a clearer delineation of the role of consolidation and retrieval effects in retrograde amnesia phenomena.

I thank Professor Linus Pauling for his valued interest in this work and for critical revision of earlier drafts. Miss Mayme Bailey and Mrs. Mary Garman carried out the experiments and Mr. Daniel Cherkin assisted with the calculations. Reprinted from *Proceedings of the National Academy of Science*, 1969, **63**, 1094–1101, by permission of the National Academy of Science.

RETROACTIVE EFFECTS OF TRANSCORNEAL AND TRANSPINNATE ECS ON STEP-THROUGH LATENCIES OF MICE AND RATS

ALLEN M. SCHNEIDER/BRUCE KAPP/CLAUDINE ARON/MURRAY E. JARVIK

Transcorneal or transpinnate ECS was delivered to rats and transcorneal ECS was delivered to mice 10 sec., 1 hr., or 6 hr. after step-through training. At the 10-sec. and 1-hr. intervals both modes of ECS decreased test latencies 24 hr. later in both species. At the 6-hr. interval only the transcorneal ECS decreased test latencies, and then only in rats. The training-ECS interval at which ECS ceased to decrease test latencies was also shown to vary directly with the length of cutoff criteria used to terminate the test trial.

As the interval between training and treatment with electroconvulsive shock (ECS) increases, impairment of performance decreases during subsequent retention tests. Attempts to identify the function relating duration of training-ECS interval to magnitude of performance decrement have produced considerable disagreement. Chorover and Schiller [1965] observed impairment with training-ECS intervals up to but not beyond 10 sec.; Kopp et al. [1966] observed impairment with a training-ECS interval as much as 6 hr. in duration. Complications arise, however, when one attempts to determine the source of variation: Chorover and Schiller [1965] used rats and transpinnate ECS; Kopp et al. [1966] used mice and transcorneal ECS. Furthermore, although both studies used passive-avoidance training, Chorover and Schiller employed a platform apparatus and terminated test trials with a 30-sec. cutoff, while Kopp et al. employed a step-through apparatus and a 300-sec. cutoff.

The present study examines the degree to which mode of ECS administration, type of species, and choice of cutoff contribute to the disparity in temporal gradients. To accomplish this the authors compared retention gradients obtained with (1) transcorneal and transpinnate ECS in rats, (2) mice and rats receiving transcorneal ECS, and (3) data analysis using 30-sec., 300-sec., and 600-sec. cutoffs.

METHOD

Two hundred and seventy-six male albino Sprague-Dawley rats, 90–100 days old, were housed three or four to a cage and were permitted ad-lib food and water. One hundred and forty-five female albino CF1 mice, 60–80 days old, were housed eight to a cage and were permitted ad-lib food and water.

The training apparatus for mice is described in detail elsewhere [Jarvik and Kopp, 1967a]. The training apparatus for rats, patterned after the one described for mice, was constructed of 6.4-mm. Plexiglas and was enlarged (64 × 28 × 6.25 cm.) to accommodate rats. It consisted of a small compartment, illuminated by a Tensor lamp (GE 93), connected to a larger dark compartment by a 28 × 6.25 cm. opening. The floor of each compartment consisted of pairs of parallel stainless-steel plates, one pair in the smaller (16 × 2.5 cm.) and two pairs in the larger compartment (23 × 2.5 cm.). Adjacent plates were spaced 1.25 cm. apart. The apparatus was trough shaped, with the width of each compartment increasing from a 6.25-cm. base to a 21-cm. top; the top of each compartment was covered with a hinged lid. The floor of the large compartment was connected to a Grason-Stadler shocker set to deliver .8-ma. footshock. Footshock (FS) was triggered by the break of a photobeam positioned in the large compartment 23 cm. from the entrance point.

Training for mice and rats The animals were placed, one at a time, in the small compartment facing away from the larger compartment and a timer was started manually. When *S* entered the larger compartment and broke the photobeam, the timer stopped, and footshock started and remained on until *S* returned to the small compartment; all *S*s were removed from the small compartment within 5 sec.

Posttraining manipulation for rats Following training the rats were randomly assigned to one of three groups and received either transcorneal, transpinnate, or sham ECS. Each of the three groups was divided into three subgroups and received its respective treatment either 10 sec., 1 hr., or 6 hr. after training; *S*s in the 1-hr. and 6-hr. groups were returned to their home cage during the training-treatment interval. The ECS (35–50 ma.) was delivered for .2 sec. and reliably produced full tonic seizures. All *S*s were held by the nape of the neck for approximately 5 sec. during the posttraining manipulation; sham *S*s were handled like

READINGS IN MEMORY CONSOLIDATION

TABLE 1 *Medians and interquartile ranges of step-through latencies (sec.) on the test trial (600-sec. cutoff) for both mice and rats*

Animals	n	\[10 sec.\] Mdn.	Range	\[1 hr.\] Mdn.	Range	\[6 hr.\] Mdn.	Range
Rats							
NT	16	5	4–6				
NS	20	196	112–600				
Sham	120	150	29–600	141	36–600	175	38–600
Corneal	60	8	4–21	37	25–58	73	22–271
Pinnate	60	12	6–23	41	28–87	206	75–498
Mice							
NT	25	7	5–13				
NS	30	600	311–600				
Corneal	90	21	16–29	330	155–600	538	236–600

(Header: *Train-ECS interval* spanning the 10 sec., 1 hr., and 6 hr. column pairs.)

ECS Ss, either with ear clips or corneal electrodes, except that no current was delivered. Two control groups were employed: one control group (NS, no sham) was trained, was given no posttraining manipulation, and was returned directly to its home cage. The other control group (NT, no treatment), neither trained nor given a posttraining manipulation, was placed in the apparatus, was allowed to step into the larger compartment and to remain for 3 sec., an interval calculated to match the mean duration FS received by trained Ss, and was then removed to its home cage. Each rat group contained 20 Ss, except that the NT group contained 16 Ss.

Posttraining manipulation for mice Following training the mice were randomly assigned to one of three groups and received transcorneal ECS either 10 sec., 1 hr., or 6 hr. after training. The ECS (20 ma.) was delivered for .2 sec. and reliably produced full tonic seizures. Two control groups were employed, identical to those (NS and NT groups) used for rats. Each mouse group contained 30 Ss, except that the NT group contained 25 Ss.

Retention test for mice and rats Step-through latencies of all groups were taken 24 hr. after training or in the case of the NT groups 24 hr. after exposure to the apparatus; if S remained in the small compartment for 600 sec., the test trial was terminated.

The Mann-Whitney U test (two-tailed) was used for statistical evaluation of the data.

RESULTS

Transcorneal, transpinnate, and sham effects in rats with a 600-sec. cutoff It can be seen from Table 1 that although STLs (step-through latencies) increased for rats in both the transcorneal and transpinnate conditions as the training-ECS interval increased, none of the STLs reached the level of the sham control groups except in the transpinnate group, and then only at the 6-hr. interval ($p > .05$). Furthermore, the transpinnate and transcorneal manipulations had virtually the same effects on STLs at the 10-sec. and 1-hr. training-ECS intervals, but not at the 6-hr. interval, where STLs for the transpinnate group were significantly greater ($p < .05$) than those for the transcorneal group.

The data from sham-transcorneal and sham-transpinnate groups were pooled at each interval, since there was no difference between the two treatments within a given interval. Although STLs appear to decrease in the sham conditions relative to the NS group, these differences failed to achieve statistical significance ($p > .05$). Interquartile ranges indicate, however, that the variance was considerably greater in each of the sham groups than in the NS group.

Comparison of transcorneal effects in mice versus rats with a 600-sec. cutoff Although mice showed significantly greater STLs than rats at each training-ECS interval ($p < .05$ for 10-sec. groups; $p < .01$ for 1-hr. and 6-hr. groups), their STLs, similar to those for the rats, did not reach the level of the trained control group except at the 6-hr. training-ECS interval. Moreover, mice also showed significantly greater ($p < .01$) STLs than rats when given training without ECS (NS groups). This suggests that the longer STLs in mice when given both training and ECS simply reflect the effects of stronger conditioning.

TABLE 2   **Effect of cutoff times (in sec.) on the apparent efficacy of ECS**

| | Training-ECS interval | | |
	10 sec.	1 hr.	6 hr.
Transpinnate rats			
600	RA*	RA†	Ret
300	RA*	RA†	Ret
30	RA*	Ret	Ret
Transcorneal (rats)			
600	RA*	RA†	RA†
300	RA*	RA†	RA†
30	RA*	Ret	Ret
Transcorneal (mice)			
600	RA*	RA†	Ret
300	RA*	Ret	Ret
30	RA*	Ret	Ret

Note   RA refers to retrograde amnesia and is defined by STLs that do not reach the level of sham (rats) or trained (mice) controls. Ret refers to retention and is defined by latencies that are not significantly different ($p > .05$) from sham (rats) or trained (mice) controls.
*$p < .01$.   †$p < .05$.

READINGS IN MEMORY CONSOLIDATION

Comparison of analyses using 30-sec., 300-sec., and 600-sec. cutoff criteria It can be seen from Table 2 that choice of cutoff determines in large part the apparent training-ECS interval at which ECS ceased to be effective. With a 30-sec. cutoff ECS appears to lose its effectiveness in rats 1 hr. after training irrespective of mode of delivery. Analyses with 300- and 600-sec. cutoff, however, give a much different picture: (1) transpinnate ECS retains its effectiveness 1 hr. but not 6 hr. after training; (2) transcorneal ECS remains effective at both the 1-hr. and 6-hr. training-ECS intervals.

Similar changes occur with varied cutoff analyses of the mice data: with the 30-sec. and 300-sec. cutoffs ECS appears to lose its effectiveness 1 hr. after training; with the 600-sec. cutoff ECS remains effective at the 1-hr. but not the 6-hr. interval.

DISCUSSION

The results of the present experiment indicate that the relationship between the training-ECS interval and test STLs varies as a function of mode of ECS administration, type of species, and choice of cutoff.

With a 600-sec. cutoff the differential effects of transcorneal and transpinnate ECS in rats were not discernible until the training-ECS interval was increased to 6 hr. At this interval transcorneal ECS induced a greater decrement in STLs than transpinnate ECS. This finding with rats is in general agreement with recent observations on mice by Dorfman and Jarvik [1968a]. Using a step-through procedure and delivering ECS 45 sec. after training, they found that mice treated with transcorneal ECS had shorter STLs on a later retention test than mice treated with transpinnate ECS. At this point we can only speculate, but one reason for this difference may be that the tissue resistance is less and thereby the current is greater with transcorneal than transpinnate ECS.

Comparing the effects of 600-sec.-cutoff transcorneal ECS on mice and rats indicates that mice show both stronger conditioning and greater resistance to ECS than rats. These data are in general agreement with recent observations by Ray and Bivens [1968], who found, when varying strength of conditioning in mice, a similar direct relation between strength of conditioning and resistance to ECS.

It is particularly noteworthy that although the present authors used the same procedure, strain of mice, and laboratory facilities as Kopp et al. [1966], we failed to obtain the decrement that they observed at the 6-hr. training-ECS interval. The specific source of this discrepancy is not clear but seems to be generally related to intershipment variability in mice. It has been observed in one of the laboratories that across shipments the 1-hr. ECS effect occurs uniformly but the 6-hr. ECS effect occurs with some variability.

Finally, it is clear that varying choice of cutoff from 30 to 300 to 600 sec. yields ECS-susceptibility gradients ranging from 10 sec. to 6 hr. in rats and from 10 sec. to 1 hr. in mice. This disparity in gradients stems from the fact that, at least with the step-through procedure, the 30-sec., the 300-sec., and perhaps even the 600-sec. responses are not asymptotic; asymptote here refers to the cutoff latency beyond which the ECS effects relative to trained controls (ECS-susceptibility gradients) do not change. Regarding the present data, it appears from comparing 300-sec. and 600-sec. analyses that such stability was achieved in both the transpinnate and transcorneal effects in rats but not in the transcorneal effects in mice.

This work was supported by National Science Foundation Grant NSF-GB-7278 to Allen M. Schneider and United States Public Health Service Grant MH-05319 to Murray E. Jarvik. Reprinted from the *Journal of Comparative and Physiological Psychology*, 1969, **69**, 505–509, by permission of The American Psychological Association.

RECOVERY OF MEMORY AFTER AMNESIA INDUCED BY ELECTROCONVULSIVE SHOCK

SHEILA ZINKIN/A. J. MILLER

Electroconvulsive shock given to rats immediately after one-trial avoidance learning produced a significant amnesic effect 24 hours later; this amnesia had largely disappeared in further retention tests 48 and 72 hours after treatment. This result puts in question a basic assumption implicit in most memory consolidation studies that such amnesic effects will be permanent.

Animals given an electroconvulsive shock (ECS) shortly after a single avoidance learning trial will show little or no evidence of learning when tested 24 hours later [Madsen and McGaugh, 1961; Heriot and Coleman, 1962; Weissman, 1963; Chorover and Schiller, 1965]. The usual interpretation of this effect is that the ECS has disrupted certain neural processes essential for the establishment of a memory trace. Such an interpretation is based on the assumption that any amnesic effects of this sort will be permanent: for, if ECS has effectively prevented the formation of a memory trace by occurring within the critical period required for this

READINGS IN MEMORY CONSOLIDATION

process, then the retention deficit observed 24 hours after treatment should be equally apparent at any other time of testing. Apart from an early experiment by Worchel and Narciso [1950] and a more recent one by Chevalier [1965], this assumption has never been systematically examined, yet it is of critical importance for memory consolidation theory.

Worchel and Narciso tested rats four days after a series of six massed ECS treatments were administered immediately after a criterion learning trial. The rats showed no impairment in relearning a 14-unit T-maze, although significant impairment had been noted when the rats were tested 24 hours after treatment [Worchel and Narciso, 1950]. While these results were attributed by the authors to the temporary retroactive effects of the treatment, they could equally well have been due to the temporary proactive effects of the massive dose of ECS used in this experiment, or to a combination of both effects. Chevalier [1965] was unable to find any differences in the extent of amnesia for a nonspecific avoidance response (reduction of locomotor activity in an apparatus where shock had been given) in different groups of mice tested 1, 7, or 30 days after a single footshock-ECS treatment; he concluded that the amnesia was permanent. However, the results of the following experiment indicate that under certain conditions there can be a dramatic recovery from the retroactive effects of ECS. In this experiment ECS was administered after footshock consequent upon a step-down response, the interval between footshock and ECS was three-fifths of a second, and all animals were tested for retention 24, 48, and 72 hours after treatment.

METHOD

Subjects in the experiment were 124 male albino rats of the Wistar strain, aged 90 to 100 days. Each cage housed four or five rats with free access to food and water. The apparatus was similar to that first described by Jarvik and Essman [1960]. It consisted of an uncovered 44-cm square compartment with walls 46 cm high, made of aluminum lined with matte black plastic. The floor was constructed of stainless steel rods (0.24 cm in diameter) set 1.27 cm apart. In the center was a 9-cm square platform raised 7.5 cm above the grid floor and illuminated from above by a collimated light source. Footshock could be delivered through the grid floor for 2.0 seconds by means of a scrambler delivering 10 pulses/sec to each rod at approximately 0.4 ma. The ECS (50 cycles a-c at 35 ma for 0.20 second) was administered by way of modified crocodile-clip ear electrodes from a constant current machine using the principle of the Pittsburgh electroshock apparatus [Russell et al., 1948].

In each daily trial earclips were attached to each rat; it was then placed on the platform and its step-down latency (that is, the time spent on the platform) was recorded to within .01 second. On the first three days preliminary training trials were given in which the rats were permitted to explore the apparatus for approximately 10 seconds after stepping down. On the fourth day differential treatment was given as follows: Group 1 (FS, $n = 34$) received 2.0-seconds footshock through the grid floor immediately on stepping down from the platform; Group 2 (FS-ECS, $n = 40$) received immediate footshock, followed 0.6 second later by ECS; Group 3 (ECS, $n = 24$) received ECS only, 2.6 seconds after stepping down; Group 4 (NT, $n = 26$) received no treatment after stepping down. All ECS animals were removed from the apparatus while still unconscious, and they recovered in their home cages; the other animals were returned to their home cages after approximately 10 seconds on the grid. On each of the three subsequent days retention trials were given with the same procedure as had been used in the preliminary training trials.

RESULTS

The usual criterion of retention in a step-down experiment is the length of time animals remain on the platform the day after footshock treatment (here termed step-down latency). In our experiment there was considerable variation in the post-treatment step-down latencies of the FS group, relatively few of these animals having the very long latencies normally reported in experiments of this sort. This may be a function of interstrain differences, and also of the time of day used for testing—in this experiment all testing was carried out at night. Because latencies for all rats in the trials before treatment were consistently short (median 1.02 seconds for trials 2 through 4), we considered that even a moderate increase over previous latencies would indicate some degree of retention. Accordingly retention was assessed in this experiment by comparing each rat's step-down latency in trials 5, 6, and 7 with its own longest latency in trials 2 through 4.[1] Increased latencies were classified according to whether they exceeded 1, 3, or 10 seconds. The percentage of rats in each treatment group meeting each of these criteria in the three retention trials is shown in Fig. 2.[2]

[1]Latencies tended to be rather longer in the first than in the following three trials and were therefore excluded from the comparison. To avoid ambiguity, we excluded from the experiment any rat having a latency of more than 5 seconds in trials 2 to 4; 14 animals were excluded for this reason.

[2]A number of animals jumped completely out of the apparatus in trials 5 to 7. This behavior, which never occurred in the trials before treatment, was considered a strong indication of retention; such responses were therefore treated as equivalent to maximum step-down latencies and are accordingly included in the 10-second criterion.

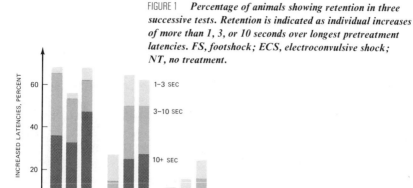

FIGURE 1   *Percentage of animals showing retention in three successive tests. Retention is indicated as individual increases of more than 1, 3, or 10 seconds over longest pretreatment latencies. FS, footshock; ECS, electroconvulsive shock; NT, no treatment.*

The effect of principal interest emerging from these results is that the retention deficit clearly apparent in the FS-ECS group on the first day after treatment has largely disappeared in the two subsequent trials. In the first retention test (trial 5), 68 percent of the FS group met the 1-second criterion, 65 percent met the 3-second criterion, and 36 percent met the 10-second criterion, as compared with only 27.5 percent, 15 percent, and 7.5 percent, respectively, for the FS-ECS group (all χ^2 significant beyond the .01 level). This result is comparable with those obtained in similar experiments when retention is tested 24 hours after treatment. There is, however, very little evidence of impaired retention in the FS-ECS group in the next two trials. By the third day of retention testing (trial 7), the proportions of these animals reaching the 1-, 3- and 10-second criteria have risen to 62.5 percent, 50 percent, and 27.5 percent, respectively. It is worth noting that of the 72.5 percent of FS-ECS animals failing to meet even the 1-second criterion on trial 5, as many as 28 percent have reached the 10-second, 58.5 percent the 3-second, and 69 percent the 1-second criteria on either or both of the subsequent trials.

The FS-ECS group as a whole shows a significant increase in step-down latency from trial 5 to trial 7, the mean latency rising from 3.42 seconds on trial 5 to 9.18 seconds on trial 7 ($t = 2.89$, $P < .01$). In contrast, the comparable increase (from 10.7 to 12.5 seconds) for the FS group is not significant ($P > .25$). As can be seen from these mean latencies, the FS-ECS animals were showing approximately the same degree of avoidance on the final day of testing as that of the FS group on the day after treatment ($P > .25$).

All ECS animals included in these results had full tonic extensor fits. The interval between footshock and ECS (0.6 second) used in this experiment was shorter than in most of the comparable studies, and the ECS intensity (35 ma) and duration (0.2 second) were similar. It would seem, therefore, that the amnesic effect regularly found by other investigators when testing 24 hours after treatment may not reflect a permanent absence of the memory trace.

It is possible that the recovery found in our study is due to a "shrinkage" of amnesia as described for retrograde amnesia following concussion [Russell, 1959]; such a shrinkage would be predicted from the model proposed by Weiskrantz [1964, 1966]. An alternative possibility is that the recovery depends on reexposure to the testing situation and that learning is taking place. Such learning would depend on there being some minimum retention of the traumatic properties of the situation on the first day of testing.

The results for the group receiving ECS only were significant. Previous studies have suggested that while a single ECS is not aversive, repeated treatments may become so [Hudspeth et al., 1964; Chorover and Schiller, 1965]; the aversive effect has been found on the third or fourth day of repeated treatments. Since we have found significantly more evidence of retention on the third day of testing than on the first ($t = 2.34$, $P < .05$), after a single ECS, it is possible that the results of the earlier studies may be due not only to the repetition of ECS, but to a latent and strengthening trace set up by the first ECS in the series.

Work supported by grants from the Medical Research Council, London. We thank Dr. L. Weiskrantz for advice. Reprinted from *Science*, 1967, **155**, 102–104, by permission of the American Association for the Advancement of Science.

PERMANENCE OF RETROGRADE AMNESIA PRODUCED BY ELECTROCONVULSIVE SHOCK

MARVIN W. LUTTGES/JAMES L. McGAUGH

The permanence of retrograde amnesia produced for a single training trial by a single electroconvulsive shock was studied. No recovery from amnesia was found with either single or repeated retention tests. Amnesic effects were found to be permanent with retention intervals as long as 1 month.

Electroconvulsive shock (ECS) can produce amnesia in animals if applied shortly after training [Duncan, 1949; McGaugh, 1965; Thompson and Dean, 1955; Pearlman et al., 1961]. It has generally been assumed that ECS produces amnesia by disrupting time-dependent processes which underlie memory storage [McGaugh, 1966; Glickman, 1961]. This interpretation has been supported by evidence that the amnesia produced by a single ECS given shortly after a single learning trial is permanent for at least one month [Chevalier, 1965].

This permanence of amnesia produced by ECS has been seriously questioned in recent reports [Zinkin and Miller, 1967; Cooper and Koppenaal, 1964]. Zinkin and Miller have reported evidence which indicates that amnesia produced by ECS may diminish when animals are given repeated retention tests. However, their data do not permit determination of the basis for the increased response latencies used to index recovery of retention. The change in performance may have arisen from several sources: repeated exposure to the test situation, passage of time after ECS treatments, or simply, nonreinforced increments in avoidance which are not directly related to ECS treatments.

The experiments reported here examine the degree of permanence of amnesia produced by ECS with single and repeated tests at retention intervals of different lengths. The amnesia did not decrease either as a function of time or as a function of repeated tests. Within the limits of these experiments, amnesia appeared to be permanent. Thus, amnesia produced by ECS continues to be most adequately explained as a consequence of interference with time-dependent processes underlying memory storage.

METHOD

Eighty male Swiss-Webster mice, 55 to 65 days old at the beginning of training, were used in each of three experiments. With the exception of the retention interval between training and testing, the procedures used in each experiment were identical. The retention intervals for the three experiments were 12 hours, 7 days, and 32 days, respectively.

As preliminary training, the 80 mice in each experiment were given one trial every 12 hours for 2 days on an inhibitory avoidance apparatus [Essman and Alpern, 1964]. Each mouse was placed on a small metal platform (2.25 by 6.25 cm) which extended from beneath a hole (3.75 cm in diameter) in the wall of a darkened box. The mouse was allowed to step from the highly illuminated platform (40-watt bulb, 19 cm above the platform) into the box and remain there for 5 seconds before it was removed to the home cage. No shock was given during preliminary trials. Training was given 12 hours after the last of these preliminary trials. Four experimental groups of 20 mice each were used in each experiment during training. The mice were housed eight to a cage, including two mice from each of the four experimental groups. Mice in the first experimental group received momentary footshock (FS) (5 ma) as they stepped from the platform into the box, followed within 15 seconds by an ECS (15 ma, 0.2 second) delivered through corneal electrodes. Artificial respiration was given until normal respiration was resumed. Mice in the second group received the footshock and were immediately removed to their cages without ECS (NECS). Mice in the third group received no footshock (NFS), but were given ECS 15 seconds after entering the box. Mice in the fourth group received neither footshock nor ECS. The retention trials, given after the appropriate interval, were identical to preliminary trials, and no further treatment was given. The time required for each mouse to step from the platform into the box was used as a retention measure. In general, mice that have received footshock require a much longer period of time than control mice or mice that have not received footshock. During the retention tests an avoidance response was recorded if the response latency exceeded 30 seconds.

RESULTS

The results of all three experiments[1] are summarized in Fig. 1. Over all the retention intervals used in the three experiments, the FS-NECS groups showed high retention with long latency scores, and none of these groups differed from the others despite differences in retention intervals.[2] By contrast, the three FS-ECS groups showed latencies that were significantly shorter (Kruskal-Wallis, $df = 3$, $P < .001$) than those of the groups receiving only footshock. Like the FS-NECS groups, the FS-ECS groups did not differ significantly from one another despite differences in retention intervals. Therefore, since the differences between the results of the FS-NECS and the FS-ECS groups are comparable over the three experiments, it appears that ECS has a stable disruptive effect on retention, independent of the interval of time between training and testing. Furthermore, comparisons of the NFS-ECS and the NFS-NECS groups showed that ECS alone did not increase response latencies on the retention test. The differential response latencies of the FS-ECS and the FS-NECS groups cannot, consequently, be attributed to a performance effect of ECS alone. This supports the hypothesis that ECS produces its effects through a direct disruption of memory storage processes.

Comparison of the latencies of the FS-ECS and the NFS-ECS

[1]Twenty mice were initially used in each group; however, mice were eliminated if full tonic extension was not produced by ECS, if initial latencies were excessive, or for other procedural reasons. No more than three mice were deleted from any group.

[2]Mann-Whitney U tests were used for all comparisons between pairs of groups. Kruskal-Wallis one-way analysis of variance was used for comparisons of more than two groups.

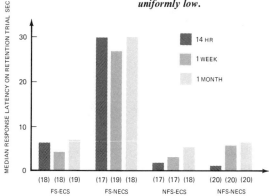

FIGURE 1 *Median response latencies for each experimental group at each different retention test interval. Response latencies for preliminary and training trials were uniformly low.*

groups over the three retention intervals gives an indication of the extent of the amnesia produced by the ECS. With the retention intervals of 12 hours and 32 days, the latencies of the FS-ECS groups were significantly longer ($P < .002$ and $P < .004$ for the two intervals, respectively) than those of the NFS-ECS group. This suggests that ECS given within 15 seconds after a single trial does not eliminate all residual memory of that trial. In the case of the 12-hour interval, this difference between FS-ECS and NFS-ECS groups disappeared when the animals were given an additional test 12 hours after the first test or a total of 24 hours after training. The fact that the residual memory did not increase but instead decreased with the passage of 12 additional hours and with the presentation of an additional trial suggests that any residual memory remaining after ECS was transient and labile.

The latencies of animals tested at 32 days were significantly ($P < .05$) longer than those of animals tested at either 12 hours or 7 days, under all four experimental conditions. Within the 32-day experiment, however, the latencies of the four experimental groups formed a pattern comparable to those found in the 12-hour and 7-day experiments. It seems likely that this overall increase in the latencies of the 32-day groups is due to the ages of these animals.

It has been suggested that repeated testing may somehow cancel the performance deficits produced by ECS [Zinkin and Miller, 1967; Cooper and Koppenaal, 1964]. The results of giving additional tests to animals originally tested at 12 hours are shown in Fig. 2. There was no evidence that the additional tests eliminated performance deficits produced by ECS. The FS-ECS animals showed the short response latencies mentioned above, and the large differences in the latencies of the FS-ECS and the FS-NECS groups remained unchanged through several additional tests at different retention intervals. Quite clearly,

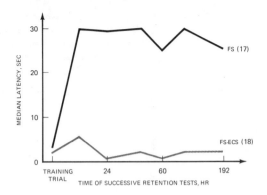

FIGURE 2 *Median response latencies for FS-ECS and FS-NECS animals on successive retention tests. Tests were conducted using procedures of preliminary trials. Testing was discontinued 192 hours after training.*

the trained animals can maintain a high level of performance over many additional tests. The stability of the learned response as well as the amnesia produced by ECS are thus equally well demonstrated.

Over the intervals examined in our experiment, retrograde amnesia produced by ECS appears to be permanent. The differences in the latencies of the FS-ECS and FS-NECS groups remained constant both over several retention trials (Fig. 2) and when tested at different times after training (Fig. 1). These findings support and extend the findings reported by Chevalier [1965].

Our data do not show the apparent recovery of retention reported by Zinkin and Miller [1967], who, using repeated retention tests, demonstrated increased response latencies over trials for most of their experimental groups. The increased latencies were somewhat greater in their ECS-trained group than in their other experimental groups; however, comparisons between groups on any single test trial suggest that the ECS-trained group apparently does not attain the performance level of the control group. Unfortunately, an evaluation of these findings is quite difficult, since highly stable retention was not obtained for the control animals. The data may be interpreted as revealing some of the transient properties of ECS treatment or as demonstrating spontaneous fluctuations of a poorly learned response. Not enough information is available for a valid interpretation.

Our findings, unlike those of Zinkin and Miller, demonstrate permanent retrograde amnesia and support the hypothesis that ECS produces retrograde amnesia by interferring with time-dependent memory storage processes.

Supported by PHS research grants MH 12526-01 and MH 10261-03. Reprinted from *Science*, 1967, **156**, 408–410, by permission of the American Association for the Advancement of Science.

RECOVERY OF MEMORY FOLLOWING AMNESIA

DONALD J. LEWIS/JAMES R. MISANIN/RALPH R. MILLER

Rats were administered foot shock on stepping off of a raised platform. Electroconvulsive shock administered immediately following foot shock produced amnesia for the shock on a retest 24 hr later. When these animals were given a second "reminder" shock 4 hr later in a different compartment and tested again 20 hr later, suppression of the stepping response was observed, indicating recovery from amnesia. Recovery was also obtained in two additional experiments, even when a much lower intensity "reminder" shock was administered.

The possible recovery of a memory which has disappeared as the result of an electroconvulsive shock (ECS) or some other amnesic agent is of considerable theoretical importance to the understanding of the process by which memories are laid down. Consolidation theory [Glickman, 1961; McGaugh, 1966] assumes that the engram remains susceptible to disruption for a period after its formation and that interference with its consolidation results in its permanent disruption. Evidence suggesting that memories can be recovered [Zinkin and Miller, 1967] is rebutted by those who hold to consolidation [Luttges and McGaugh, 1967]. If memories are not permanently destroyed by the administration of amnesic agents, a revision of consolidation theory will be necessary.

Memories may be laid down within a few seconds of the penetration of information, although there may be interference with their retrieval [Lewis et al., 1969]. If this is true, it should be possible to devise procedures which will result in the return of a memory, following amnesia produced by an ECS.

A simple stepdown platform is often used in studying memory formation and amnesia. A rat is placed on a platform raised a few inches above a grid floor and when it steps down it receives a foot shock followed by ECS. The ECS produces a deficit for the memory of the foot shock; the rat steps rapidly off the platform the next time it is put there. Control rats which do not receive ECS after the foot shock usually remain on the platform. If the memory is not thoroughly destroyed by the ECS, it should be possible to remind the animal that it has been punished and thus produce a memory return. In four experiments we have given a reminder by administering another foot shock several hours after the rats had recovered from the effects of the convulsion.

In our first experiment we randomly assigned 40 albino rats to four types of treatment. After three adaptation trials, on stepping off the raised platform one group received approximately 1.6 mA of current through the feet for 5 s, followed immediately by ECS administered through alligator clips attached to the ears. The second group did not receive foot shock but were convulsed for 5 s after stepping off the platform. The third group received the foot shock but not the convulsive current, and the fourth group received neither foot shock nor ECS. All rats were returned to the apparatus 20 h later to determine whether amnesia had been produced. Subsequent analysis showed that it had.

Four hours after this test all rats were placed in a small compartment, quite different from the one in which the experimental treatment had been administered, and given another 5 s 1.6 mA foot shock. They were returned to the stepdown apparatus 20 h later to see if a reminder effect had been produced. The measure of response was the time it took each rat to step off the platform on the second test trial compared with the first. Analysis showed there was no significant change in the group which received ECS alone or in the group given no treatment. The group receiving initial foot shock alone showed an increase in suppression significant at the 0.05 level, and the group receiving initial foot shock followed by ECS (the amnesic group) showed an increase in suppression significant at the 0.01 level (two-tailed). These results show that foot shock followed by ECS produces an amnesia from which partial recovery occurs after a reminder shock.

A second experiment entailed a $2 \times 2 \times 2$ factorial design in which the presence and absence of ECS, foot shock, and reminder shock were varied in groups each of twenty animals. An analysis of variance showed a significant foot-shock effect ($P < 0.001$), a significant reminder shock effect ($P < 0.001$), and a significant foot shock by ECS interaction ($P < 0.003$). The reminder effect should show up in the triple interaction. This interaction just fails ($P = 0.08$) to be significant by a traditional two-tailed criterion, but the fact that it is repeatable in successive experiments testifies to its reliability.

Figure 1 shows the results with the triple interaction. We interpret this to mean that foot shock produces a response suppression if it is not followed by ECS, and if it is followed by ECS the suppression occurs only if a reminder shock is given. The ECS blocks the memory of the initial foot shock unless a reminder shock is given later. This interpre-

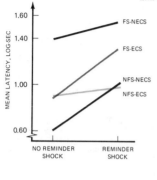

FIGURE 1 *Mean log latency for test trial stepdown with and without reminder shock, illustrating the source of the three-way interaction. Individual two-tailed t tests between groups receiving and not receiving reminder shock yield P < 0.005 (FS-ECS), P > 0.30 (FS-NECS), P > 0.30 (NFS-ECS), and P < 0.02 (NFS-NECS).*

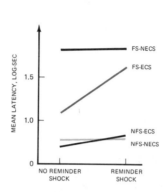

FIGURE 2 *Mean log latency for test trial stepdown with and without weak reminder shock, illustrating the source of the three-way interaction. Individual two-tailed t tests between groups receiving and not receiving reminder shock yield P < 0.005 (FS-ECS), P > 0.70 (FS-NECS), P > 0.90 (NFS-ECS), and P > 0.30 (NFS-NECS).*

tation is supported by t tests between individual groups. The P values of these tests are shown in Fig. 1. The smallest P value is associated with the foot-shock and ECS group, which indicates a reliable memory return.

Perhaps one reason why there is such a strong reminder shock effect is that we used a fairly intense current. We therefore set up a small control experiment using a reminder shock with an intensity setting at 0.6 mA instead of the 1.6 mA used before, but then we did not obtain a significant effect of the reminder shock alone. Again the reminder shock significantly reduced the amount of amnesia that had been produced by the previous ECS—a third replication of memory return.

In the final experiment, design and procedure were identical to those of the second experiment, and an analysis of variance of logarithmetically transformed data revealed similar results. Further, there was no significant difference ($P > 0.30$) between the group receiving only the original learning foot shock and the group that was made amnesic and then reminded of the first foot shock. In this case memory return was almost complete. In this experiment, the memory shock alone had no significant effect ($P > 0.30$) compared with a group that received no treatment. Figure 2 is a graph of these data.

Our experiments indicate that a post-amnesic foot shock can serve as a reminder for the return of a memory which had been inhibited by ECS. This indicates that at least part of the memory remained, but that its retrieval was prevented by ECS.

This research was supported by a grant from the U.S. National Institutes of Health. We thank Mr. Norman Richter for assistance. Reprinted from *Nature*, 1968, **220**, 704–705, by permission of MacMillan (Journals) Ltd., London.

LONG TEMPORAL GRADIENT OF RETROGRADE AMNESIA FOR A WELL-DISCRIMINATED STIMULUS

RUDOLF KOPP/ZDENEK BOHDANECKY/MURRAY E. JARVIK

This experiment tested the general validity of recent findings that retrograde amnesia can be produced by electroconvulsive shock only if the shock is administered within 10 to 30 seconds after the learning trial. Precautions were taken to avoid confusion of other shock effects with retrograde amnesia. A temporal gradient of electroconvulsive shock-produced retrograde amnesia, extending up to at least 1 hour, for a well-discriminated stimulus, was demonstrated in mice in a one-trial learning passive avoidance situation.

Recently Quartermain et al. [1965] reported that retrograde amnesia could be produced in rats by electroconvulsive shock (ECS) if the shock was administered within 30 seconds after a learning experience, but not later. The brevity of this temporal gradient strongly substantiated findings of Chorover and Schiller [1965], who were unable to obtain any retrograde amnesic effect from ECS administered more than 10 seconds after the learning trial.

Quartermain et al. [1965] suggest that retention deficits after much longer ECS delays, as reported by other investigators [Heriot and Coleman, 1962; Weissman, 1964; Davis et al., 1965; King, 1965] may be the results of different task and procedural variables. They point out that studies which have shown significant effects of ECS administered after long delays have generally used learning tasks in which the subjects have received considerable training under deprivation of food or water before the punishing shock was administered.

Chorover and Schiller [1966] offer an alternative explanation for ECS effects observed when ECS is administered more than 10 seconds after one-trial passive avoidance learning, referring to an effect on "the locomotor inhibitive component of a generalized conditional emotional response (CER)" established in the course of the learning procedure. They feel that if certain precautions are taken in a passive avoidance test this CER component can be minimized and that under such circumstances ECS has no effect on retest performance if administered more than 10 seconds after the training trial. They seem to imply that this effect of ECS on the CER shows no temporal gradient.

The findings of Chorover and Schiller [1965] and Quartermain et al. [1965] cast doubt on results of investigators who have reported ECS effects on retest performance after delays much longer than 10 to 30 seconds [Heriot and Coleman, 1962; Weissman, 1964; Davis et al., 1965; King, 1965]. If the effect of an ECS administered after a long delay were due to an effect on a "generalized CER" established in the course of the learning procedure (as suggested by Chorover and Schiller [1966], implying that this effect on retest latencies had nothing to do with retrograde amnesia), the interpretations of the results of investigators reporting such ECS effects after long delays would have to be seriously questioned.

The present experiment was designed to test the general validity of the findings of Chorover and Schiller [1965] and Quartermain et al. [1965], taking the precautions recommended by these authors to avoid confusion of other ECS effects with retrograde amnesia, especially in the case of a long delay. In determining the time within which retrograde effects of an ECS could be obtained in a one-trial learning situation we used animals that had not been subjected to pretraining and ascertained that the avoidance response produced by the punishing shock was discriminatory.

METHOD

Female CF1 mice approximately 60 days of age were trained in a two-chambered box where they could receive a single punishing shock (800 volts a-c through 2 Mohm in series, causing approximately 320 μa r.m.s. $\pm$ 15 percent flow through the animal for 0.8 second) for stepping spontaneously from a small lighted compartment into a larger darkened one. This one-trial learning procedure (registration) generally took less than 20 seconds. Electroconvulsive shock (800 volts a-c through 40 kohm in series causing approximately 15 ma r.m.s. $\pm$ 20 percent to flow through the animal for 0.2 second) producing full tonic seizures was administered outside the apparatus, transcorneally, to different groups of mice, 5, 20, 80, 320 seconds, 1 hour, or 6 hours after learning.

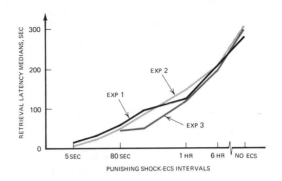

FIGURE 1   *The temporal gradient of retrograde amnesia following ECS in mice. Each data point represents the retrieval test latency median of seven to eight animals.*

A control group received no ECS after registration. A second control group received no punishing shock but ECS. Approximately 24 hours after the learning trial the animals were again placed in the brightly lighted compartment for retest and the latencies of stepping into the darkened chamber were measured (retrieval test). Animals tarrying longer than 300 seconds were removed.

RESULTS

It is clear from Fig. 1, which is based on three independent experiments, that the longer the ECS treatment is delayed the smaller is its effect upon a subsequent retrieval trial. Table 1 contains the pooled data of three experiments. It can be seen that the difference between 5 minutes and 1 hour is still significant ($p < 0.01$).[1] The difference between 1 hour and 6 hours just misses significance ($p > 0.05$). The difference between the latencies of the 6-hour group and of the control group receiving punishing shock without ECS is significant ($p < 0.01$). Table 1 includes a control group which did not receive a punishing shock in the step-through box but which received a single ECS outside the box 10 seconds after having stepped into the second compartment. The low retest latencies indicate that the single ECS is not punishing.

These results support the view that consolidation processes may extend over minutes and perhaps even hours or days [Heriot and Coleman, 1962; Weissman, 1964; Davis et al., 1965; King, 1965; Glickman, 1961; Flexner et al., 1963]. The discrepancy between our results and those of Chorover and Schiller [1965] and Quartermain et al. [1965] may be related to different species used (rats versus mice) or to the intensity of the punishing shock. There is a suggestion in the data of Chorover and Schiller that a retrograde amnesic effect may have been

[1]The Wilcoxon Rank Sum Test was used for statistical evaluation of the data.

produced by ECS administered 30 seconds after foot shock when the duration of the punishing shock was diminished to 0.5 second.

Beyond 1 hour the gradient appears to level off and differences between groups that received ECS 1 and 6 hours after the learning trial versus unconvulsed animals may be due to a proactive disinhibitive effect of the ECS on retrieval test performance. The time course of proactive disinhibitive effects of ECS cannot be determined from the present results.

In order to check the possibility suggested by Chorover and Schiller [1966] that ECS effects obtained after long delays might be due to an action on a generalized CER established in the course of the learning trial, we examined the generalizability of the punishment. A group of animals was trained in the apparatus in the usual way, except that upon stepping into the inner compartment they were immediately removed and put into a small restraining device, an electrode was applied to the base of the tail, and a strong electric shock was administered (800 volts a-c through 40 kohm in series causing approximately 2.5 ma r.m.s. $\pm$ 30 percent to flow through the animal for 0.8 second).

TABLE 1   *Retest latency decrements when ECS was given at different intervals after learning*

ECS administered after learning trial	Mice, no.	Retest latency medians, sec	Interquartile range, sec	Probabilities of differences between groups
5 seconds	16	9.3	6.3 to 16.2	
20 seconds*	16	27.8	17.6 to 46.2	$p < 0.005$
80 seconds	23	50.3	36.5 to 87.0	$p < 0.025$
320 seconds*	23	82.8	35.3 to 119.0	Not significant
1 hour	23	127.7	97.3 to 174.9	$p < 0.01$
6 hours*	16	195.0	98.6 to 251.6	Not significant
No ECS	24	< 300.0	188.0 to < 300.0	$p < 0.01$
No punishing shock; ECS 10 seconds after stepping through	9	5.0	3.5 to 11.1	

*Twenty seconds versus 320 seconds, $p < 0.005$; 320 seconds versus 6 hours, $p < 0.005$.

TABLE 2   *Effect of punishment, inside the apparatus versus outside, on retest latencies*

Group	Received punishing shock	Mice, no.	Median of retest latencies, sec	Interquartile range, sec
A	Inside box	9	290.5	216.4 to > 300
B	Outside box	25	7.0	5.8 to 20
C	No punishing shock	24	6.7	4.3 to 13.6

Under these conditions all animals squeaked and appeared to experience intense pain. It can be seen in Table 2 that group *B*, which received such a strong punishment outside the box, showed retest latencies that were essentially the same as those of unpunished control animals (group *C*) and were significantly lower ($p < 0.005$) than those of animals shocked in the box (group *A*). This indicates that the mice discriminated the stimuli of the avoidance situation and it implies that ECS lowered retest latencies by producing retrograde amnesia to a well-discriminated painful experience.

Reprinted from *Science*, 1966, **153**, 1547–1549, by permission of the American Association for the Advancement of Science.

RETROGRADE AMNESIA: PRODUCTION OF SKELETAL BUT NOT CARDIAC RESPONSE GRADIENT BY ELECTROCONVULSIVE SHOCK

BROMFIELD HINE/RONALD M. PAOLINO

Rats given a single electroconvulsive shock immediately after but not 60 seconds after an aversive conditioning trial exhibited behavioral retention deficits 24 hours later in a one-trial passive avoidance task. In contrast to these differential performance deficits, similar heart rate changes, indicative of fear retention, were seen in punished animals irrespective of the time of delivery of the shock. These data suggest retention of a generalized fear to the training experience that was not revealed by the behavioral measure. The potential usefulness of concomitant behavioral and physiological response assessment in consolidation research is discussed.

Rats given an electroconvulsive shock (ECS) shortly after training in single-trial learning tasks exhibit behavioral performance deficits when tested for retention 24 hours later. The gradient generated by the inverse relation between the magnitude of these deficits and the training-ECS interval has generally been attributed to a retrograde amnesia resulting from disruption of memory consolidation [McGaugh, 1966]. Some investigators, however, have applied this interpretation only to situations where training-ECS intervals on the order of seconds are used [Spevack and Suboski, 1969; Chorover and Schiller, 1966], while others discount effects of ECS on memory consolidation entirely [Adams and Lewis, 1962a; Adams and Peacock, 1967].

Assessment of autonomic changes in ECS studies where punishment is applied should facilitate evaluation of behavioral data, but such measures have seldom been used in single-trial tasks. In one such study where heart rate was measured, it was reported that ECS, when presented within 6 seconds of a single buzzer-shock pairing, did not modify the bradycardia produced to the conditioned stimulus during a retention test 24 hours later [Mendoza and Adams, 1969]. Although behavior was not reported for this task, the authors suggested that the cardiac data argued against consolidation disruption as an explanation of ECS effects. We think, however, that any interpretation of the data of Mendoza and Adams with respect to the memory consolidation hypothesis is unwarranted, since this study employed (1) familiarization to the training environment before training, (2) no independent behavioral measure of memory, and (3) only one training-ECS interval. The importance of measuring behavior and using more than one training-ECS interval in amnesia experiments is emphasized by the report that familiarization of rats to the training apparatus may decrease the period of vulnerability of memory fixation to ECS disruption to less than 0.5 second after training [Lewis et al., 1969].

We report here the effects of ECS on one-trial aversive learning with both behavioral and heart rate responses as indices of retention under conditions that have, in our previous experience, repeatedly and consistently produced reliable, short behavioral gradients of retrograde amnesia [Paolino et al., 1969; Quartermain et al., 1965; Paolino and Kovachevich, unpublished]. Two training-ECS intervals were investigated to ascertain the time dependency of these effects—one which consistently produces behavioral retention test deficits, the other which produces no such deficits. Cardiac responses, suggestive of fear retention, were seen under conditions where behavioral evidence of amnesia was confirmed.

METHOD

We used 108 male rats (Holtzman strain, 90 to 120 days old). The animals were caged together until surgery and then were placed in individual wire-mesh cages with free access to food and water, which was available throughout the experiment. Two days before the first habituation session, animals were anesthetized with ether. Stainless steel surgical wire (Ethicon stranded) was inserted through the skin behind each pinna and tied flush to the skin. A third wire lead was implanted subcutaneously just above the sternum and exited on the dorsal surface of the neck between the two pinna leads, where it was sewn into the skin. "Wire form" subminiature female pin contacts (Amphenol Co.) were soldered to 5-mm extensions of these leads to make connection with male contact pins soldered to ECS delivery and heart rate recording wires. These wires were enclosed in a shielded cable suspended from a counter-balanced, overhead boom which allowed free movement of the animal throughout the apparatus. The electrocardiogram (EKG), monitored between one of the pinna leads and the sternum lead, was recorded on an E & M physiograph. The ECS was delivered by way of the pinna leads from a Hans model 2-C seizure apparatus.

The one-trial passive avoidance apparatus [Quartermain et al., 1965] consisted of a small opaque Plexiglas compartment (SC) connected to a larger compartment (open field with grid floor) by a guillotine door. An opaque guillotine door was used during habituation and training sessions, and a clear Plexiglas door was used during retention testing.

Animals were habituated to the SC in four separate 3-minute sessions.[1] Two sessions were given per day for two consecutive days, with sessions within a day separated by approximately 5 hours. During habituation, the opaque guillotine door was in place to prevent entrance into the open field. The animal, with recording leads attached, was placed in the SC, and the EKG was recorded for 3 minutes. The animal was then returned to its home cage.

A single training trial was given the day after the last habituation session, followed 24 hours later by a 3-minute retention test. During training, each animal, with its leads attached, was placed in the SC. After the guillotine door was opened, latency for placing all four paws into the open field was recorded to the nearest 0.1 second. The door was then closed, and one of five treatments was applied. For the three experimental groups, entry into the open field initiated the presentation of a 1.5-ma 1.5-second footshock (FS) through the grid floor. In the FS learning group ($N = 18$), animals were removed 3 minutes after receiving FS and were returned to home cages. In the other two groups ($N = 18$ each) a single ECS (100 ma for 0.5 second) was administered either immediately (FS-ECS immed.) or 60 seconds (FS-ECS 60 sec) after FS termination. Two control groups were trained. One group of animals (NFS-NECS) received no shocks. Each animal was returned to its home cage 3 minutes after entering the open field. A second group (ECS) received only ECS after entering the open field. In all groups that received ECS, recovery from the resultant tonic flexion or extension convulsions occurred in the home cage. Animals that failed to enter the open field within 180 seconds were discarded.

For the retention test, recording leads were attached and the animal was placed in the SC. With the exception of the FS-ECS 60 sec group, heart rate and latency data were collected separately for each training group in order to obtain cardiac data which were free from confounding effects of performing the behavioral response. Accordingly,

---

[1]It is important to note that animals were habituated to the SC only and not to the large compartment where training to FS took place.

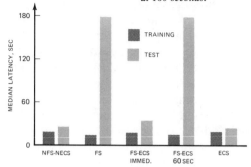

FIGURE 1   *Median latencies to enter the open field during training and retention test sessions. Timing of latency to enter the open field during both sessions was terminated at 180 seconds.*

each training group was divided into subgroups of equal sizes. Animals in each subgroup were either confined to the SC for heart rate recording (clear Plexiglass guillotine door in place) or given access to the open field area (guillotine door opened). The EKG was recorded for 3 minutes. Neither FS nor ECS was administered.

RESULTS

Median latencies to enter the open field during training and retention sessions for the five nonconfined groups are presented in Fig. 1. Every animal in both FS and FS-ECS 60 sec groups remained in the SC for 180 seconds,[2] indicating maximum retention for the FS animals and failure of ECS to disrupt retention when delayed 60 seconds after FS administration. While not significantly different from either the NFS-NECS or ECS control groups, animals convulsed immediately after FS did differ significantly from both the FS learning group and FS-ECS 60 sec group [Kruskal-Wallis analysis of variance on retention latencies: $H = 29.2$, d.f. $= 4$, $P < .001$; significant Mann-Whitney comparisons: FS-ECS immed. versus FS and FS-ECS 60 sec ($U = 4.5$), NFS-NECS and ECS versus FS and FS-ECS 60 sec ($U = 0.0$), all $P < .001$]. No significant differences were found between latency scores of the groups during training. These results confirm previous findings of a short behavioral gradient for this task [Paolino et al., 1969; Quartermain et al., 1965; Paolino and Kovachevich, unpublished].

Heart rate data were tabulated as number of beats per minute in six alternate 15-second epochs of the 3-minute test sessions. A trend analysis of variance performed on the intrasession retention data for the confined FS and NFS-NECS groups revealed significant heart rate changes ($F = 9.90$, d.f. $= 5/80$, $P < .005$). When compared with the

---

[2]Since the variability of these groups' latencies was zero, nonparametric (distribution-free) statistics were used for the analysis of the latency data.

nontreated control group, these changes, manifested as a decrease in rate for the FS group, were limited to the first two epochs ($t = 2.38$, d.f. $= 16$, $P < .025$) when habituation-retention group differences were analyzed. This conditioned bradycardia in shocked animals should be contrasted with the significant increase in heart rate in response to the FS in the training session. The training tachycardia was seen in all FS animals and lasted for most of the 3-minute recording period. The increase in rate during the first epoch after FS, when compared with a similar period during the last habituation session) was significant ($t = 2.86$, d.f. $= 8$, $P < .05$). During this post-FS period locomotor activity within the open field decreased markedly from preshock levels and was, in most animals, entirely absent. These results suggest that mechanisms responsible for the production of bradycardia to conditioned and tachycardia to unconditioned stimuli during classical aversive conditioning and conditioned suppression training in rats [Fitzgerald and Teyler, 1970; de Toledo and Black, 1966] as well as conditioned suppression training in monkeys [Zeiner et al., 1969] may also be operating in a passive avoidance task, where the training environment acquires aversive cue properties.[3]

DISCUSSION

The following discussion of heart rate data refer to those rates produced during the first 15-second epoch of a session. Since between-group averages for the last habituation session were not statistically different, these scores were equated. Retention scores were expressed as average rate changes from habituation scores for each group (Fig. 2). Analysis of variance of difference scores ($F = 115.8$, d.f. $= 5/45$, $P < .005$) and multiple comparison tests revealed that significant retention deficits occurred between groups that received FS during training and those for which FS was absent, irrespective of the presence or absence of ECS. That is to say, bradycardia with respect to cardiac responses of non-FS controls was produced for groups receiving ECS immediately as well as

[3]Additional evidence for single-trial cardiac conditioning was provided by the data from a shock-sensitization control group of nine rats. These animals were habituated and tested for retention in exactly the same manner as the other confined groups. On the training day, each animal was removed from the apparatus 1 minute after entering the open field from the SC, and was then returned to its home cage. One hour later, a 1.5-ma 1.5-second alternating current shock was delivered to the tail of the restrained animal. The shock was administered outside of the training apparatus, and the rat was returned immediately to its home cage. The retention test was given 24 hours after tail shock. During retention testing, these animals exhibited an average increase of 17 beats per minute with respect to rates produced during the last habituation session (the group mean of 413 beats per minute for the habituation session was not significantly different from other habituation group means). This increase was similar in direction to that displayed by nonshocked and ECS controls. The retention heart rate of these sensitization controls was significantly greater than that of the FS learning group ($t = 1.61$, d.f. $= 16$, $P < .05$, one-tailed).

60 seconds after FS, thus demonstrating the absence of a performance gradient with this measure. The fact that heart rate changes for the ECS group were similar in magnitude and direction to those of nontreated controls provides further support for the lack of aversiveness of ECS in this task. Lack of significant differences between FS confined and nonconfined groups suggests minimum influence of stimulus change, with respect to the presence or absence of the plexiglass door, during retention testing.

The major finding of this study, then, is the presence of an amnesic gradient when response latency is measured, but the lack of a gradient when heart rate is monitored. Assuming that both heart rate and response latency are valid measures of retention, cardiac responses may be more sensitive to training effects. While the underlying basis for the differences between the two measures is not known, the following speculation is offered for heuristic purposes. The bradycardia observed in animals that received ECS immediately after FS may actually reflect retention of a generalized fear. A possible mechanism that might account for this "sparing" effect is that fear conditioning to general environmental cues proceeds at an extremely rapid rate and that a longer time is required for the formation of associations with specific cues within the environment. Thus, placing animals back into the apparatus on the retention trial would reactivate a generalized fear response as measured by heart rate. However, the minimum association

FIGURE 2 *Mean change in heart rate from the last habituation session to the retention test session. All groups, with the exception of the nonconfined (NC) FS group, were confined (C) to the small compartment during both sessions. Responses between the groups during the last habituation trial were not significantly different and were therefore equated.*

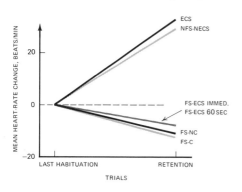

between pain produced by footshock and specific cues of the open field would not be sufficient to inhibit entrance into the open field.[4] Indirect evidence for such "sparing" of memory in a task where a short training-ECS interval was used is provided in a study reported by Dawson and McGaugh [1969a]. In their study of ECS effects on conditioned suppression of licking behavior in rats, these authors reported that animals which exhibited ECS-produced inhibition of suppression to the CS displayed significantly increased latencies to make a fixed number of licks during a pre-ECS period.

The questions raised by this study are important for several reasons. The use of a single dependent variable in consolidation research, while providing apparently unambiguous data, may actually mask the observation of important relationships. For example, the presence or absence of retention deficits may be inferred from our data, depending on the variable one chose to examine. The potential usefulness of both autonomic and behavioral variables in consolidation research might be applied to the problem of determining the nature of the process or processes that are disrupted by ECS, and whether "task" or "emotional" components, or both, of memory processes are being modified by ECS in aversive tasks.

Some of the current controversy about the concept of consolidation appears to be directed more to describing the range of conditions under which behavioral disruption will be produced by traumatic agents than to the assessment of the validity of the concept itself. Perhaps, even the question of validity will disappear as more specific postulates about memory mechanisms are developed. Both the judicious use of behavioral techniques and concurrent study of physiological mechanisms seem necessary if this goal is to be successfully approached.

Supported by Purdue Research Foundation predoctoral fellowship to B.H. and NIMH grant MH-15352. Reprinted from *Science*, 1970, **169**, 1224–1226, by permission of the American Association for the Advancement of Science.

[4]While this report was in press, Quartermain et al. [1970] independently proposed a similar mechanism to account for the finding that a reminder shock would produce recovery of an ECS-disrupted passive avoidance response. According to these authors, however, the basis for the retained fear is an incomplete weakening, by ECS, of the association between specific training cues and fear, rather than the inability of ECS to disrupt a rapidly conditioned generalized fear response, as we suggest.

RETROGRADE AMNESIA PRODUCED
BY ANESTHETIC AND CONVULSANT AGENTS

CHESTER A. PEARLMAN, JR./SETH K. SHARPLESS/MURRAY E. JARVIK

Rats were trained to press a bar for water and then administered a shock through the bar which produced subsequent avoidance of the bar. Ether anesthesia induced within 5, but not 10, min. and sodium pentobarbital administered within 10, but not 20, min. of the learning trial produced significant amnesia for the shock. A single pentylenetetrazol convulsion administered four days after the shock also resulted in significant interference with retention.

The striking ability of electroconvulsive shock and other agents to impair retention of an acquired response has been the subject of numerous investigations. In general, it has been shown that the memory deficit is most extensive if the treatment is administered within a short time after the learning trial. The effective agents include concussion [Russell, 1959], convulsions [Zubin and Barrera, 1941], anoxia [Thompson, 1957a], and direct electrical stimulation of specific brain structures [Glickman, 1958; Thompson, 1958a]. It is agreed that the interval during which such agents can exert significant retrograde effects is relatively short, a few hours at most. The concept of a consolidation process has been proposed to account for this period during which a memory is vulnerable, implying the perseveration of some form of neural activity after the learning trial which results in an increased stability of the memory trace.

The effects of anesthesia on recent memory are controversial. Although Leukel [1957] showed some impairment of learning in a water maze when thiopental was administered 1 min. after each daily trial, at least one author has expressed the opinion that rapidly induced anesthesia does not affect recent memory [Burns, 1958]. According to this view, the process of consolidation can take place even when central synaptic transmission is severely depressed by anesthetic agents.

In studying the consolidation process, it is desirable to have precise control over the interval between the learning experience and the memory-disrupting event. This control is difficult to achieve in experiments involving practice and repetition of learning trials. Glickman [1958] adapted the one-trial avoidance learning procedure of Hudson [1950] to study the effects of brain stimulation on consolidation. In the present experiment, a similar design was used to compare the effects of convulsant and anesthetic drugs on consolidation. Additional control of the interval between learning experience and drug treatment was achieved by administering the drugs, where appropriate, through permanently indwelling intravenous catheters.

METHOD

Eighty-five naive male rats of the Sprague-Dawley strain were used. They were received in four separate samples; animals in each sample were 90 to 120 days old at the beginning of the experiment.

Training   The procedure involved the suppression of a previously learned bar-pressing response as the result of a single electric shock administered through the bar. The animals were trained to press a bar for water on a continuous reinforcement schedule. They were maintained on a $23\frac{1}{2}$-hr. water-deprivation schedule and trained for 10 min. a day until a stable rate of pressing was attained. The criterion of stability was that the number of presses on the final day of training should not deviate by more than 10% from the mean of the previous three days. On the day after achievement of the criterion, an avoidance response was established by electrifying the bar and reward nozzle with 750 v. through 750,000 ohms after the animal had been in the apparatus for 5 min.

Treatment   In some animals, chronically indwelling catheters were inserted in the external jugular vein and then run subcutaneously to an incision just below the base of the skull. A more detailed description of the procedure appears elsewhere [Sharpless, 1959]. Since the catheters remained patent for about two weeks, the animals were allowed two days of rest after the operation and then tested for retention of the stability criterion before being subjected to the avoidance training.

The *S*s were divided into groups of five animals for treatment. Three groups were anesthetized with ether at approximately 10 sec., 5 min., and 10 min. after the shock, respectively. Anesthesia was induced by placing the rat under an inverted beaker containing cotton saturated with ether. Surgical anesthesia was produced in about 35 sec., and the animals recovered to their normal state of arousal within 10 min.

Sodium pentobarbital (30 mg/kg) was administered through the intravenous catheters to four groups, at approximately 20 sec., 5 min., 10 min., and 20 min. after the shock. Surgical anesthesia was produced within 10 sec. after the injection and persisted for about an hour. An attempt was made to produce roughly equivalent depths of anesthesia in all groups, as indicated by superficial (conjunctival and pinna) reflexes.

In five groups, pentylenetetrazol (Metrazol, 20 mg/kg) was injected through the catheters about 20 sec. after the shock or intraperitoneally 2 hr., 4 hr., 8 hr., and 4 days after the shock. All injections of pentylene-

TABLE 1 *Rate of bar-pressing during test for retention of avoidance response after drug treatment, expressed as percentage of initial rate of pressing (mean values for groups of five; SD in parentheses)*

Time interval between shock and drug treatment	Ether	Pento-barbital	Pentylene-tetrazol	Control (no drugs)
Control (no shock)	100 (3)	98 (5)	99 (3)	—
10 sec.	36 (4)*	76 (5)*	100 (6)*	2 (2)
5 min.	17 (6)*	48 (4)*	—	—
10 min.	4 (2)	23 (4)*	—	—
20 min.	—	1 (1)	—	—
2 hr.	—	—	94 (8)*	—
4 hr.	—	—	98 (5)*	—
8 hr.	—	—	92 (7)*	—
4 days	—	—	70 (19)*	1 (1)†

*Significantly different from the untreated control group ($p < .01$).
†These two groups were tested for retention five days after the shock. Other groups were tested 24 hr. after the shock.

tetrazol produced a clonic-tonic-clonic seizure in which the clonic activity persisted for about 4 min.

Retention The experimental groups were tested for retention of the avoidance response 24 hr. after the shock, with the exception of the group receiving pentylenetetrazol four days after the shock. These animals were tested for retention one day after being convulsed (i.e., five days after the original avoidance learning). Loss of the avoidance response was measured by expressing each animal's performance as a percentage of its normal rate of pressing. The latter value was calculated by averaging the results of the last four days of training before the shock.

Controls As shown in Table 1, five groups served as controls. The animals in three of these groups received no shock but were given the various drugs and tested 24 hr. later to determine whether there were any delayed effects of the drugs on the bar-pressing response which might obscure the results. The remaining two groups were given the shock but no drug. They were tested either one day or five days later in order to measure the retention of the avoidance response in the absence of pharmacological interference.

The statistical significance of the data was evaluated by the Mann-Whitney U test.

RESULTS

The mean value for each group is shown in Table 1. Failure to avoid (i.e., loss of memory due to drug treatment) is indicated by a high rate of pressing and a high percentage score.

Animals given ether within 5 min. and those given pentobarbital within 10 min. after the shock show significantly less avoidance than the unanesthetized controls, and each pentobarbital group shows significantly less avoidance than the corresponding ether group ($p < .01$).

Pentylenetetrazol given up to 8 hr. after the shock completely suppressed the avoidance response. Animals convulsed as long as four days after the shock still showed significantly less avoidance than untreated controls tested after the same interval ($p < .01$).

DISCUSSION

Anesthesia induced within a few minutes after a learning trial impaired retention of an avoidance response acquired during that trial. Moreover, the effect was graded, dependent upon the time elapsing between the learning experience and the induction of anesthesia. Pentobarbital was more effective than ether in impairing retention and was effective for a longer time after the learning trial.

The greater potency of pentobarbital anesthesia in interfering with recent memory may be due to the longer sleeping time induced by this agent—about an hour as compared with 10 min. for ether. Russell [1959] observed that the extent of retrograde amnesia following head injury was roughly correlated with the duration of posttraumatic amnesia, which may be a measure of the duration of abnormal cerebral function. It is difficult to judge depth of anesthesia by superficial reflexes, however, and it is possible that the initial level of anesthesia was deeper with pentobarbital than with ether.

Previous evidence concerning the effects of anesthetic agents on memory is ambiguous. Artusio [1955] has shown that there is a stage of anesthesia with ether at which patients are unable to form new memories although their mental function is intact as measured by response to spoken voice, problem solving, old memory, etc. Orkin et al. [1956] reported similar results with thiopental. In the experiment of Leukel [1957], referred to previously, intraperitoneal injection of thiopental 1 min. after each daily trial produced impairment, whereas thiopental given 30 min. after the trial had no such effect.

On the other hand, Summerfield and Steinberg [1959] report that the anesthetic gas nitrous oxide actually improves memory for nonsense syllables when it is given after learning and continued until just before recall. Ether [Hunt et al., 1953] and pentobarbital [Siegal et al., 1949] have been reported to protect against some of the amnesic effects of electroconvulsive shock.

It is probable that a general anesthetic can have two effects on memory. When given after consolidation is more or less complete, the anesthetic may reduce interference and retroactive inhibition and thus conserve the memory trace; when given within a few minutes after the learning experience, it may block the consolidation process before the

READINGS IN MEMORY CONSOLIDATION

memory has attained stability and permanence. In addition, the observations of Artusio [1955] suggest that the consolidation process may be selectively impaired in the absence of generalized depression of cerebral function.

In the present study, very marked impairment of retention was produced by a single pentylenetetrazol convulsion 8 hr., and even *four days*, after the learning trial. This is in contrast with the results with anesthesia, where the maximum interference time was approximately 15 min. It is difficult to avoid the conclusion that the mode of interference is different when the disturbing event occurs within a few minutes of the learning trial and when it occurs days later. In the first case, the disturbing event disrupts a consolidation process, which requires only a few hours at most to bring the memory to a stable, permanent condition. In the case of impairment of memory by a single convulsion or multiple convulsions days after the initial learning, it is likely that a different process is involved. It would be in accord with both clinical experience and previous experimental studies to expect that in the latter case, the memory impairment would be temporary and concomitant with the confusional state that comes as the aftermath to convulsant therapy [Brady, 1952; Kalinowsky and Hoch, 1946].

In previous studies, if convulsive treatment was not begun until a day or more after the acquisition of an emotional response, many convulsions were required to produce significant impairment of retention. Why a single convulsion was so effective in the present experiment is an interesting question. Perhaps the emotional response acquired in this situation was relatively weak since it was established in a single trial by an easily escaped shock from the bar of the Skinner box rather than the customary inescapable grid shock repeated several times. The fact that the convulsion was induced by pentylenetetrazol rather than electric shock may also be relevant, but clinical experience suggests that there is no difference in the degree of memory impairment produced by the various convulsant agents [Kalinowsky and Hoch, 1946].

SUMMARY AND CONCLUSIONS

Rats were trained to press a bar for water. They were then taught to avoid the bar in a single trial during which they received a shock through the bar when they touched it. At various intervals after learning the animals were subjected to ether or pentobarbital anesthesia or a pentylenetetrazol convulsion. A day later, they were tested for retention of the avoidance response with the following results:

1. Surgical anesthesia severely impaired retention of the avoidance response if the anesthesia was induced within 10 to 15 min. after the learning trial.

2. Intravenous pentobarbital was more effective than ether in producing this retrograde amnesia.

3. A single pentylenetetrazol convulsion abolished the avoidance response when as much as 8 hr. intervened between learning and treatment and markedly depressed the response even when the interval between learning and convulsion was increased to four days.

4. It was concluded that the consolidation process, at least in its initial stages, is incompatible with a state of surgical anesthesia.

5. Interference with memory by convulsions occurring hours or days after the learning trial probably depends upon a different mechanism, related to the clinically observed sequelae of convulsive treatment, which are characterized by various transient derangements including confusion and memory lacunae.

This work was supported by Interdisciplinary Grant 2M-6418, National Institute of Mental Health; United States Public Health Service Grant M-1225; and National Science Foundation Grant G-4459. Reprinted from the *Journal of Comparative and Physiological Psychology*, 1961, **54**, 109–112 by permission of the American Psychological Association.

MEMORY IN MICE AS AFFECTED BY INTRACEREBRAL PUROMYCIN

JOSEFA B. FLEXNER/LOUIS B. FLEXNER/ELIOT STELLAR

The antibiotic puromycin caused loss of memory of avoidance discrimination learning in mice when injected intracerebrally. Bilateral injections of puromycin involving the hippocampi and adjacent temporal cortices caused loss of short-term memory; consistent loss of longer-term memory required injections involving, in addition, most of the remaining cortices. Spread of the effective memory trace from the temporal-hippocampal areas to wide areas of the cortices appears to require 3 to 6 days, depending upon the individual animal. Recent reversal learning was lost, while longer-term initial learning was retained after bilateral injections into the hippocampal-temporal areas.

The suggestion has become increasingly frequent during recent years that nucleic acids or proteins may be concerned with learning and memory. We were led to investigate the effects of the antibiotic puromycin on these aspects of behavior by the discovery of Yarmolinsky and de la Haba [1959] that puromycin produces profound inhibition of protein synthesis in a cell-free system and by the later demonstration that it efficiently suppresses protein synthesis in vivo [Gorski et al., 1961]. In an earlier paper with de la Haba and Roberts [Flexner et al., 1962] we reported studies on mice which received the maximum amount of puromycin which could be tolerated in a single subcutaneous injection. Although this treatment appeared to suppress the rate of protein synthesis in various parts of the brain to 80 percent of the control value for a period of 6 hours, it was without effect on the learning and retention of simple or discrimination avoidance responses.

The experiments to be reported here have been made with intra-cerebral injections of puromycin. The amounts injected were smaller than previously used [Flexner et al., 1962], so that disorientation of the animal at the time of testing was avoided. With this intracerebral approach, we have found that memory can be consistently destroyed, difference in the effective loci of recent and longer-term memory apparently established, and the time factor concerned in modification of the effective locus determined. Upon recovery, animals were capable of learning again. We cannot now relate these behavioral effects to sup-pression of protein synthesis, since our biochemical studies are not yet complete.

METHOD

Adult white mice were trained in a Y-maze with a grid floor through which shock could be applied. The animal was placed in the stem of the Y. To avoid shock the mouse had to move into the correct arm within 5 seconds. If it entered the incorrect arm, it received shock until it moved to the correct arm. Training was continued in one session of about 20 minutes to a criterion of 9 out of 10 correct responses, thus avoiding overtraining. The same procedure was used in testing for memory of the training experience, shock having been given for errors of perfor-mance except as noted. In this type of training we have found mice to behave essentially like rats and to retain excellent memory of the training for at least 5 weeks. Intracerebral injections of puromycin, each injection of a volume of 0.012 ml, were made through small holes in the skull, as previously described [Flexner et al., 1962].

From one to three injections of puromycin were made into each hemisphere, all at a depth of 2 mm from the surface of the skull. Bilateral injections were made through holes placed (1) just above the angle between the caudal sutures of the parietal bones and the origins of the temporal muscles—these are here designated temporal injections; (2) 2 mm lateral to the sagittal suture and 2 mm rostral to the caudal sutures of the parietal bones—these are here designated ventricular injections; and (3) 4 mm rostral to these last holes and 1 mm lateral to the sagittal suture—these are here designated frontal injections. At the present time we are dependent upon control injections of a solution of fluorescein to estimate the spread of puromycin; more refined studies, using other techniques, are not yet complete. Animals which received injections of fluorescein were sacrificed 1 hour after the injection.

RESULTS
Results with four of the seven types of injections are shown in Fig. 1. This shows that the area around the caudal rhinal fissure was stained with temporal but spared with ventricular injections. The three types of injection not shown in the figure consisted of combined ventricular and temporal injections, of combined ventricular and frontal injections, and of combined temporal and frontal injections. The distribution of fluorescence in these combined injections was essentially the sum of the individual injections as shown in Fig. 1.

The effects of intracerebral injections of puromycin on memory of the training experience are given in Table 1, which shows the number of animals in which memory was lost, impaired, or retained after puromycin injection. In the legend of the table, the means and standard deviations of the percentage savings in retention are given for the three categories of memory. Percentage savings in retention tests were calculated for both trials and errors by subtracting the number to criterion in the retention test from the number to criterion in the learning experience, dividing by the number in the learning experience, and multiplying by 100. Retention tests were given usually 3 days after puromycin, to allow ample time for recovery of the animal. At the time of testing, any weight loss had commonly been regained and feeding, general locomotor activity, and reactions to the maze were normal.

Our first observations were made on mice trained to criterion on one arm of the maze and injected with puromycin 1 day later (Table 1, "Short-term memory"). After combined bilateral temporal, ventricular, and frontal injections, retention tests showed that memory of the training experience had been completely lost. An effort was then made to localize this effect. Memory was also completely lost with high consistency when puromycin was given in bilateral temporal injections. By contrast, bilateral frontal, ventricular, or combined frontal and ventricular injections were essentially without effect.

The next series of observations was made on mice trained to criterion and injected with puromycin 11 to 43 days later (Table 1, "Longer-term memory"). Only combined, bilateral temporal, ventricular plus frontal injections consistently destroyed memory in these animals. Bilateral temporal or frontal or ventricular injections were without effect. Three combinations of two injections (combined ventricular and

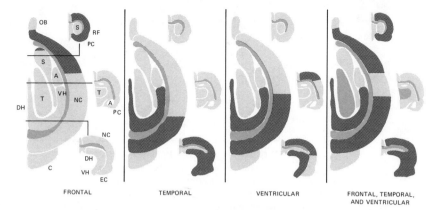

FRONTAL   TEMPORAL   VENTRICULAR   FRONTAL, TEMPORAL,
AND VENTRICULAR

FIGURE 1 *Spread of fluorescein after intracerebral injection. The larger sections in each diagram are views from the top after removal of a horizontal section of the hemisphere; the small ones are cross sections (frontal) of the hemispheres at the level indicated for frontal injections. Relative intensity of staining is indicated for each type of injection. With all injections there was intense staining (not shown) of the corpus callosum. A, amygdaloid nucleus; C, cerebellum; DH, dorsal hippocampus; EC, entorhinal cortex; NC, neocortex; OB, olfactory bulb; PC, pyriform cortex; RF, rhinal fissure; S, corpus striatum; T, thalamus; VH, ventral hippocampus.*

TABLE 1 *Effects of different sites of injection of puromycin on short- and longer-term memory. T, V, and F refer, respectively, to temporal, ventricular, and frontal injections, all given bilaterally.*

| | Puromycin injections | | No. of mice in which memory was* | | |
| | Days after | | | | |
Site	learning	Milligrams	Lost	Impaired	Retained
Short-term memory					
T + V + F	1	0.03 to .06	7	0	0
T	1	.09	8	0	0
T	1	.06	14	3	1
V	1	.09	0	0	5
F	1	.09	0	0	5
V + F	1	.09	0	1	2
Longer-term memory					
T + V + F	18 to 43	0.03 to .06	7	0	0
T	11 to 35	.06 to .09	0	0	7
V	12 to 38	.06 to .09	0	0	3
F	16 to 27	.06 to .09	0	0	3
V + F	28	.06 to .09	0	2	2
V + T	28 to 43	.09	1	1	2
T + F	28	.09	0	0	3

*For the 37 mice with loss of memory, the means and standard deviations for percentages of savings of trials and of errors were, respectively, 1 ± 3 and 2 ± 6; for the seven mice with impaired memory, 26 ± 29 and 39 ± 12; and for the 33 mice with retention of memory, 90 ± 14 and 90 ± 9. Negative savings in the group with lost memory have been designated zero so that the mean for this group is an overestimation of savings.

129

Injections, days after learning	No. of mice in which memory was*		
	Lost	Impaired	Retained
2	3	0	0
3	4	0	1
4	0	1	1
5	0	1	2
6	0	0	3

*For the seven mice with loss of memory, the means and standard deviations for percentages of savings of trials and of errors were, respectively, 1 ± 4 and 0 ± 0; for the seven mice with retention of memory, 85 ± 19 and 93 ± 7. In one mouse with impaired memory the percentages of savings for trials and errors were, respectively, 38 and 20; for the other, 39 and 55.

TABLE 2   *Effect of bilateral temporal injections of puromycin on memory of increasing age. Each injection contained 0.09 mg of puromycin.*

temporal, or ventricular and frontal, or temporal and frontal) into each hemisphere were without effect in the majority of animals, even though the total amount of puromycin in all but two of eleven of these was at the maximum level tolerated and twice that amount injected in six of the seven experiments with combined temporal, ventricular, and frontal injections. There was consequently a clear distinction between recent and longer-term memory; recent memory was lost when puromycin was introduced through temporal injections into hippocampi and caudal cortices, including the entorhinal areas, while loss of longer-term memory required puromycin additionally in a substantially greater part of the cortex and possibly in the thalamus also.

How long does it require for this modification of the locus of the effective memory trace? As shown in Table 2, bilateral temporal injections consistently destroyed memory 2 days after training but were consistently without effect 6 days after training. Results were variable at 3, 4, and 5 days. It consequently appears that the enlarged locus of longer-term memory in the type of learning experience we have used with the mouse becomes completely effective in from 3 to 6 days, depending upon the individual animal.

We proceeded from these observations to experiments in which the animal received reversal learning 3 weeks after its first training in the Y-maze, that is, the mouse was first trained, for example, to move from the stem of the Y into its left arm; then 3 weeks later was retrained to move from the stem of the Y into its right arm. Was it possible to destroy memory of reversal learning 24 hours after reversal training, spare the longer-term memory of the initial training experience given 3 weeks earlier, and in consequence have the mouse perform the task for which it was first trained?

To test this possibility bilateral temporal injections were made 24 hours after reversal learning and 3 weeks after initial learning in seven animals. Shock was omitted in the retention trials 3 days after puromycin injection, since there was, within the design of the test, no right or wrong choice. As shown in Table 3, on testing for memory the first choice of all animals was consistent with the first learning experience, as were the large majority of subsequent choices. In view of consistent results with numerous untreated animals on various schedules of learning and reversal learning, only two control animals (Table 3) were used in this series. All these untreated animals, in sharp contrast to the experimental group, made choices consistent with their second, or reversal, learning. Because the experimental animals were able to perform the older position habit efficiently and consistently, this experiment offers strong evidence that the effect of puromycin in

TABLE 3 *Differential effect of bilateral temporal injections of puromycin on recent and longer-term memory. Each injection had a volume of 0.012 ml and contained 0.06 or 0.09 (experiment 71) mg of puromycin. Choices of the arm of the Y-maze by an animal after injection were scored as "1" if consistent with initial learning, and as "2" if consistent with reversal learning. For various reasons trials were continued irregularly beyond the 10 originally planned.*

			Trials to 9/10 criterion	
Experimental animals			*Reversal learning*	
Expt. no.	*Animal no.*	*Initial learning*	*3 weeks later*	*Choice or arm of Y-maze**
86	26A	13	22	1,1,1,1,1,1,1,1,1,1,1,1,1,1,1
86	24A	7	10	1,1,2,1,1,1,1,2,1,1,1,1,1,1,1,1,1,1,1,1,2,1,1,1
86	25A	8	10	1,1,1,1,2,1,1,1,1,2,1,2,2,1,2
86	22A	9	8	1,2,2,1,1,2,1,2,1,2,1,1,1,1,1,1,1,1,1,1,1,1
86	23A	13	4	1,1,1,1,1,1,1,1,1,1,1,1
71	49	22	9	1,1,2,2,1,1,1,1,2,1,1,1,1,2,1,1,1,1,1,1,1,1,1,1
86	27A	12	5	1,1,1,1,1,1,1,1,1,2,1
Control animals				
86	58A	10	14	2,2,2,2,2,2,2,2,2,2,2,2,2,2
86	60A	10	12	2,2,2,2,2,2,2,2,2,2,2,2

*The experimental animals made their choices 3 days after temporal injections of puromycin, which were given 24 hours after reversal learning. The control animals made their choices 4 days after reversal learning, no puromycin being injected. Neither group received shock.

destroying a recent habit is not due to disorganization or incapacitation of the animal.

A beginning has been made in testing for the specificity and reversibility of the puromycin effect. Numerous control injections of saline, of subliminal concentrations of puromycin, and of puromycin hydrolyzed at the glycosidic bond were without effect on memory. Most animals treated with effective doses of puromycin were demonstrated to be capable of relearning after loss of memory, though the process of relearning, particularly with high doses of puromycin, often required considerably more trials than in the initial training experience. This aspect of the effects of puromycin will be reported more extensively at a later time.

Although the effective locus of short-term memory clearly appears different from that of longer-term memory we cannot now define the difference with precision. It does appear that the area around the caudal rhinal fissure, likely entorhinal cortex, carries the short-term memory trace, since short-term memory was retained with ventricular injections but lost with temporal injections. The part played by the hippocampus will not become evident until experiments are performed which provide for exposure of the entire temporal cortex to puromycin while the hippocampus is spared. Similarly, we cannot state whether the locus of longer-term memory is confined to the cortex or whether other parts of the brain, principally the hippocampus, are also involved. It can only be said that our observations are consistent with the evidence and conclusions of others [Milner and Penfield, 1955; Scoville and Milner, 1957; Stepien et al., 1960], that the hippocampal zone is the site of recent memory and, that an extensive part of the neocortex is concerned with longer-term memory.

It must be emphasized that our results, although apparently clear-cut in important particulars, should be interpreted at this time with caution. We are in the process of obtaining more precise information, for example, on the localization of puromycin after intracerebral injection. Histological studies on the cells of the hippocampus and cortex must be completed. Determinations must be made of the degree of suppression of protein synthesis, and, particularly in view of the negative behavioral results with subcutaneous puromycin [Flexner et al., 1962], the possibility must be kept in mind that loss of memory after intracerebral injection of puromycin may be owing to effects not related to changes in protein synthesis. Further, it remains to be shown that other learning situations, currently being investigated, and other animals are comparable to the mouse in the training experience we have used.

Supported by grants NB-00514 and MH-03571 from the U.S. Public Health Service. We are indebted to the Lederle Laboratories for our supply of puromycin. Reprinted from *Science*, 1963, **141**, 57–59, by permission of the American Association for the Advancement of Science.

CHEMICAL STUDIES ON MEMORY FIXATION IN GOLDFISH

BERNARD W. AGRANOFF/ROGER E. DAVIS/JOHN J. BRINK

Puromycin and acetoxycycloheximide, antibiotics known to block selectively protein synthesis, also block the formation of memory of shock avoidance in the goldfish.

A striking characteristic of this decade in biochemistry is the introduction of selective blocking agents as tools for research. A major area of application has been in studies on nucleic acid and protein synthesis. As findings in diverse areas are correlated, the details of the selective nature of these toxic substances become known, adding to their value.

The use of selective blocking agents in behavioral experiments has been reported by several laboratories. Dingman and Sporn [1961] injected 8-azaguanine intracisternally into rats in an attempt to block learning. Chamberlain et al. [1963] reported that intraperitoneally injected 8-azaguanine prolonged the time during which asymmetry of the limbs of rats became fixed following section of the spinal cord. Barondes and Jarvik [1964] recently found that intracerebral injection of actinomycin D into mice had no specific behavioral effect. These reports were of interest because of the putative role of 8-azaguanine and actinomycin D in blocking the synthesis of RNA. In 1963, Flexner et al. reported an effect of puromycin on memory in mice. This study will be discussed later in connection with work in our laboratory with goldfish. Puromycin is a naturally occurring nucleoside-amino acid which has been reported to block selectively protein synthesis. A mechanism has been proposed for its action which is based on the structural similarity between puromycin and the aminoacyl-adenosine terminus of transfer-RNA [Yarmolinsky and de la Haba, 1959]. Experimental results indicate that the forming peptide chain combines with puromycin instead of the next aminoacyl-transfer-RNA and that the forming peptide is released from the ribosome prematurely as peptidyl puromycin [Horner et al., 1961; Morris et al., 1962].

Interest in memory at the biological laboratories of the Mental Health Research Institute was stimulated to a large extent by Ralph W. Gerard, former director of laboratories, whose continued interest in this work is gratefully acknowledged. For the past two years, we have been studying biochemical correlates of memory in *Carrassius auratus*, the goldfish. From the literature, we learned that goldfish were capable of learning shock avoidance as well as other tasks, and appeared to have long-term memory of their training [Horner et al., 1961]. This animal has several other experimental advantages. Since teleosts are poikilotherms, it becomes easy to investigate the effect of temperature on behavioral phenomena. The small size of the goldfish makes it potentially suitable for autoradiographic studies, since the exposure time for development of histologic sections is largely a function of the amount of isotope injected per unit body weight. The goldfish brain is easily exposed for surgical procedures, and surgery is well-tolerated. We were able to devise a simple technique for the rapid injection of drugs intracranially (over, not into, the brain) without the use of anesthetics [Agranoff and Klinger, 1964].

METHOD

In the experiments presented here, we used a shuttle box similar to one described by Bitterman [Horner et al., 1961]. Goldfish are placed in individual tanks divided into two compartments by an underwater barrier (Fig. 1). At the start of a trial, a light is turned on at the end of the tank in which the fish has been placed. Twenty sec later, an intermittent electric shock is applied to the illuminated end of the tank for an additional 20 sec. During this period, fish that have not already swum over the barrier do so, escaping further shock. Forty sec after the start of the trial, light and shock are both terminated. After 20 sec of intertrial interval, in which there is no light or shock, the opposite end of the tank is illuminated and the procedure is repeated. Fish receive five trials in 5 min. A block of five trials as outlined in Fig. 1 is followed by 5 min of rest in darkness. In this way fish receive 20 trials in 40 min on the first day of the experiment. If a fish swims over the barrier with the light stimulus alone and thus avoids being shocked, a correct response is scored for that trial. Groups of fish usually score up to 30% correct responses during the first 10 trials and improve during the second 10 trials. If they are immediately given an additional set of 10 trials, they do still better. If we now interpose a time interval between trial 20 and 21 such as an hour, a day, a week, or a month, there is little effect on the scores for the last 10 trials. Thus we see that the goldfish has good memory of the task. In our experiments, we use an interval of 3 days between trial 20 and 21. Fish receive 20 trials on day 1 and 10 trials on day 4. In our initial studies, we compared the effect of

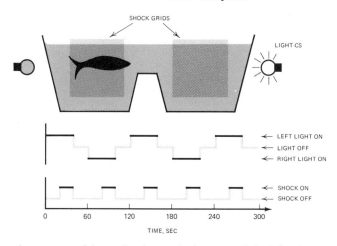

electroconvulsive shock and intracranial injections of puromycin following the 20 trials on day 1 on the performance observed on day 4. We found that each of these agents produced a partial memory deficit if given immediately after trial 20, but had no effect if given 2 h later [Davis and Agranoff, 1965; Davis et al., 1965]. In each instance, memory was measured as the performance for the 10 trials on day 4. Using electroconvulsive shock as the agent which blocks memory fixation, we studied the effect of water temperature during the period immediately following trial 20 on the rate of memory fixation. We found that cooling extended the period of time during which electroconvulsive shock can block memory [Davis and Agranoff, 1965; Davis et al., 1965]. This result is similar to that reported in mammals [Ransmeir and Gerard, 1954], but is of particular interest in that we used a poikilotherm, simplifying interpretation of the results.

During the course of these experiments, we introduced a regression analysis for the evaluation of memory on day 4. The regression of the total day 1 score on the day 4 score, derived from data for 129 control fish, is used to predict day 4 scores for experimental fish. The predicted score (P) of a fish is subtracted from the score the fish achieves (A) on day 4, and the result is called the *retention score* $(A - P)$; a retention score of zero signifies normal memory. This technique compensates for uncontrolled differences in levels of responding between fish. Conclusions reached by evaluating retention scores or raw day 4 scores have been identical, but the retention scores have been more consistent.

RESULTS

We have recently found that by increasing the amount of puromycin injected we can obliterate memory of the avoidance response on day 4

TABLE 1   *Effect of puromycin injected after training on memory*

| | Trials day 1 | | | | Trials day 4 | Retention |
No.	1–10	11–20	Treatment	21–30 A	21–30 P	score (A − P)
72	2.3	3.4	Uninjected	5.3	5.3	0
36	2.5	3.8	Puromycin dihydrochloride, 170 µg, immediate	2.7	5.4	− 2.7
35	2.5	4.6	Puromycin dihydrochloride, 170 µg, 60 min delay	5.5	5.6	− 0.1

TABLE 2   *Effect of puromycin moieties on memory*

| | Trials day 1 | | | | Trials day 4 | Retention |
No.	1–10	11–20	Treatment	21–30 A	21–30 P	score (A − P)
23	2.0	3.2	Puromycin aminonucleoside, 90 µg, immediate	5.1	5.0	+ 0.1
81	2.5	3.5	O-Methyltyrosine hydrochloride, 70 µg, immediate	5.2	5.4	− 0.2

TABLE 3   *Effect of puromycin injected before training on memory*

| | Trials day 1 | | | | Trials day 4 | Retention |
No.	1–10	11–20	Treatment	21–30 A	21–30 P	score (A − P)
39	3.0	3.8	Puromycin dihydrochloride, 170µg, 1 min pretrial	3.3	5.5	− 2.2
35	2.4	3.3	Puromycin dihydrochloride, 170 µg, 20 min pretrial	4.2	5.2	− 1.0

(the score for the 10 trials on day 4 is not significantly different from the score in the first 10 trials on day 1) [Agranoff et al., 1965]. Injection of 170 µg of puromycin immediately after trial 20 on day 1 produces a complete memory deficit on day 4. If we wait 1 h after trial 20 before injecting, the drug has no detectable effect on memory (Table 1). The dramatic change in susceptibility of memory on day 4 to puromycin injected during the hour following the trials on day 1 is indicated by the graph of retention scores in Fig. 2. These results indicate that memory on day 4 depends on a fixation process occurring after the trials on day 1 which is disrupted by puromycin. The effect of different amounts of puromycin injected immediately after trial 20 is also shown in Fig. 2. Injection of 50 µg or less has no significant effect, while 90 µg or more produces memory deficits. Memory is not affected by injection of physiological saline, nor is it affected by puromycin aminonucleoside or

O-methyltyrosine (methoxyphenylalanine), two moieties which comprise the puromycin molecule (Table 2).

Puromycin can be injected into fish rapidly and without anesthesia. There is no transient drowsiness or other evidence of neurological disorder. We have found that fish given puromycin shortly *before* the 20 trials on day 1 show the usual increase in correct responses from trials 1–10 to 11–20, while their memory on day 4 is deficient (Table 3). Thus puromycin does not affect that aspect of memory which is manifested in the improvement in performance on day 1, that we define as short-term memory. We see then that puromycin produces deficits in memory on day 4 by acting specifically on the process by which long-term memory is fixed. A summary on these experiments is seen in Fig. 3.

A question before us is what is the relationship between the behavioral effect of puromycin and its role as an inhibitor of protein synthesis? We have performed experiments in which puromycin was injected intracranially into groups of fish and then at various times later, leucine-³H was injected intraperitoneally. Thirty minutes after the leucine injection, the brains were removed and analysed for protein radioactivity. While we see a marked inhibition of leucine incorporation into brain protein for hours after the puromycin injection, we cannot as yet claim a simple correlation between the biochemical and behavioral effects of puromycin. These experiments must be tempered by such questions as whether puromycin acts as a specific locus, and whether a specific protein mediates the behavioral effect. We measure total acid precipitable protein, and do not see the dynamic effect of the drug on the family of proteins turning over in the brain, each with a unique

FIGURE 2   *Effect of injection time and dosage on the retention score. At left, 170 µg of puromycin injected at various intervals after trial 20. At right, various doses of puromycin injected immediately after trial 20.*

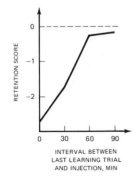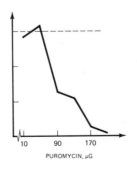

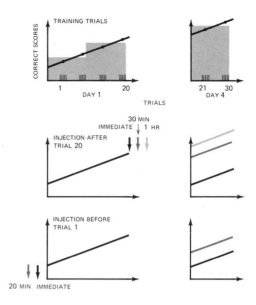

FIGURE 3 *Diagrammatic summary of experiments on memory. At top, fish are given 20 trials on day 1, in blocks of five, and 10 trials on day 4. The shaded areas represent each 10 trials for which means and standard errors are determined. A predicted score for trials 21 to 30 is subtracted from the achieved score. At center, puromycin injected immediately after trial 20 reduces performance on day 4 to the naive level (lower line at right), puromycin injected 30 min after trial 20 results in intermediate retention, and puromycin injected 1 hr after trial 20 has no effect on retention measured the next day. At bottom, puromycin injected immediately before trial 1 appears to have no effect on the increase in performance on day 1 (short-term memory) but blocks memory fixation and subsequent retention measured on day 4 (lower line at right); puromycin injected 20 min before trial 1 leaves acquisition unimpaired but blocks some fixation.*

time constant. We have evidence that another *in vivo* inhibitor of brain protein synthesis, acetoxycycloheximide, also causes a memory deficit (Table 4). 0.1 μg of the drug produces a partial memory deficit, but blocks incorporation of leucine-^{3}H into protein more profoundly than 170 μg of puromycin. This apparent difference between two potent inhibitors of protein synthesis may prove to be an important tool in the elucidation of the behavioral effect of puromycin.

More significant is the fact that two structurally unrelated substances, both of which exert their antibiotic effect by selectively blocking protein synthesis, affect memory. Thus protein synthesis is further implicated as an obligatory step in memory formation.

A few words about memory and time constants. In studies with mice, Flexner et al. report that recent, or short-term memory can be destroyed by bilateral temporal injections into the brain substance of puromycin 3 to 6 days after a learning experience, while older memory can be destroyed 6 weeks after learning by injections into bilateral frontal and ventricular sites as well [Flexner et al., 1965; Flexner et al., 1963]. Comparison of these studies with our work on goldfish are complicated by differences between the mouse and goldfish nervous system, the mode of injection, and the training tasks. In the mouse, short- and long-term memory are distinguished by differences in the effective site of puromycin injection. Both short- and long-term memory are reportedly destroyed by puromycin. Short- and long-term memory in the goldfish are distinguished by puromycin susceptibility during formation. Short-term memory may be measured in days, but it cannot be transferred to long-term memory after an hour following training. Formed long-term memory does not appear to be puromycin-susceptible in our experiments. Long-term memory in goldfish, once formed, does not appear to turn over, but rather, like genetic and immunological information, it is stored in what appears to be a metabolically inert form.

Text of a talk presented at the 132nd meeting of the American Association for the Advancement of Science, Berkeley, Calif. (U.S.A.), December 27, 1965. The research was sponsored by a grant from the National Science Foundation. Reprinted from *Brain Research*, 1966, **1**, 303–309, by permission of the Elsevier Publishing Company.

TABLE 4 *Effect of acetoxycycloheximide* injected after training on memory*

No.	Trials day 1 1–10	Trials day 1 11–20	Treatment	21–30 A	Trials day 4 21–30 P	Retention score $(A - P)$
30	1.7	2.7	Acetoxycycloheximide, 0.1 μg, immediate	3.2	5.1	−1.9
36	0.89	2.2	Acetoxycycloheximide, 0.1 μg, 6 h delay	4.8	4.7	+0.1

*Generously donated by Dr. T. J. McBride, Chas Pfizer Co., Maywood, N.J. (U.S.A.).

AROUSAL AND THE CONVERSION OF "SHORT-TERM" TO "LONG-TERM" MEMORY

SAMUEL H. BARONDES/HARRY D. COHEN

Mice whose cerebral protein synthesis was markedly inhibited by cycloheximide during training learned normally, remembered normally for the following 3 hours, but had markedly impaired "long-term" memory. Impaired "long-term" memory was observed even though "short-term" memory persisted through the time when the capacity to synthesize cerebral protein had largely returned. Brief foot shock, amphetamine, or corticosteroids given 3 hours after training induced the formation of "long-term" memory, but this effect was blocked by resumption of inhibition of cerebral protein synthesis. Cognitive information, an intact capacity for cerebral protein synthesis, and an appropriate degree of "arousal" are all apparently necessary for the establishment of "long-term" memory.

We have reported that mice trained while their cerebral protein synthesis was markedly inhibited by acetoxycycloheximide learned normally and remembered normally for more than 3 hours after training but had markedly impaired "long-term" memory [Barondes and Cohen, 1967, 1968a; Cohen and Barondes, 1968a].[1] These studies suggest that learning and "short-term" memory are not dependent on cerebral protein synthesis, but that it is necessary for the establishment of "long-term" memory. Acetoxycycloheximide was found to be maximally effective in impairing the formation of "long-term" memory if it was given prior to training so that inhibition of cerebral protein synthesis was established during training. The drug was slightly effective if given immediately after training [Barondes and Cohen, 1968a] and completely ineffective if given 30 minutes later. This suggests that the cerebral protein synthesis apparently required for "long-term" memory normally occurs during training or within minutes after training, or both.

In the previous experiments, it was not possible to determine

[1]Since mice that learned while cerebral protein synthesis was markedly inhibited remember normally for at least 3 hr but less than 6 hr, we have for convenience chosen to refer to memory for 3–6 hr as "short-term" memory and memory for 6 hr or more as "long-term" memory.

whether "short-term" memory could lead to the formation of "long-term" memory at times later than a few minutes after training. Although "short-term" memory persisted for hours after training, inhibition of cerebral protein synthesis by acetoxycycloheximide also persisted for this period of time. Therefore, "conversion" of "short-term" memory to "long-term" memory hours after training would presumably be blocked by the persistent action of the inhibitor of cerebral protein synthesis. Recently, we have found that cycloheximide inhibits cerebral protein synthesis as intensely but more transiently than acetoxycycloheximide, and shares with it the ability to prevent the formation of "long-term" memory [Cohen and Barondes, 1968b]. In the present experiments, the doses of cycloheximide that were used inhibited approximately 95 per cent of cerebral protein synthesis during training but permitted very marked recovery within 3 hours after training. Despite the extensive recovery of the capacity of the brain to synthesize protein at a time when "short-term" memory still remained, "long-term" memory was not spontaneously established. However, the introduction of manipulations that generate "arousal" led to the development of "long-term" memory if introduced at a time when "short-term" memory persisted (i.e., 3 hours after training). The reestablishment of marked inhibition of cerebral protein synthesis prior to the onset of the "arousal"-producing manipulation blocked the establishment of "long-term" memory.

METHOD

Male Swiss albino mice weighing approximately 30 g were obtained from the Charles River Breeding Corp. They were trained to escape shock by choosing the lighted limb of a T-maze to a criterion of five out of six consecutive correct responses as described previously [Cohen and Barondes, 1968a]. In other experiments, they were trained to choose the left limb of a T-maze for water reinforcement to a criterion of three out of four consecutive correct responses as described previously [Cohen and Barondes, 1968b]. From 12 to 15 mice were used for each time point in the behavioral studies. Savings were calculated as described previously [Barondes and Cohen, 1967]. Statistical analysis of the data was made with the Mann-Whitney U test.

The drugs used were obtained from commercial sources, except that acetoxycycloheximide was the gift of Dr. T. J. McBride, John L. Smith Memorial for Cancer Research, Charles Pfizer and Co., Maywood, N.J. (supported by contract PH-43-64-50). Drugs were dissolved in 0.15 M saline and injected subcutaneously on the back. Dextroamphetamine was used where indicated and is referred to as amphetamine. The corticosteroid mixture contained 5 mg each of hydrocortisone and corticosterone per ml of dimethylsulfoxide. Incorporation of valine-1-C^{14} into protein and inhibition of incorporation by cycloheximide were

Injection	Time tested	Per cent savings
Saline	3 hr	75
	6 hr	73
	7 days	76
Cycloheximide	3 hr	73
	6 hr	28
	7 days	31

Mice were injected with 0.12 g/kg cycloheximide 30 minutes before being trained to escape shock by choosing the lighted limb of a T-maze to a criterion of five out of six consecutive correct responses [Cohen and Barondes, 1968a, Barondes and Cohen, 1968a]. Savings were calculated as described previously [Barondes and Cohen, 1967]. Groups of 15 mice were tested for retention at the indicated times. The cycloheximide-injected mice did not differ significantly from controls if tested 3 hours after training but differed significantly ($P < 0.01$) if tested at 6 hours or 7 days.

TABLE 1   *Effect of cycloheximide on "short-term" and "long-term" memory*

determined as described previously [Barondes and Cohen, 1967, 1968a]. At least three separate determinations were made at each time point. The degree of inhibition of protein synthesis is somewhat overestimated by this method of calculation as indicated previously [Barondes and Cohen, 1968a], and this is particularly true when the calculated degree of inhibition is small.

RESULTS

Administration of 0.12 g/kg cycloheximide subcutaneously inhibited approximately 95 per cent of cerebral protein synthesis within the first 30 minutes after injection. With the dose used, inhibition subsided fairly rapidly. In the interval between 3 and $3\frac{1}{2}$ hours after injection, only 19 per cent of cerebral protein synthesis was inhibited and in the subsequent 30-minute interval, an average of 9 per cent inhibition was found. Mice injected with this dose of cycloheximide 30 minutes before training learned normally and remembered normally 3 hours after training but had markedly impaired memory 6 hours after training and thereafter (Table 1). Therefore, "long-term" memory was not formed despite marked recovery of the capacity for cerebral protein synthesis at a time when "short-term" memory remained. However, the slight inhibition of cerebral protein synthesis that remained 3 hours after training (in the range of 9 to 19 per cent inhibition) might be sufficient to prevent the formation of "long-term" memory, although inhibition of at least 90 per cent of cerebral protein synthesis during training was previously found to be necessary for significant interference with the establishment of "long-term" memory [Barondes and Cohen, 1967].

Attempts were then made to determine whether or not "long-term" memory could be induced by various manipulations of cycloheximide-injected mice 3 hours after they were trained. The effect of the administration of a brief foot shock at this time was studied. Mice trained 30 minutes after injection of cycloheximide were removed from their home cage at several times after training, placed on an electric grid, and given a 0.5-ma shock of 0.5-second duration. If foot shock was administered 3 hours after training, the mice had an average of 63 per cent savings when tested 7 days later and differed significantly ($P < 0.01$) from a cycloheximide-treated group that received no foot shock and that had 27 per cent savings 7 days after training. In contrast, administration of foot shock 6 hours after training, a time when "short-term" memory had terminated, did not significantly induce "long-term" memory. This group had an average of 22 per cent savings when tested 7 days after training. Therefore, a single foot shock without any additional discriminitive training, if given while "short-term" memory persisted, could lead to the establishment of "long-term" memory.

The mechanism by which the foot shock led to the establishment of "long-term" memory could not be determined from this experiment. Several aspects of foot shock were considered. First, the foot shock resembled the shock received during training and might thereby act as a "reminder." It has been reported that a "reminder" shock, given prior to testing to animals which received electroconvulsive shock after training, improves retention [Koppenaal et al., 1967], but the experimental design differed so markedly from the one we used that this phenomenon may have little relationship to that reported here. A second possibility is that foot shock aroused the animal and that this state of "arousal" might be necessary for the formation of "long-term" memory. To evaluate the possible role of "arousal," the effect of dextroamphetamine and corticosteroids, two drugs that produce "states of arousal" [Goodman and Gillman, 1965], was studied. Controls were handled identically and injected with either 0.15 M saline or with dimethylsulfoxide.

Cycloheximide-treated mice injected with amphetamine 3 hours after training showed much greater memory than controls when tested either 3 hours or 7 days later (Table 2). Amphetamine injected 3 hours after training in 15 saline-injected mice had no effect on performance measured 7 days later. Therefore, this drug had no discernible action if "long-term" memory was established normally. Injection of amphetamine 6 hours after training in cycloheximide-injected mice had no significant effect on memory tested 3 hours or 7 days later (Table 2). Injections of amphetamine 3 hours before testing had no effect on memory at 7 days (Table 2). Likewise, injections of amphetamine 30 minutes before training along with the cycloheximide had no effect on memory when tested 7 days after training (Table 2). These experiments indicate that if amphetamine injections are given at a time when cerebral protein synthesis inhibition is slight and when "short-term" memory remains, "long-term" memory is formed. Administration of the amphetamine after "short-term" memory has terminated (at 6 hours in this situation) is ineffective.

Similar results were found when a mixture of corticosteroids was used. Administration of 0.1 ml of the corticosteroid mixture 3 hours after cycloheximide-injected mice were trained significantly improved "long-term" memory. The mice injected with cycloheximide 30 minutes before training and with corticosteroids 3 hours after training had 58 per cent savings when tested at 6 hours, and 60 per cent savings when tested at 7 days. Controls that received only dimethylsulfoxide 3 hours after training had 29 per cent savings 7 days later. However, cycloheximide-treated mice injected with corticosteroids 6 hours after training, a time when "short-term" memory had markedly declined, had 30 per cent savings when tested 9 hours after training and 22 per cent

TABLE 2 *Effect of amphetamine on memory in cycloheximide-treated mice*

Time amphetamine given	Time tested	Per cent savings
—	7 days	31
3 hr	6 hr	54
3 hr	7 days	62
6 hr	9 hr	32
6 hr	7 days	39
7 days	7 days + 3 hr	28
− 30 min	7 days	25

Mice (12 in each group) were injected with cycloheximide 30 minutes before training as indicated in the legend of Table 1. Dextroamphetamine (1m/kg) was injected subcutaneously at various times after training or 30 minutes before training as indicated. The group that received no amphetamine was injected with saline 3 hours after training. The mice were tested at the indicated times after training. Mice injected with amphetamine 3 hours after training had significantly more savings ($P < 0.01$) than any of the other groups.

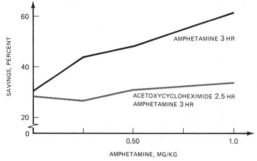

FIGURE 1   *Antagonism of the amphetamine effect by injection of acetoxycycloheximide. All mice (each point represents a group of 12) were injected with 0.12 g/kg of cycloheximide 30 min before training. Acetoxycycloheximide (8 mg/kg) was injected 2½ hr after training, where indicated. In the ensuing 30 min, 93% of cerebral protein synthesis was inhibited. The indicated dose of dextroamphetamine was administered 3 hr after training. All mice were tested for retention seven days later.*

savings when tested at 7 days. The group injected with corticosteroids 3 hours after training differed significantly ($P < 0.01$) from the controls, whereas the group injected with corticosteroids at 6 hours had no significant enhancement of savings.

Administration of 0.12 g/kg of cycloheximide or 8 mg/kg of acetoxycycloheximide $2\frac{1}{2}$ hours after training, so that 95 per cent inhibition of cerebral protein synthesis was again established when the amphetamine was administered, markedly antagonized the amphetamine effect (Fig. 1). Acetoxycycloheximide was found to be somewhat more effective than cycloheximide. This may be due to its longer duration of action, whereby inhibition of cerebral protein synthesis persisted throughout the period when the arousing effect of amphetamine remained.

To evaluate the hypothesis that the amphetamine was exerting its effect through "arousal," the effect of administration of 40 mg/kg of pentobarbital concurrently with 1 mg/kg amphetamine was determined. This combination produced sedation. The 15 cycloheximide-treated mice injected 3 hours after training with a combination of amphetamine and pentobarbital had 34 per cent savings 7 days later. This was significantly less than the savings of the mice treated with amphetamine alone. Therefore, sedation obliterates the action of amphetamine. Neither cycloheximide nor acetoxycycloheximide administered subcutaneously has any sedative effects on mice, and indeed their behavior appeared quite normal at a time when maximal inhibition of cerebral protein synthesis was achieved. Therefore, the inhibitors of protein synthesis do not antagonize the amphetamine effect by producing sedation.

Since large doses of protein synthesis inhibitors are known to produce illness [Barondes and Cohen, 1967], the possibility that amphetamine or corticosterone antagonize this illness must be considered. This might be particularly true of the corticosteroids that have multiple, potentially therapeutic properties. However, the dose of cycloheximide used in the present studies produced no significant signs of illness. Furthermore, it would be difficult to ascribe such therapeutic properties to amphetamine or to foot shock. Nevertheless, this possibility cannot be excluded. A possible stimulation of cerebral protein-synthesizing capacity by amphetamine injections in cycloheximide-treated mice was also considered. Injection of amphetamine with cycloheximide had no significant effect on inhibition of cerebral protein synthesis observed in the ensuing hour. Injection of amphetamine 3 hours after cycloheximide injection did not significantly stimulate cerebral protein synthesis measured in the following 30-minute interval. However, the degree of inhibition was already small and varied between about 5 and 25 per cent. Therefore, a relatively small change might not be readily detectable.

The shock escape task that we used would be expected to cause the release of large amounts of catecholamines and corticosteroids during training. The injection of amphetamine or corticosteroids might, therefore, produce a state reminiscent of training. Because of this, it seemed of interest to determine the effects of injections of amphetamine on memory in cycloheximide-treated mice trained in an appetitive task. Mice were injected with cycloheximide or saline 30 minutes before being trained to choose the left limb of a maze for water reinforcement, as described previously [Cohen and Barondes, 1968b]. The saline-injected mice had 73 per cent savings when tested 7 days later, whereas the cycloheximide-injected mice had 33 per cent savings. Therefore, cycloheximide had an amnesic effect in this appetitive task, as observed previously [Cohen and Barondes, 1968b]. Cycloheximide-treated mice injected with 1 mg/kg amphetamine 3 hours after training had 56 per cent savings 7 days later and differed significantly ($P < 0.05$) from controls. Cycloheximide-treated mice injected with amphetamine 6 hours after training had only 31 per cent savings. Therefore, the effectiveness of amphetamine is not confined to a shock-motivated task but is quite similar in a task in which water reinforcement is employed. Nevertheless, there is "arousal" during training in this appetitive task, and the amphetamine may be acting as a "reminder" in this situation as well. The "reminder," if this is what it is, is effective only if administered while "short-term" memory persists.

DISCUSSION

The mechanisms for "short-term" and "long-term" memory are not known. There is evidence, from studies in which disruptive manipulations are made at different times after training, that "long-term" memory is "consolidated" during a time period of seconds to hours after training [McGaugh, 1966]. A number of drugs, particularly analeptics, enhance "long-term" memory if given within minutes after training [McGaugh, 1966], presumably by facilitating "consolidation." Although amphetamine injections have usually produced no significant effect on memory in normal animals, some enhancement has been observed in multiple-trial avoidance training when the drug was given within 4 hours after each training session [Doty and Doty, 1966]. The fact that the enhancing effects of drugs and the disruptive effects of electroconvulsive shock may, under certain circumstances, occur when these manipulations are made within several hours of training has suggested that "short-term" memory may be available for "consolidation" for this relatively prolonged period. There is also evidence that the time when such "consolidation" begins can be influenced by the environment and presumably the state of the organism [Davis and Agranoff, 1966].

The present studies have permitted a dissection of "short-term" memory and "long-term" memory by producing conditions in which "short-term" memory is established and persists for hours without the ultimate development of "long-term" memory. These studies suggest that if the establishment of "long-term" memory is prevented by inhibitors of cerebral protein synthesis administered prior to training, it will not subsequently develop spontaneously, despite persistence of the information in "short-term" memory concurrent with the marked recovery of the capacity for cerebral protein synthesis. However, manipulations that are thought to act by producing "arousal" will lead to the development of "long-term" memory. The view which emerges from these studies is that both the persistence of the cognitive information acquired from training and an intact cerebral protein synthesis capacity are insufficient for the production of "long-term" memory. An appropriate state of "arousal," which appears to specifically direct the establishment of "long-term" memory, also seems necessary. Livingston has speculated on the possible role of "arousal" in ordering the memory stage system to "Now print!" [Livingston, 1967].

This work was supported by grant MH-12773 and by Career Development Award K3-MH-18232 from the U.S. Public Health Service. This is communication no. 139 of the Joan and Lester Avnet Institute of Molecular Biology. Reprinted from *Proceedings of the National Academy of Science*, 1968, **61**, 923–929, by permission of the National Academy of Science.

RETROACTIVE IMPAIRMENT OF PASSIVE-AVOIDANCE LEARNING BY STIMULATION OF THE CAUDATE NUCLEUS

EVERETT J. WYERS/HARMAN V. S. PEEKE/JOHN S. WILLISTON/MICHAEL J. HERZ

Highly trained rats received a single brief and intense footshock through a lever they were depressing for a liquid reward. Single-pulse bilateral electrical stimulation of the caudate nuclei, or of the ventral hippocampal dentate regions, produced retroactive interference with passive avoidance of the lever 24 hr later. Stimulation at a number of other brain sites did not produce retrograde impairment of passive avoidance. Control electrode placements negated current peripheral effects mediated by internal capsular fibers as significant influences in the mediation of the retention deficits obtained. The retention deficit obtained was essentially the same with footshock–brain-stimulation intervals as long as 30 sec.

Numerous investigations have demonstrated that electroconvulsive shock (ECS) can interfere with learning in a wide variety of situations [Glickman, 1961; McGaugh, 1966]. For the most part, the effects of posttrial ECS have been interpreted as resulting from interference with time-dependent processes underlying memory storage [McGaugh, 1965]. However, the gross and widespread disturbance of brain function and resulting overt behavioral seizures make it extremely difficult to assess the role of discrete brain structures during the critical period, the initial phase of memory storage.

An alternative to ECS, low-intensity posttrial stimulation of specific brain sites, would provide information for further delineation of structure-function relationships. The effect of single-pulse stimulation of the caudate nucleus, as well as several other brain sites, on retention of a passive-avoidance task was studied in the following experiment.

METHOD

One hundred and twenty-five male albino rats 100 to 250 days old were used in the experiment. Each rat was housed individually and maintained at 85 percent of its initial weight on a water-deprivation schedule. The apparatus consisted of a 60-cm unpainted wooden runway, 12 cm wide and 25.5 cm high, leading to a counterbalanced copper lever at one end. The floor was constructed of 10-mm brass rods spaced 13 mm apart. A 3-mm-high wooden platform treadle switch occupied the first 20.3

cm of the runway floor. Each lever press actuated a liquid pump that delivered 0.02 ml of a saccharin solution (0.1 percent) to a small plastic cup. Footshock could be delivered by passing a current from a constant-voltage d-c power supply set at 350 volts through the lever, the rat's body, and the grid floor for a maximum of 40 msec.

After being shaped to lever press, each rat was trained to run from the treadle platform and press the lever 100 times; three such daily runs (each followed by 100 lever presses) were presented in immediate succession. Daily training continued until the mean time required for a run and 100 lever presses was 184 sec or less on two successive days; this required less than 14 days for all subjects. The next day one foot-shock was delivered on the fifty-first lever press after a single run. For most animals the footshock was of sufficient intensity (10 to 30 ma) to produce an upward and backward leap. The rat was removed from the apparatus 30 sec later. On the next day the animal was returned to the apparatus and was either run as in training or, if it did not return to lever, removed after 9 min. Training began prior to electrode implantation and was resumed after a one-week recovery period.

On at least two separate occasions in the course of training, but independent of the training apparatus and procedures, ECoG records were made and the effects of electrical stimulation were observed. Single monophasic pulses from a Grass S-4 stimulator, isolated from ground with a Grass stimulation isolation unit, were delivered bilaterally to the caudate nuclei to determine parameters for production of "caudate spindles" at the frontal poles of the cerebral cortex. These values were used in later behavioral tests. The pulse duration and voltage used to produce spindles varied from animal to animal. Duration was .03 to 0.5 msec. Voltages were used that resulted in current values of approximately 180 to 900 μa. This amount of current was divided between the two hemispheres, and since the output of a single stimulator (Grass S-4) was paralleled to a pair of stimulating electrodes with relatively similar resistances, each hemisphere received approximately half the current. The stimulating electrodes were concentric bipolar depth electrodes, with 0.25 mm bared on both the tips and the barrels, implanted bilaterally and stereotaxically oriented to either the caudate nuclei or another subcortical structure. In the latter case the stimulating parameters were 0.5 msec duration and 750 μa of current. The active cortical recording electrodes were two silver balls placed on the dural surface. One was placed on the frontal pole of each hemisphere, just posterior to the olfactory bulb, and a third silver-ball electrode was placed posteriorly over the occipital cortex to serve as reference.

RESULTS

A retention score was devised by comparing the value obtained for the individual rat on the first posttreatment retention test run with his last pretreatment performance. All behavioral results are presented in terms of the total time required to traverse the runway and press the lever 100 times. In each case the largest of the two daily first-run values obtained on the two criterion training days was subtracted from the posttreatment value. With this score, retention of the effects of the footshock (passive avoidance) is indicated by a large positive value. Lower values (sometimes negative) of the score indicate the degree of retention deficit.

Nonparametric Kruskal-Wallis and Mann-Whitney U tests were used in the statistical evaluation of the data presented [Siegel, 1956]. All differences described are significant at the $p = .05$ level or less by a two-tailed test.

Retention deficit and caudate-stimulation delay If ECS impairment of passive-avoidance learning is critically dependent on disruption of caudate function, a temporal gradient for retention deficit similar to that for ECS might be found with caudate stimulation. Although the caudate nucleus is known to be highly resistant to seizure induction, it seems unlikely that the occurrence of full tonic-clonic behavioral seizure that usually accompanies ECS would not involve it. In addition, the form of stimulation used produced the caudate spindle in the frontal-pole cortex. Such spindles could be interpreted as indications of brief localized episodes of seizurelike activity in the cortex and elsewhere. Thus, if this assumption is correct, the occurrence of a retention deficit with some range of temporal delays of caudate stimulation would not be surprising. It would be expected that such retroactive effects would fall within the range of those produced by ECS.

Figure 1 represents the approximate loci of the electrode tips and their dispersion of the 55 animals with histologically confirmed [Guzman et al., 1958] electrode placements in the caudate nuclei. The animals fell into four different delay-of-stimulation groups: 0.1 sec ($n = 25$), 1.0 sec ($n = 10$), 5.0 sec ($n = 11$), and 30.0 sec ($n = 9$). Figure 2 compares their median retention-deficit scores with that for a control group of 22 nonstimulated animals. No differences appear among the delay groups, but each shows a retention deficit (0.1 sec, -2.6; 1.0 sec, 7.85; 5.0 sec, 9.0; and 30.0 sec, -4.8) in relation to the nonstimulated control group (121.2). The control group included eight implanted animals which were treated (footshocked) with their electrode cables attached. These animals did not differ from the unimplanted controls.

From these data it appears that although caudate stimulation produced a deficit, a temporal gradient of increasing retention with longer footshock–caudate-stimulation intervals either similar to or

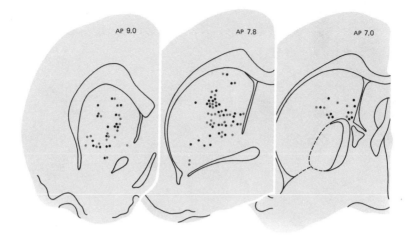

FIGURE 1 *Drawings of sections taken at three different anterior-posterior levels according to De Groot [1959] to illustrate the placements of paired electrodes in the caudate nuclei of 55 animals. The light circles represent points in the left caudate and the dark circles represent points in the right caudate.*

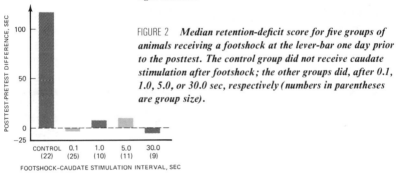

FIGURE 2 *Median retention-deficit score for five groups of animals receiving a footshock at the lever-bar one day prior to the posttest. The control group did not receive caudate stimulation after footshock; the other groups did, after 0.1, 1.0, 5.0, or 30.0 sec, respectively (numbers in parentheses are group size).*

shorter than that found with ECS did not appear. The deficit is essentially uniform up to a learning-trial–stimulation interval of at least 30 sec. This result is quite surprising in view of the recent studies demonstrating a brief graded interference effect with ECS, with little or no retention deficit at 30 sec [Chorover and Schiller, 1965, 1966; Quartermain et al., 1965; Schiller and Chorover, 1967]. In addition, even in experiments evidencing longer amnesic gradients, with significant deficits produced at learning-trial–ECS intervals as long as 1 hr or more, a graded effect is usually observed over the initial 30 sec [Alpern and McGaugh, 1968; Kopp et al., 1966]. Although the present results suggest the possibility that caudate stimulation produces more complete interference with the initial stages of memory storage than does ECS, differences in procedure and task may also account for the discrepant findings among various investigations. The results also suggest that much important information

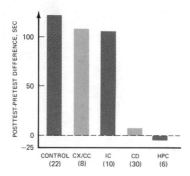

FIGURE 3 *Median retention-deficit score for five groups of animals receiving a footshock at the lever-bar one day prior to the posttest. Control, no brain stimulation after footshock; CX/CC, delayed stimulation in subcortical white matter and/or corpus callosum; IC, delayed stimulation in internal capsule; CD, delayed caudate stimulation; HPC, delayed stimulation in ventral hippocampus.*

could be obtained by directly comparing the effects of ECS and caudate stimulation in the same experimental setting. Of course, these data concerning the effective learning-trial–caudate-stimulation interval do not rule out the possibility that other sites may be important in producing retention deficits.

Retention deficit and noncaudate sites of stimulation Thirty-six animals had bilateral electrodes oriented to brain sites other than the caudate nuclei. These fall into four subgroups defined by anatomic locus of the electrodes: ventral hippocampus ($n = 6$); subcortex and corpus callosum ($n = 8$); internal capsule ($n = 10$); and seven other diversified sites ($n = 12$).

Hippocampal stimulation Stimulation oriented to the hippocampus produced a retention deficit, as indicated in Fig. 3. The six animals comprising this group did not differ from any of the four caudate-stimulation groups (represented in Fig. 2), although they differed markedly from the nonstimulated control group ($p < .01$), the internal-capsule control ($p < .01$), and the cortical-callosal control ($p < .01$). Their median score was -3.0 and their individual scores were -11.0, -6.0, -14.5, 0.0, 1.0, and 3.9. The stimulation-pulse delay was 0.1 sec for the first five animals and 1.0 sec for the sixth one. All electrodes were clustered in the posteroventral hippocampus at the approximate level of the junction of the medial and lateral geniculate bodies. With one exception, all were placed medially in the hippocampus, and together they formed a line of curvature through the dentate gyrus and around the lateral aspect of the lateral geniculate body.

TABLE 1 *Retention-deficit scores, electrode placements, and brain-stimulating delay in seconds, for 12 animals identified by brain structure containing the electrode tips*

				Stereotaxic coordinates*					
	Retention	Stimulus		Left			Right		
Brain structure	deficit	delay	AP	L	H	AP	L	H	
Accumbens	257.4	1.0	9.0	2.0	−2.0	9.0	2.0	−2.0	
Accumbens	403.6	1.0	9.0	3.0	−1.1	9.0	1.0	−1.1	
Accumbens	−0.8	1.0	8.2	2.2	−2.5	8.2	2.6	−2.5	
Lateral septum	13.8	1.0	8.2	0.8	1.5	8.2	0.8	1.5	
Lateral septum	114.8	1.0	7.8	0.0	0.5	7.8	1.0	0.5	
Ventral thalamus	49.4	30.0	4.2	2.2	−0.2	3.2	2.2	−0.2	
Piriform cortex	62.0	1.0	9.2	5.0	−1.0	9.7	5.0	−1.0	
Substantia nigra	75.0	.1	2.8	2.5	−3.5	2.4	2.8	−2.5	
Substantia nigra	86.0	.1	2.2	2.75	−1.0	2.2	3.0	1.0	
Globus pallidus	∞	.1	6.8	3.0	−1.0	6.8	3.5	0.0	
Dorsal hippocampus	233.5	.1	3.8	2.0	2.5	3.8	2.0	2.5	
Dorsal hippocampus	405.0	.1	4.4	2.0	2.0	4.4	2.5	2.0	

*Stereotaxic coordinates as defined in De Groot [1959].

In the rodent, fibers arising from this region of the hippocampus project subcortically to the nucleus accumbens, ventral and subjacent to the caudate nucleus [Carman et al., 1963]. Thus it may be possible that the caudate retention-deficit effect is a result of antidromic excitation of this pathway back to the dentate regions of the hippocampus. This possibility would seem more likely if electric field effects of the single-pulse caudate stimulation were such as to cause excitatory current flow in such fibers or their synaptic endings. That this is unlikely is indicated by the results reported below.

Other subcortical stimulation Twelve animals had bilateral electrodes oriented to other brain structures close to, adjacent to, and more or less surrounding the medial, ventral, and caudal extents of the caudate nucleus. These sites included the following nuclei: accumbens ($n = 3$), lateral septum ($n = 2$), substantia nigra ($n = 2$), dorsal hippocampus ($n = 2$), globus pallidus ($n = 1$), piriform cortex ($n = 1$), and ventral thalamic nuclei ($n = 1$). Table 1 lists the 12 animals by site of stimulation and shows their individual retention-deficit scores, the stimulus delay used, and the stereotaxic coordinates based on the De Groot atlas, which specifies more precisely the histological site of electrode placement. The approximate locations of the electrodes in 9 of these 12 animals are shown in Figs. 4 and 5.

As a whole, this group of animals did not differ from the non-stimulated controls in their retention-deficit scores (median 100.4). However, it is evident from Table 1 that the individual variation in the scores does not allow us to conclude that stimulation of each or any one

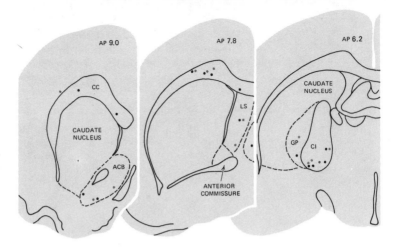

FIGURE 4 *Drawings of sections taken at three different anterior-posterior levels according to De Groot [1959] to illustrate the placements of paired electrodes in corpus callosum (CC), nucleus accumbens (ACB), lateral septum (LS), globus pallidus (GP), and internal capsule (CI). Light circles represent placements in the left hemisphere and the dark circles represent placements in the right hemisphere.*

of the sites actually fails to produce a retention deficit. For example, one of the three nucleus-accumbens animals and one of the two lateral-septal animals do show retention-deficit scores comparable to the medians of the caudate-stimulated groups. What the grouped results do mean is that stimulation oriented to a number of sites close to the caudate nucleus does not produce the retention deficit that would be expected if generalized current spread were a significant factor in the retention-deficit effect of caudate stimulation. If this were the case, a similar spread of current and retention deficits would be anticipated from stimulation of nearby sites. That excitation within the caudate nucleus itself is the critical factor is further indicated by the following results of subcortical-callosal and internal-capsular stimulation.

If antidromic excitation from nucleus accumbens to hippocampus were in fact the case, 9 of the 12 animals would be expected to show a retention deficit—specifically, all animals but those with globus-pallidus, ventral-thalamic, and piriform-cortex placements, since the rest had placements either in or near the nucleus accumbens, in the hippocampus itself (anterodorsal), or in the substantia nigra region near the critical hippocampal stimulation zone. Instead these nine animals had a median retention-deficit score of 114.8, differing from the caudate-stimulation groups ($p = .05$) but not from the nonstimulated control group. Although the possibility of antidromic effects cannot be definitely excluded on the basis of these data, they are inconsistent with this explanation.

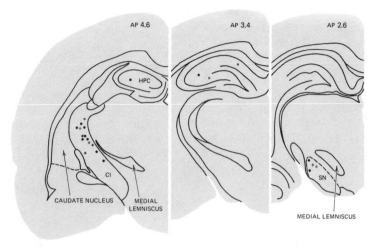

FIGURE 5   *Drawings of sections taken at three different anterior-posterior levels according to De Groot [1959] to illustrate paired-electrode placements in dorsal hippocampus (HPC), internal capsule (CI), and substantia nigra (SN). Light circles represent placements in the left hemisphere and the dark circles represent placements in the right hemisphere.*

Subcortex-callosal and internal capsule stimulation   Fibers arising from the rat cortex of the frontal poles of the hemispheres pass through the subcallosal fasiculus and perforate the caudate nucleus [Webster, 1961]. More posteriorly, after exciting the caudate, these fibers combine with others arising in the cortex and form the internal capsule. The fibers arising from the frontal poles have collaterals that end in the region of the caudate nucleus to which our electrodes were oriented. This type of representation of the cortex in the caudate-putamen complex by collaterals of fibers of passage is extensive and topographically arranged [Carman et al., 1963; Webster, 1961]. This anatomic situation permits another type of comparison bearing on the localization of stimulation effects.

Figure 3 illustrates results for three groups of rats stimulated following learning in areas structurally related to the caudate putamen. One group (*CX/CC*) had electrodes located in the white matter subjacent to the cortex or in the corpus callosum immediately over the anterior and dorsal surfaces of the caudate. Stimulation here should excite fibers arising from the frontal poles. The approximate loci of the tips of 10 of the 16 electrodes implanted in this group are represented in Fig. 4. The other six electrode tips were located more anteriorly over the convexity of the head of the caudate nuclei. Another group, IC, had electrodes that were clearly in the internal capsule posterior to the head of the caudate. Stimulation here would also excite fibers arising from the frontal poles, as well as fibers arising from many other regions of the cortex. The sites in the internal capsule where the electrode tips were clustered are pictured in Figs. 4 and 5. The retention-deficit scores of these two groups were compared with those of a group of 20 caudate animals formed by combining the three subgroups stimulated at delays of 1 sec or more (Fig. 2).

There was no difference between the CX/CC group (median 108.4) and the IC group (median 107.2) or the nonstimulated control group (median 121.2). All three groups differed from the caudate-stimulated group (median 7.0). This pattern indicates that the caudate-stimulated retention deficit was not due to antidromic disruption of cortical activity associated with excitation of fibers of passage perforating the caudate nucleus, nor was it due to spread of current to the cortex. Moreover, it was not a consequence of downstream effects mediated by internal capsule and elicited by excitation of fibers of passage in caudate nucleus.

Step-down task and caudate stimulation In order to examine the generality of this method of retroactive interference with learning, and as a first approach to the question of task and procedural differences it was determined to establish the occurrence of caudate-produced retention deficit in a step-down task. More specific questions regarding the differences between step-down tasks themselves were left to the future, as was the determination of differential retention-deficit gradients between lever pressing and step-down passive avoidance.

The animals used in this experiment were 25 caudate implants from the previous study and 24 unimplanted controls. The animals were required to step down 5 cm from a small compartment, which confined them closely, into a larger compartment which permitted freedom of movement. The larger compartment consisted of cardboard walls enclosing an area approximately 45 cm square. The smaller compartment was approximately 15 cm square. It also had cardboard walls, with a movable partition at the rear which was used to crowd the animals up against the door leading to the larger compartment. Two single trials on two successive days were given in this apparatus. An electrode cable leading to the stimulation isolation unit and the brain stimulator was attached on both days. On day 1 the animal's stepping latency from opening of the door was determined. Upon stepping, a single brief shock (estimated at 10 to 13 ma) was administered to the forefeet. One hundred msec after termination of the footshock the caudate animals received a single bilateral pulse to the caudate nuclei at the parameters previously established for the individual animal. On the second day stepping latency was determined in the absence of footshock and brain stimulation. The control animals received only the footshock on day 1 and were tested as the caudate animals were on day 2: all animals were given a 60-sec interval in which to step and were then removed from the apparatus.

The results of the step-down test are shown in Fig. 6. All animals stepping with a latency of more than 30 sec on day 1 were excluded. Five animals in the caudate group and one in the control group were excluded on this basis. Thus the results are based on 20 caudate-stimulated animals and 23 control animals. The two groups did not differ in step-down latency on day 1 (the control median was 9.0 sec and the caudate median was 7.0 sec). The left portion of Fig. 6 shows the median stepping latency for the two groups on both days. The caudate-stimulated group did not differ in stepping latency from day 1 to day 2. The control-group latency on day 2 differed both from the caudate-group day-2 latency and its own day-1 latency (Wilcoxon test, $p < .05$). The day-2 median latency was 17.0 sec for the caudate group and more than 60 sec for the control group. Eighteen of the 23 control animals did not step within 60 sec on day 2, while only 6 of the 20 caudate-stimulated animals failed to step within 60 sec. This fact is illustrated in the righthand portion of Fig. 6.

These results indicate that a retroactive passive-avoidance retention deficit can be produced by delayed caudate stimulation in a step-down as well as a lever-press task. As such they provide a degree of confidence in the generality of the effect of caudate stimulation within passive avoidance tasks. Although they provide little information regarding the temporal gradient of retention deficit, they do suggest a communality of site of influence of ECS and caudate stimulation. This does not mean that disruption of caudate function is the only possible site of influence

FIGURE 6   *At left, median stepping latency on days 1 and 2 for a delayed-caudate-stimulation group (100-msec delay) and a nonstimulated group. At right, the percentage of each of the two groups failing to step within 60 sec on day 2.*

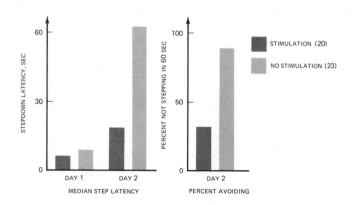

of ECS, nor does it mean that the caudate is the critical site of influence of electrical stimulation oriented to that nucleus.

DISCUSSION

The results of the present study demonstrate that retention deficits similar to those produced by ECS can be obtained with discrete and brief electrical stimulation of the caudate nucleus and hippocampus, and that the temporal gradient of these deficits in the case of caudate stimulation is quite different from that resulting from ECS in at least some situations [Chorover and Schiller, 1965, 1966; Quartermain et al., 1965; Schiller and Chorover, 1967].

Little can be said concerning the exact nature of the involvement in memory storage of neural structures affected by electrical stimulation oriented to the caudate nucleus. However, the data obtained in the present experiment suggest two points. In the rat, as in other vertebrates, the caudate nucleus is penetrated by fibers of passage. That the retention deficit associated with caudate stimulation was due to the effects on nuclear tissues in the caudate rather than on fibers of passage is indicated by the lack of such a deficit with stimulation oriented to the internal capsule and other adjacent or nearby structures, especially the corpus callosum and white matter subjacent to frontal cortex. Also, in the rat, as in other mammals, the caudate nucleus receives afferents from the thalamus. It remains a possibility that the retention deficit was due to antidromic excitation of such cells, since they participate with the caudate in a system that modulates and checks inputs ascending to the cortex [Buchwald et al., 1962].

The retention deficit obtained with hippocampal stimulation is not surprising in view of the results of lesion studies [Douglas, 1967; Milner and Penfield, 1955]. The failure to find a deficit in two animals with electrodes oriented to the dorsal hippocampus may be somewhat surprising in view of Douglas' theoretical formulation [Douglas, 1967], but it fits with other findings indicating differentiation of function between the dorsal and the ventral hippocampus [Siegal and Flynn, 1968]. In any case, the present results tell us little about the relationship between hippocampal and caudate functions as related to memory storage and retrieval. The form of stimulation used produces neither seizure activity in hippocampus nor spindle activity there or elsewhere when oriented to the hippocampus [Buchwald et al., 1961c].

Kesner and Doty [1968] have reported retroactive impairment of passive avoidance in cats administered electric stimulation of the amygdala and dorsal hippocampus, but no impairment with stimulation of the ventral hippocampus. The reversal of the effects of dorsal and ventral hippocampal stimulation between the Kesner and Doty study and the present one is surprising. However, their use of high-frequency trains of much more intense electric pulses (1.0 to 2.0 ma) and of a species possibly differing markedly in the nature of its information-processing functions offer opening wedges for future penetration of the problem posed by the contradictory results.

This study was supported in part by National Science Foundation Research Grants G-18891 and GB-4363 to the University of Southern California, Grant GB-5634 to the State University of New York at Stony Brook, and by USPHS Fellowship MH 22269 from the National Institute of Mental Health to M. J. Herz. The authors would like to express their appreciation to Michael Dawson for aid in data collection during the early stages of this investigation. An earlier version of this article appeared in *Experimental Neurology*, 1968, **22**, 350–366. Reprinted by permission of Academic Press.

RETROGRADE AMNESIA: TIME-DEPENDENT EFFECTS OF RHINENCEPHALIC LESIONS

WILLIAM J. HUDSPETH/WILLIAM E. WILSONCROFT

Retrograde amnesia produced by posttrial lesions of the anterior limbic field in mice was found to be inversely related to trial-lesion intervals. Control experiments demonstrated that the amnesia was not due to response bias, seizures, spreading depression, or generalized electrical stimulation. Damage of the motor cortex failed to produce amnesia. The results support the contention that small lesions of the anterior limbic field selectively interfere with memory-storage processes without disrupting retrieval of memory.

The biological characteristic of retaining information depends on hypothetical memory-storage processes which are initiated by experience and endure for brief periods of time [McGaugh and Petrinovich, 1965; McGaugh, 1966]. Evidence for this hypothesis is typically provided by the observation that electroconvulsive shock (ECS) treatments given shortly after training interfere with retention. In general, the shorter the interval between training and the ECS treatment, the greater the retrograde amnesia during retention tests [e.g., Hudspeth et al., 1964].

Although ECS treatments are commonly thought to produce a massive "neurological storm," it may well be that convulsions impair memory by functionally ablating selected central nervous system structures [Vanderwolf, 1964; Hudspeth and Gerbrandt, 1965]. This suggestion is consistent with electrophysiological evidence showing that particular limbic system structures are susceptible to seizure induction [French et al., 1956; Gastaut and Fischer-Williams, 1959] and a consequent reduction in excitability [Flynn et al., 1961]. Histological material from animals given several ECS treatments is consonant with this interpretation in that neurons of the hippocampal formation, as well as other areas, undergo atrophic change [Hartelius, 1952].

The present research investigates the effect of circumscribed brain damage produced shortly *after* training (i.e., during memory storage) on the retention of an avoidance response. Unlike studies of the acquisition of prelesioned animals, this procedure provides for each animal to be neurologically intact during training. This assures that perceptual, motivational, and related factors do not affect the quality of the learning experience, and that differences in retention will be related more directly to changes in memory-storage processes.

The decision to explore the anterior limbic field [Rose and Woolsey, 1948] was based on behavioral and neuroanatomical considerations. Destruction of two anatomically related areas [Glees et al., 1950], the anterior limbic and orbitofrontal fields in primates, results in deficient performance on tasks requiring short-term memory [Whitty and Lewin, 1960; Jacobsen, 1931]. Similarly, rats with homologous lesions are impaired in the acquisition of avoidance responses [Thompson and Langer, 1963; Hudspeth, 1966].

METHOD

Ninety-six (48 male and 48 female) 75- to 76-day-old Swiss-Webster albino mice, weighing 23 to 35 g, were maintained on *ad libitum* food and water in a vivarium with controlled temperature and light-dark cycle. Eighty-eight (44 male and 44 female) Ss were anesthetized with an intraperitoneal injection of pentobarbital sodium (65 mg/kg). The Ss heads were shaved, cleaned with benzylchonium chloride, and mounted in a Baltimore Stereotaxic Instrument. A longitudinal incision was made over the midsaggital suture, and the skin and fascia were reflected and then retracted with small hooks. Two small burr holes were drilled 2.0 mm anterior from lambda, with centers separated by 2.0 mm. A single burr hole was made in the nasal bone to accommodate a small skull screw.

Electrodes were made of .009-in. stainless-steel wire formed into an inverted Y shape, with the arms parallel and separated by 2.0 mm. A female pin connector was crimped on the single leg. The two-point monopolar electrodes were electropolished [Green, 1958] to a conical shape, with the tips approximately 50 to 75 μm in diameter. The electrodes were lowered into the burr holes and placed 1.25 to 1.50 mm below the dura. A single skull screw was then turned into the nasal bone. The entire package was encapsuled in dental acrylic.

A modified version of a step-through inhibitory avoidance box, 20.5 × 20.5 × 20.5 cm, was manufactured of $\frac{1}{4}$-in. plywood and painted flat black. An aluminum platform, 4.0 × 7.0 cm, was centered on the box front below a 2.5-cm opening to allow access into the box. The floor of the apparatus consisted of an aluminum plate which, in conjunction with the small platform, provided the anode-cathode source for delivering a 5.0-ma footshock. The apparatus was placed on a table, with the platform extending over the edge, at a distance of 80 cm from the floor. During testing the room lights were out and a surgical lamp was focused on the platform.

A Nuclear-Chicago (model 7150) constant-current stimulator was used for both lesions and stimulation. The current-time parameters used to produce lesions were 0.1 ma for 20.0 sec (electrode anode and skull-screw cathode). The energy developed in each arm of the electrode was calculated to be 0.1 mcoul and produced a lesion area of $.062^3$ to .294 mm^3 (median .1345 mm^3). Stimulation parameters were set to approximate those of the lesion values. Anodal pulses of 0.5 msec duration were delivered at the rate of 1 per sec for a period of 20 sec.

Main experiment Eighty (40 male and 40 female) mice were assigned randomly (except as noted below) to 10 conditions of a 2 × 5 factorial design. Half the subjects were trained with footshock (FS) punishment, and the remaining half received no footshock (NFS). Under each of these treatments were four conditions specifying the interval between the first training trial and the production of a lesion: 24 hr before, 0 sec after, 10 min after, and 45 min after. In addition, two nonlesioned control groups (one FS and one NFS) were used as baseline controls. Limitations on randomization included the equalization of males and females within each subgroup, and the fact that half the Ss within both of the nonlesioned control groups (FS-C and NFS-C) were implanted with electrodes as sham operates.

Twenty-four hours before the first trial all Ss in the FS-24 and NFS-24 conditions were individually attached to counterbalanced lesion cables, placed within the apparatus, lesioned, and then returned to their home cages. On day 1 each S was individually connected to the lesion cables and placed on the small platform. As it stepped into the interior of the box, appropriate treatments were carried out. The latency of each S was recorded, and the S was then returned to its home cage. All lesions were produced while the Ss were within the apparatus. However, Ss in both the 10- and 45-min posttrial groups were first returned to their home cage to await the appropriate interval and were then brought back to the apparatus for lesioning.

On day 2 each S was again placed on the small platform, with shorted lesion cables connected, and its step-through latency was recorded. No further treatments were given. After 23 days of rest the Ss were given a second retention test under conditions identical to those of the 24-hr retention test.

Control series Two groups of eight Ss each were used to determine whether either lesions of the motor cortex or stimulation of the anterior limbic field delivered immediately (0 sec) after an FS trial would alter performance on a 24-hr retention test. The procedures for training these Ss were identical to those used in the main experiment. The eight implanted Ss from the FS-C and NFS-C groups were used to determine whether electrocoagulation of the anterior limbic field produced after-discharges or seizure activity. Prelesioned records (Grass Model 6 EEG instrument) were taken for 5 min, and at the end of that period a switch was thrown to connect the lesion terminal outputs and isolate the preamplifier inputs. Immediately upon termination of the lesion current the S's electrode cables were again switched back to the EEG inputs for a period of 5 to 10 min.

Histological One week after the last retention test all experimental Ss and two Ss each of the motor-cortex-lesion and anterior-limbic-stimulation control groups were anesthetized with an intraperitoneal injection of pentobarbital sodium (75 mg/kg). The thorax was opened quickly, a small (27-gauge) scalp-vein catheter was introduced into the left ventrical, and perfusate of 10 percent formalin buffered with sodium acetate was pumped through the catheter at a pressure of 120 mm Hg. After 1 min the pressure was reduced to 60 mm Hg, and the perfusion was continued for another 4 min. Each brain was placed on a metric grid and photographed, and measures of electrode localization at the cortex surface were recorded for all Ss. The brains were sectioned at 40 μm and stained with thionin. Each S's lesions were completely reconstructed, and measurements of volume (mm^3) were determined. Anterior-posterior placement of lesions was calculated from sections, with the anterior horn of the capsula externa as a zero reference.

Since the lesions were made in cortical areas, their placement and extent were determined by thalamic retrograde cell degeneration. Photomicrographs of sections through the midline thalamic nuclei were taken from eight experimental and two control Ss to assist in identifying areas of cell atrophy and/or loss.

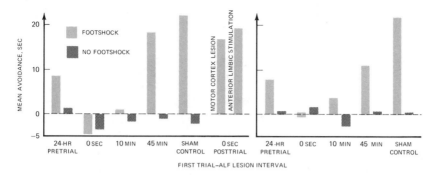

FIGURE 1 *Avoidance latencies expressed as the difference between the training trial and the retention test. Positive values indicate an increase in avoidance duration on the retention test; negative values indicate a decrease. At left, the mean avoidance of each group on the 24-hr retention test (difference between trial 1 and trial 2); at right the mean avoidance of each group on the 3-week retention test (difference between trial 1 and trial 3). Results of the 24-hr retention test for the anterior-limbic-stimulation and motor-cortex-lesion control groups are shown at the center.*

RESULTS

Main experiment Each group's first-trial mean or median latencies were separated by a range of no more than 5.5 sec. An analysis of variance of these measures (or their reciprocals) showed that the means were comparable ($F = 1.26$, $w/df = 9/20$, $p = ns$). Subsequent analyses of the results were based on differences between each S's first-trial latency and its latencies on the 24-hr or three-week retention tests (the quantity and direction of latency change from day 1).

As may be seen in Figure 1, the degree of retention depended on both the presence of footshock and the interval between footshock and destruction of the anterior limbic cortex. An analysis of variance of these data was inefficient owing to the heterogeneity of variance among groups. Reliable differences were found between the major FS and NFS conditions ($F = 7.74$, $w/df = 1/20$, $p < .025$), but no statistical differences were noted for different lesion intervals ($F = 1.76$, $w/df = 4/70$, $p > .05$) or within the interaction ($F = 1.64$, $w/df = 4/20$, $p > .05$). The inflated error term of the analysis of variance was used in Duncan's Multiple Range test [Edwards, 1960] for a conservative estimate of differences among treatment means. The results of these tests showed that the FS-45 and FS-C groups were similar in performance, while all other groups had significantly shorter response latencies ($p < .05$). Furthermore, the data demonstrate a retrograde amnesic effect in that the FS-0 and FS-10 groups show significantly poorer retention ($p < .05$) than both the FS-45 and FS-C groups. All NFS groups were highly similar in performance, regardless of when lesions were produced.

It was important to determine whether the observed amnesia was attenuated or disappeared in time, as measured on a long-term retention test. The results of a three-week test are also shown in Figure 1; as can be seen, the groups did not change their relative positions. An analysis of variance for repeated measures showed no reliable difference between the 24-hr and three-week tests, or between the repeated measures and their interactions with the main treatments (all F ratios 1.0).

Behavioral control series While electrocoagulation of the anterior limbic cortex produced retrograde amnesia, several other interpretations were tenable, and appropriate observations were made to evaluate their plausibility. First, the amnesic effect may have been due to general excitation or polarization of tissue. However, as may be seen in Figure 1, repetitive anodal stimulation of the anterior limbic field did not result in amnesia on a 24-hr retention test. A second possibility was that amnesia might result from the destruction of *any* cortical field. The evidence of this was clearly negative (Figure 1) in that motor cortex lesions of comparable volume failed to block memory storage. Finally, there was the possibility that seizures evoked by electrocoagulation had produced the observed amnesia. No behavioral components of convulsive activity were observed in any S during or after the passage of lesion current. In addition, EEG records taken before or immediately and 24 hr after lesions gave no evidence of seizure or afterdischarge activity.

Histological The anterior-posterior and lateral placements of lesion electrodes were measured from photographs of each brain on a metric grid. Lateral placements were quite restricted, having a range of 0.6 mm. Anterior-posterior placements varied somewhat, having a range of 1.8 mm. The possibility was noted that the lesion groups might differ with respect to electrode placement. However, all the groups were quite similar in terms of mean anterior-posterior location, so that there is no basis for suspecting that the experimental findings were due to systematic electrode placement.

Eight lesioned Ss were selected for analysis of retrograde thalamic degeneration. Degenerative changes were characterized by loss of neuron soma and relative increase in glial elements within the area of cell loss. Additional evidence of degeneration was adduced from the serial continuity of the atrophic pattern through the thalmic nuclei.

Lesions of the anterior cortex were of similarly small proportion, although there was a slight difference in anterior-posterior placement. Retrograde cell loss was readily traced through the ventromedial borders of the thalamic nuclei anteromedialis and paratenialis. Experimental lesions extended ventrally through layer VI of the motor cortex and ran parallel to layer VI of the anterior limbic field. In addition, the inter-hemispheric cortex bordering the lesion typically contained pyknotic or disintegrating pyramidal cells within layer V. No such cells were noted either in the motor cortex or on the lateral side of the lesion. These histological observations, as well as earlier studies of rabbit thalamocortical projections [Rose and Woolsey, 1948], led to the conclusion that the experimental ablations represented rather small lesions within the anterior limbic field.

Although the experimental lesions destroyed a portion of the motor cortex, ablations restricted to this area alone had no effect on learning performance, nor was retrograde cell atrophy observed in the nucleus anteromedialis. Motor cortex damage was evidenced by gliosis [Meyer et al., 1947] emerging from the lesion area, which then perforated the corpus callosum and was subsequently traced into the myelinated fibers of the internal capsule. Marchi material from rats with similar lesions has shown an identical pattern of degeneration, which continues through the middle and midlateral portion of the basis peduncularis [Hudspeth, 1967). These observations are presumed to result from damage to the corticospinal (pyramidal) system.

DISCUSSION

The results of the present experiments clearly show that small posttrial lesions of the anterior limbic cortex interfere with memory-storage processes. The severity of retrograde amnesia is inversely related to the amount of time between training and destruction of the anterior limbic area. In addition, the amnesia produced by this lesion does not disappear over longer retention intervals. In all, our results are consistent with the consolidation hypothesis [Müller and Pilzecker, 1900], which contends that the neural activity initiated by experience must persevere unin-terrupted for a period of time before a viable or stable memory trace is formed. The hypothesis says nothing of memory being localized in the central nervous system; nor, in fact, do our data substantiate such a notion. However, the present results do support the position that specific structures participate in memory storage, but not in memory retrieval. This conclusion is clearly supported by the fact that Ss lesioned 45 min after training showed no impairment of retrieval. The specificity of structure underlying consolidation is also supported by the finding that brain damage alone (motor cortex) is not sufficient to block memory formation. This finding is consistent with other observations of the specificity of neuroanatomic structures in short-term memory processes [Mahut, 1962; Goddard, 1964; Wyers et al., 1968; Kesner and Doty, 1968].

Many lesion studies purporting to demonstrate the role of specific brain structures in learning and memory processes eventually become translated into concepts involving performance capacities. For example, orbitofrontally damaged primates are not deficient in short-term memory; they are, rather, inattentive [Nissen et al., 1938; Finan, 1942; Malmo, 1942] or hyperreactive [Richter and Hines, 1938; Orbach and Fischer, 1959]. Similarly, brain-damaged rats do not fail to learn avoidance responses; rather, their performance is impaired owing to damage of postulated mechanisms controlling response inhibition [McCleary, 1961; Douglas, 1967], internal inhibition [Kimble, 1968], or release and control of freezing [Thomas and Slotnick, 1962; Schwartzbaum et al., 1964; Vanderwolf, 1964]. Although such mechanisms are important to our understanding of behavior, lesion studies consistent with these conceptual mechanisms do not necessarily lead to understanding of memory processes [Gerbrandt, 1965]. It seems clear that the deficient performance reported here is due to impaired memory processes, since the same lesion produced 45 min after training did not impair the Ss' ability to "inhibit responses" (or memory, for that matter).

Since unitary mechanisms are inconsistent with the present data, a logical alternative is a variable process which mimics the time-dependent function associated with retrograde amnesia (concepts dealing with reinforcement or conditioning of lesion-produced cues). However, this alternative does not appear to be likely, since the retention scores of nonpunished (NPS) groups lesioned at different intervals after training do not differ. Clearly, response latencies are not directionally biased merely because of the lesion, or because of lesions made at different periods after a trial.

Any notion that the anterior limbic area is unique in memory storage must be tempered by the observation that 24-hr pretrial lesions do not completely block storage and subsequent retention. However, it is not clear just what information is stored. For example, all pretrial-lesion Ss were familiarized with the apparatus (during lesions) before training, but this was not the case for Ss lesioned after training. Recent experiments in our laboratory have shown that Ss given 24-hr pretrial lesions in their home cage (no familiarization) are as amnesic as those given a 0-sec posttrial lesion; that is, no storage occurs [Hudspeth and Weening, 1968]. In view of this control, it may well be that the anterior limbic cortex is more critical for memory storage than the present data suggest. It is important to note, however, that other structures may be equally critical for memory storage, but may differ in terms of temporal organization because of connections within or between them.

This research was supported by NIMH Training Grant 5-TI-MH-6415 and in part by Grant NB-4578 from the National Institutes of

READINGS IN MEMORY CONSOLIDATION

Health (USPHS). Partial support was also provided by an Interim Grant AP-312 from the National Research Council of Canada. Appreciation is expressed to Drs. Michael J. Herz, James L. McGaugh, and Lawrence Kruger for their respective contributions to our work. Thanks are due to Miss Arlene Koithan for her excellent histological preparations and to Miss Keiko Tani and Mr. Barry Burns for their careful preparation of the drawings. An earlier version of this article appeared in the *Journal of Neurobiology*, 1969, **1**, 221–232. Reprinted by permission of John Wiley & Sons, Inc.

DRUG FACILITATION OF LATENT LEARNING

WILLIAM H. WESTBROOK/JAMES L. McGAUGH

Rats were injected with 17571.S. (1-5-diphenyl-1-3-7-diazadamantan-9-ol) or a control solution immediately after each daily trial in a 6-unit alley U maze. Half the animals received food reward after each trial. Drug-injected rats made significantly fewer errors than controls in the rewarded condition. When injections were discontinued and food reward was given to the previously non-rewarded animals, the subjects which had received 1757 I.S. injections made significantly fewer errors than rats previously injected with the control solution. The results were interpreted as providing further support for the hypothesis that 1757 I.S. improves learning by enhancing storage processes.

A number of recent investigations have shown that, in rats, learning is facilitated by injections of several compounds, including picrotoxin, strychnine, and the strychnine-like compound 1-5-diphenyl-3-7-di-azadamantan-9-ol (1757 I.S.)[1] [Kelemen and Bovet, 1961; McGaugh and Petrinovich, 1959; McGaugh et al., 1961; Petrinovich, 1963]. These findings have been interpreted as indicating that the drugs improve performance by enhancing memory storage or consolidation. This interpretation is strengthened by evidence that retention is facilitated by injections of CNS stimulants if the injections are administered within a few minutes *after* the training trials [Breen and McGaugh, 1961; McGaugh et al., 1962a; McGaugh et al., 1962b; Paré, 1961; Stratton and Petrinovich, 1963]. Although these latter findings provide strong support for a view that the drugs used improve performance by enhancing memory storage, an alternative possibility that the posttraining injections are rewarding has not as yet been excluded. If the improvement found with posttrial injections is due to a rewarding effect in place of, or in addition to, an effect on memory storage, rats given only drug injections

---

[1] In previous publications this compound was termed 5-7-diphenyl-1-3-diazadamatan-6-ol (1757 I.S.).

and no other reward following each training trial in a maze should show improvement in performance from trial to trial. If the drug acts only to enhance memory storage, however, the subjects should learn more, in comparison with control subjects, about the features and plan of the maze but should not improve in performance until a relevant reward (e.g., food or water) is given at the end of the trial. Further, following the introduction of the reward the performance of the subjects previously given posttrial drug injections should be superior to controls: that is, they should exhibit greater latent learning. To test these interpretations the present study investigated the effect of posttrial injections of the CNS stimulant 1757 I.S. on learning under rewarded or non-rewarded followed by rewarded ("latent learning") conditions. The "latent learning" training procedure was similar to those used by Blodgett [1929] and Tolman and Honzik [1930]. Longo et al. [1959] reported that 1757 I.S. affects CNS activity in a manner highly similar to that of strychnine. The dose used in the present study has been found to facilitate learning in several previous studies (cited above), and is comparable to the doses of strychnine and picrotoxin previously found to influence learning.

METHOD

Forty-eight rats, 24 males and 24 females, from the S_1 strain and 48 rats, 24 males and 24 females, from the S_3 strain were used in this study. Twelve additional subjects (8 S_1 males, 2 S_1 females, 1 S_3 male, and 1 S_3 female) were eliminated for failure to complete all stages of training. All subjects were between 70 and 85 days of age at the beginning of the experiment. The S_1 and S_3 strains are decendents of the Tryon maze-bright and maze-dull strains maintained at the University of California, Berkeley. The subjects used in this study were all reared in the animal laboratory at San Jose State College.

The learning task was a six-unit alley U maze. Each main unit of the maze was 10 cm wide, 12.7 cm high, and 50.8 cm long. The two arms extending forward from each main unit were 10 cm wide, 12.7 cm high, and 17 cm long. A 25.4 cm starting-alley connected the starting-box to the first main unit. The goal-box was connected directly to the correct arm of the last unit. The walls and floor of the maze were painted a dull medium grey. Units were separated by guillotine doors. The doors in both arms of each unit were raised at the beginning of each trial to prevent any differential visual cues for the two arms. The incorrect arms were blocked by a false door placed behind the guillotine door. Guillotine doors were also placed between the starting-box and the starting-alley, the starting-alley and the first unit, and the last unit and the goal-box. Two narrow white lines were painted on the floor of each unit 5 cm from the sides of the entrance to the unit. The correct alleys were, in sequence, L R L R R L. Mirrors suspended from a wooden frame over the maze provided a clear view of each unit. The maze was situated in a partitioned section of a large room and was centered under a large covered light which provided adequate illumination in all units.

The subjects were first placed on a 22-hour food and water deprivation schedule for five days. Each subject was allowed access to water for 2 hours daily and was given sufficient wet mash to maintain body weight at 85 percent of the subject's weight on the second day. This schedule was maintained throughout the experiment.

Following the adaptation period, the subjects were divided into four groups, each consisting of 24 subjects, six males and six females of each strain.

All subjects were given one trial per day for 10 days in the maze. Errors were recorded whenever a subject's head crossed the white line in front of a blind alley. Two of the groups were given wet mash in the goal-box and were allowed 1 minute of eating after each trial. These two groups will be referred to as Reward-Reward Experimental (RRE) and Reward-Reward Control (RRC). The subjects in the other two groups were also deprived of food and water but received no reward in the goal-box for the first four trials. On the fifth and succeeding trials they were rewarded with wet mash. Thus each subject in these latter groups had five trials with *no* prior reward and five trials *with* prior reward. These two groups will be referred to as Non-reward-Reward Experimental (NRE) and Non-reward Control (NRC).

All subjects were given an intraperitoneal injection immediately after each daily trial. Subjects in the experimental groups in each reward condition (RRE and NRE) received 1.0 ml/kg of a 1.0 mg/ml solution of 1757 I.S. after each of the first five trials. Following each of the last five trials, they received 1.0 ml/kg of a citrate buffer control solution. Subjects in the two control groups (RRC and NRC) received the control solution after each trial.

RESULTS

The means and standard deviations of errors made by subjects in each subgroup on trials 2 to 5 and trials 6 to 10 are shown in Table 1. Figure 1 shows the mean errors made by subjects in each of the four experimental groups (ignoring strain and sex) on each trial. Only initial errors were used because of the variability of repetitive errors during the non-rewarded trials. As can be seen, the RRE subjects made fewer errors that the RRC subjects throughout the training. An analysis of variance of errors made by subjects in these groups on trials 2 to 10 indicated a significant drug effect ($F = 13.9$, $df = 1/40$, $p < .005$) but no significant strain or sex differences and no significant interactions.

| | Strain S_1 | | Strain S_3 | | Combined |
	Male	Female	Male	Female	mean
Trials 2 to 5					
RRC	14.5 (4.3)	13.3 (1.8)	13.8 (1.9)	15.3 (2.0)	14.2
RRE	13.0 (1.5)	11.0 (1.7)	13.7 (2.4)	12.7 (2.3)	12.6
NRC	15.2 (1.2)	15.7 (2.7)	15.0 (2.1)	17.5 (3.0)	15.8
NRE	14.8 (1.9)	17.7 (1.1)	16.7 (2.5)	15.8 (1.6)	15.5
Trials 6 to 10					
RRC	12.3 (4.0)	12.7 (3.4)	12.3 (2.6)	15.7 (3.2)	13.2
RRE	11.7 (2.1)	8.7 (2.1)	9.2 (2.7)	8.7 (2.5)	9.5
NRC	13.8 (1.7)	14.7 (2.9)	12.2 (2.0)	12.2 (2.3)	13.2
NRE	9.0 (2.2)	11.8 (2.4)	9.0 (3.2)	11.0 (2.1)	10.2

TABLE 1 *Means and standard deviations of initial errors made by subjects in each subgroup on trials 2 to 5 (prior to reward introduction) and trials 6 to 10 (after reward introduction)*

During the first five trials the mean errors of the two rewarded groups decreased, while those of the non-rewarded subjects remained fairly constant. An analysis of variance of the errors of all subgroups on trials 2 to 5 indicated a significant drug effect ($F = 3.95$, $df = 1/80$, $p < .05$), a significant strain effect ($F = 4.29$, $df = 1/80$, $p < .05$), and a highly significant reward effect ($F = 20.01$, $df = 1/80$, $p < .005$). Fisher t tests indicated that on trials 2 to 5 the mean of the RRE subjects was significantly lower than that of the RRC subjects ($t = 2.29$, $df = 46$, $p < .05$), but the means of groups NRE and NRC did not differ significantly ($t = 0.5$). Sign tests indicated that in these latter groups, the performance of subjects on trial 5 was not significantly different ($p > .05$) from that on trial 1. These analyses indicate that the drug effect on performance in the first five trials was limited to the rewarded subjects.

Following the introduction of reward and termination of the drug injections all subjects were treated alike. As Fig. 2 and Table 1 show, however, on trials 6 to 10 the means of groups RRE and NRE were lower than those of groups RRC and NRC. An analysis of variance of the errors made on trials 6 to 10 indicated a significant drug effect ($F = 32.11$, $df = 1/80$, $p < .005$). The effect of condition of prior reward was insignificant ($F < 1$). The effect of the drug depended upon the sex and prior reward of the subjects ($F = 5.59$, $df = 1/80, p < .025$); in groups RRC and NRC male subjects made fewer errors than female subjects, while females were superior in group RRE and males were superior in group NRE. No other main effect (strain and sex) or interaction approached significance. Fisher t tests indicated that on trials 6 to 10 group RRE made significantly fewer errors than group RRC ($t = 3.45$, $df = 46$, $p < .01$) and that group NRE made significantly fewer errors than group NRC ($t = 3.90$, $df = 46$, $p < .01$). Sign tests indicated that both non-rewarded groups improved significantly ($p <$ .01) between trials 5 and 6 (i.e., following the introduction of reward).

The findings indicate that posttrial injections of 1757 I.S. facilitate latent learning as well as conventional (rewarded) maze learning. The performance of the consistently rewarded groups was similar to that of comparable groups in previous posttrial injection studies which have used different tasks and testing procedures [McGaugh et al., 1962b].

The results of the subjects which received five trials prior to reward introduction provide additional evidence bearing on the question of the basis of the facilitating effect of 1757 I.S. on maze performance. During the non-rewarded trials the performance of the control subjects was similar to that of the subjects receiving posttrial injections of 1757 I.S.; there was no evidence of improvement in maze performance in either group. This finding is evidence against the interpretation that the drug-control difference in performance is due either to a rewarding effect of the drug or a punishing effect of the control solution. Further evidence against these latter interpretations is provided by subjects' performance on the last five trials, when all subjects received food reward and post-trial control injections. If the drug affects performance only because it is rewarding, all groups would be expected to perform alike on the last few trials. This was clearly not the case. On the last trials the subjects previously injected with 1757 I.S. made significantly fewer errors than subjects that had received only the control solution. Further, the performance of subjects on the last five trials was not significantly influenced by the presence or absence of reward on the earlier trials: the mean errors of the two 1757 I.S. groups were similar and the mean errors of the two control groups were identical.

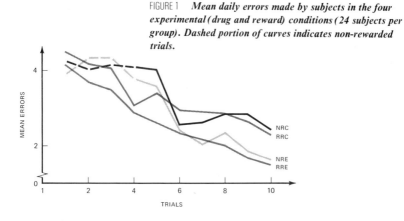

FIGURE 1 *Mean daily errors made by subjects in the four experimental (drug and reward) conditions (24 subjects per group). Dashed portion of curves indicates non-rewarded trials.*

In general, the effects of condition of reward and drug were similar for males and females of the two strains. The only exceptions to this were a strain difference in errors made during the early trials and a drug by sex by condition of prior reward interaction in the later trials. The significance of these effects is obscure.

The findings of this study, as well as those of other recent studies using other CNS stimulants are most consistent with the hypothesis that posttrial injections of CNS stimulants improve learning by facilitating memory storage. Since facilitation has been found with a variety of tasks and drugs it seems likely that the facilitation is due to a common excitatory effect of the agents on the CNS. An understanding of the process or processes underlying drug facilitation of learning will require additional knowledge of the common CNS effects of the effective compounds.

SUMMARY

Male and female rats of the S_1 and S_3 strains (descendants of the Tryon strains) were injected with either 1.0 mg/kg of 1757 I.S. (1-5-diphenyl-3-7-diazadamatan-9-ol) or a control solution immediately after each daily trial in a six-unit alley U maze. One half of the rats received a food reward in the goal box and one half was not rewarded. The non-rewarded drug and control rats did not improve in performance. Both of the rewarded groups improved, and the 1757 I.S.-injected rats made significantly fewer errors than the controls. The drug injections were then discontinued and all rats were given five rewarded trials (one per day), each followed by a control injection. On the last five trials the mean errors of the rats previously given posttrial 1757 I.S. injections were significantly lower than those of the controls. Further, performance on the last five trials was not influenced by the reward condition on the first five trials. These results were interpreted as providing further support for the hypothesis that 1757 I.S. improves learning by enhancing memory storage processes.

This study was conducted in the Psychology Department Animal Laboratory of San Jose State College and was supported by Research Grants MY-3541 and MH 07015 from the National Institute of Mental Health, United States Public Health Service. We would like to express our appreciation to Professor Daniel Bovet for providing the 1757 I.S. Reprinted from *Psychopharmacologia*, 1964, **5**, 440–446, by permission of Springer-Verlag.

STRYCHNINE AND THE INHIBITION OF PREVIOUS PERFORMANCE

JOSEPH J. FRANCHINA/MARK H. MOORE

The injection of strychnine sulfate into rats inhibits a hurdle-crossing response. Hurdle-crossing tends to decrease with increasing strychnine doses. The data are interpreted as being consistent with consolidation theory.

Studies of maze learning [McGaugh et al., 1962a], visual discrimination [Hudspeth, 1964], and active avoidance learning [Bovet et al., 1966] have shown that injections of subconvulsive doses of strychnine sulfate facilitate learning which involved the emission of locomotor responses. These findings have been attributed to strychnine's enhancement of the consolidation of persisting memory traces which were initiated by training trials.

While there is considerable evidence [McGaugh and Petrinovich, 1965] for strychnine's facilitation of locomotor behavior, there are no data on whether or not strychnine will similarly affect learning which involves the withholding (that is, inhibition) of a previously performed response. In order to provide this information, we investigated the effects of strychnine on rats' holding back from reentering a situation where a noxious stimulus (shock) had been previously experienced.

METHOD

The apparatus consisted of a white start box (8 by 9 by 10 cm) separated from a black shock box (29 by 22 by 15 cm) by a guillotine door and a hurdle, 2.5 cm high. The start-box floor was Plexiglas; the shock-box floor consisted of 22 stainless steel rods placed 0.64 cm apart and wired to a Grason-Stadler shock generator (model E 1064GS).

Fifty-four male Holtzman albino rats were used. On each of the first four days of the experiment, each rat was placed in the start box and allowed to explore both boxes for 120 seconds. A 0.01-second timer measured the amount of time which elapsed before the rat's first hurdle-crossing on each day to provide an operant index of this behavior.

On the fifth day, each rat was placed directly in the shock box and, after 5 seconds, was administered two 1-second presentations of inescapable shock (0.2 ma), separated by 4 seconds. Ten seconds after the end of the second shock, the rat was returned to his home cage, and 15 minutes later received an intraperitoneal injection of either strychnine (0.2 mg/kg, 0.1 mg/kg, 0.05 mg/kg, 0.025 mg/kg, or 0.0125 mg/kg) or

95 percent saline. Nine rats were randomly assigned to each injection condition.[1]

Beginning on the next day, each rat was administered one test trial on each of seven days. A test trial began with the rat's being placed in the start box. Five seconds later the guillotine door was raised, starting a 0.01-second timer. When the rat crossed the hurdle into the shock box the timer stopped, yielding a measure of how much time had elapsed before hurdle-crossing occurred. (Henceforth this measure will be referred to as delay of hurdle-crossing.) The rat was returned to his home cage 10 seconds after crossing the hurdle or after 120 seconds in the start box without crossing, whichever came first. In the latter case a latency of 120 seconds was recorded for that trial. No shock occurred during test trials.

After the end of this first experiment, a second experiment evaluated the possible aversive effects of strychnine injections alone on hurdle-crossing behavior. This experiment replicated the procedures and injection conditions (N = five rats per group) of the first experiment except for the procedures on the shock day (the fifth day). On this day, in the second experiment, the rat was placed in the shock box but no shock occurred. Thus, test-trial performance presumably reflected the effect of the injection conditions alone.

RESULTS

Figure 1 shows the results of the first experiment. Mean delay of hurdle-crossing is presented for all groups for the last exploratory (the pretest) trial and over all test trials.

Since maximum strychnine effects might reasonably be expected on the test trial immediately following injection, data for trial 1 were analyzed separately. The treatment effect was reliable ($P < .05$). Scheffé comparisons [Edwards, 1960] showed no reliable differences among strychnine-dose groups, but each such group, except the 0.0125 mg/kg dose group, showed reliably longer delays in crossing the hurdle than did the saline group ($P < .05$ or better). The effects of strychnine over all tests trials were evaluated with a repeated measures analysis of variance [Lindquist, 1956]. Only a reliable treatment effect was obtained ($P < .05$). Scheffé comparisons showed that delays of hurdle-crossing for the 0.2 and 0.1 mg/kg dose groups were reliably longer than those of the 0.0125 mg/kg and saline groups ($P < .05$). The 0.05 mg/kg dose

[1]Strychnine solutions were prepared by placing a weighed amount of strychnine in a liter volumetric flask, filled to capacity with isotonic saline. All rats received an injection of 1 ml/kg of body weight.

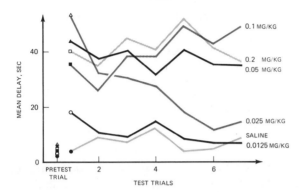

FIGURE 1 *Mean delay of hurdle-crossing in seconds for each injection condition on the last pretest trial and over all test trials.*

group's delay of hurdle-crossing was also reliably longer than that of the saline group ($P < .05$) but only marginally longer than that of the 0.0125 mg/kg dose group ($P = .05$ to .10).

In the second experiment, test-trial performance of all groups was slightly and nonsignificantly below that of the saline group shown in Fig. 1. Analyses over all the second experiment's data showed no reliable effects of injection conditions.

Since hurdle-crossing behavior in the second experiment showed no reliable effects of injection conditions alone, the results of the first experiment suggest that strychnine injections facilitated the rats' learning to inhibit reentry into the situation where they were previously shocked. These data were consistent with expectations from a consolidation viewpoint. Presumably, memory traces of the shock experience were enhanced by strychnine injections in the first study.

However, the facilitative effects of strychnine seemed to have been regulated by the dosages used. Inhibition of hurdle-crossing was reliably shown over all test trials (relative to saline controls) following 0.2 mg/kg, 0.1 mg/kg, and 0.05 mg/kg injections. Following a 0.025 mg/kg injection, however, inhibition was reliably shown on test trial 1 but decayed thereafter; a 0.0125 mg/kg injection provided no reliable evidence for inhibition at all. These results suggested that strychnine dosage determined both the initial appearance and the apparent maintenance of response inhibition. The finding of a dose-response relationship here was consistent with previous findings with Metrazol [Irwin and Banuazizi, 1966] and strychnine [McGaugh and Petrinovich, 1965] in similar hurdle-crossing situations.

Reprinted from *Science*, 1968, **160**, 903–904, by permission of the American Association for the Advancement of Science.

THE EFFECT OF STRYCHNINE ADMINISTRATION DURING DEVELOPMENT ON ADULT MAZE LEARNING IN THE RAT II: DRUG ADMINISTRATION FROM DAY 51 TO 70

HARMAN V. S. PEEKE/BURNEY J. LEBOEUF/MICHAEL J. HERZ

Strychnine sulphate administered to rats during development from day 51 to day 70 affected the rate of maze learning in adulthood. Rats given the drug in a rich environment learned the maze at a faster rate and with fewer errors than rats treated with the same drug but raised in small laboratory cages. The performance of rats given no drugs was intermediate to that of the drug-rich and drug-caged groups.

A number of previous investigations have demonstrated that learning is facilitated by the injection of central nervous system stimulants [e.g., Petrinovich et al., 1965; Breen and McGaugh, 1961]. More recently, LeBoeuf and Peeke [1969] studied the effects of daily administration of strychnine sulphate to rats from weaning (21 days) to day 50 while the rats were maintained in either an enriched or an impoverished environment. They found that drug treatment interacted with the environment to produce adult rats that were good learners (drug plus enriched environment) or poor learners (drug plus impoverished environment) when compared with controls that were reared in the same environments but not given the drug. Although these results clearly showed an environment-drug interaction at this early stage of development, no conclusion could be made regarding such interactions during other developmental periods. It was the purpose of this investigation to replicate LeBoeuf and Peeke [1969] at a different age period during development. The period 51 to 70 days was selected because it begins at the end of the period used in the previous study and ends approximately at puberty. Failure to find a drug-environment interaction would suggest a "sensitive developmental period" for the effect within the developmental span encompassed by the first study. Positive findings would reflect a more general effect with no pre-pubertal differentiation in terms of gross sensitivity to the drug-environment experience.

METHOD

Fifty male Long-Evans rats (excluding albinos) were assigned to each of four groups: (1) Drug-Rich (DR), daily strychnine injections in a rich environment ($N = 14$); (2) Drug-Caged (DC), daily strychnine injections in a caged environment ($N = 12$); (3) Water-Rich (WR), daily water injections in a rich environment ($N = 12$); and (4) Water-Caged (WC), daily water injections in a caged environment ($N = 12$).

The rich environment consisted of a cage 4 ft. wide × 4 ft. long ×

2 ft. high with wire mesh sides, the interior of which was furnished with various black and white painted objects patterned on those employed by Krech et al. [1960]. The position of the objects was changed daily in an attempt to maximize the complexity of the environment. The subjects in groups DC and WC were raised in stainless steel laboratory cages 10 in. wide × 12 in. long × 8 in. high, the bottoms of which were covered with sawdust. The cages were solid metal except for a wire ceiling, which permitted only a view of the shelf above, and slits in the front of the cage, which faced a black curtain.

The subjects were housed and treated in these environments from day 51 to day 70. During the treatment phase, each subject in groups DR and DC received a daily intraperitoneal injection of 0.05% solution of strychnine sulphate in distilled water suspension, 2.0 cc/kg of body weight or 1.0 mg/kg of body weight. One mg/kg is the dose previously found to facilitate learning in the rat [e.g., McGaugh and Petrinovich, 1959; Petrinovich et al., 1965]. Groups WR and WC were similarly injected with distilled water (the drug vehicle), the amount adjusted to body weight as with the strychnine.

On day 71, treatment was terminated and all subjects were placed in laboratory cages identical to those previously described until testing began.

Prior to maze learning trials, subjects were put on a $23\frac{1}{2}$ hr. food deprivation schedule that was maintained throughout the experiment. Once the animals were down to 85% of their original, pre-deprivation weight, they were pretrained in a 12 in. runway that led from a start box to a goal box containing wet mash (made from ground dry food pellets mixed with water). Pre-training was continued for three days. After weights reached 85% they were maintained at that level by adjusting the amount of food fed each animal after the day's session. Daily trials in a 4-unit, 8-cul Lashley III alley-maze to a wet mash reward began when the subjects were 110 days old. Initial and repetitive errors per trial and time per trial were recorded. The criterion of learning was four out of five errorless runs. An error was scored each time one-half or more of the animal's body extended into a cul. The number of different culs entered at least once per trial (initial errors) and the trials to criterion are reported.

RESULTS

Adult maze performance was affected by administration of strychnine sulphate during development (see Fig. 1). The direction of the effect,

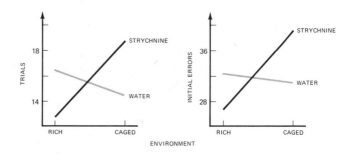

FIGURE 1   *Interaction of drug with environment for mean trials to criterion and mean initial errors to criterion.*

i.e., enhancement or impairment, varied as a function of the treatment environment.

Comparisons of all three measures were made between groups DR and DC. It was hypothesized that the results would be in the same direction as the previous study; i.e., that the WR and WC groups would not be different and that the interaction would appear as a DR versus DC difference. Mann-Whitney U tests were used for all comparisons. These expectations were borne out by all three measures. In terms of trials to criterion, group DR was faster than group DC ($p < 0.05$; all probability levels determined by one-tailed tests); in terms of both initial errors and total errors to criterion the same relationship was found ($p < 0.01$ in both cases). None of the other group comparisons reached significance.

Although the pattern of differences between groups in the present study is identical with that reported by LeBoeuf and Peeke [1969], the absolute magnitude of the difference is less. Although the basis of this difference is yet unclear, there is the possibility that it reflects a strain difference between the LeBoeuf and Peeke study (University of California K strain) and the present one.

DISCUSSION

Strychnine sulphate, administered daily from the day 51 to day 70, interacted with the environment in which the animals were raised to produce effects on their maze-learning ability long after the administration of the drug had been terminated.

This finding, combined with the previous work reported by LeBoeuf and Peeke [1969], in which animals were similarly treated, but from day 21 to day 50, suggests that the drug-environment interaction is not a phenomenon restricted to any particular pre-pubertal developmental epoch, but may reflect a more general developmental plasticity.

Finally, it should be noted that in the present study, as well as the one by LeBoeuf and Peeke, the enriched and deprived environmental treatment alone (saline groups) did not differentially affect adult learning ability. It would therefore appear that strychnine administered during environmental treatment periods can significantly shorten the time required to produce modifications in adult learning ability by such treatments.

This research was supported in part by General Research Support Grant FR 05550 from N.I.M.H. to Langley Porter Neuropsychiatric Institute, and in part by Mental Health Training Grant 5-TI-MH-7082-07 to the University of California at San Francisco. Reprinted from *Psychopharmacologia*, 1971, **19**, 262–265, by permission of Springer-Verlag.

PART THREE

BIBLIOGRAPHY

Abt, J. P., Essman, W. B., and Jarvik, M. E., 1961 Ether-induced retrograde amnesia for one-trial conditioning in mice. *Science*, **133**, 1477–1478.

Adams, H. E., and Lewis, D. J., 1962*a* Electroconvulsive shock, retrograde amnesia and competing responses. *J. Comp. Physiol. Psychol.*, **55**, 299–301.

Adams, H. E., and Lewis, D. J., 1962*b* Retrograde amnesia and competing responses. *J. Comp. Physiol. Psychol.*, **55**, 302–305.

Adams, H. E., and Peacock, L. J., 1967 ECS and one-trial learning: Retrograde amnesia or disinhibition? *Physiol. Behav.*, **2**, 435–437.

Agranoff, B. W., 1968 Biological effects of antimetabolites used in behavioral studies. In D. H. Efron et al. (eds.), *Psychopharmacology: A review of progress, 1957–1967*, PHS Publ. 1836, pp. 909–917. Washington, D.C.: U.S. Government Printing Office.

Agranoff, B. W., Davis, R. E., and Brink, J. J., 1965 Memory fixation in the goldfish. *Proc. Nat. Acad. Sci.*, **54**, 788–793.

Agranoff, B. W., Davis, R. E., and Brink, J. J., 1966 Chemical studies on memory fixation in goldfish. *Brain Res.*, **1**, 303–309.

Agranoff, B. W., Davis, R. E., Casola, L., and Lim, R., 1967 Actinomycin blocks formation of memory of shock-avoidance in goldfish. *Science*, **158**, 1600–1601.

Agranoff, B. W., and Klinger, P. D., 1964 Puromycin effect on memory fixation in the goldfish. *Science*, **146**, 952–953.

Albert, D. J., 1966*a* The effect of spreading depression on the consolidation of learning. *Neuropsychologia*, **4**, 49–64.

Albert, D. J., 1966*b* The effects of polarizing currents on the consolidation of learning. *Neuropsychologia*, **4**, 65–77.

Alpern, H. P., 1968 Facilitation of learning by implantation of strychnine sulphate in the central nervous system. Doctoral dissertation, University of California, Irvine.

Alpern, H. P., and Kimble, D. P., 1967 Retrograde amnesic effects of diethyl ether and bis(trifluoroethyl) ether. *J. Comp. Physiol. Psychol.*, **63**, 168–171.

Alpern, H. P., and McGaugh, J. L., 1968 Retrograde amnesia as a function of duration of electroshock stimulation. *J. Comp. Physiol. Psychol.*, **65**, 265–269.

Appel, S., 1964 A critical appraisal of the role of RNA information storage in the nervous system. In J. Gaito (ed.), *Symposium on the role of macromolecules in complex behavior*. Manhattan, Kans.: Kansas State University Press.

Artusio, J. F., 1955 Ether analgesia during major surgery. *J. Amer. Med. Assn.*, **157**, 33–36.

Avis, H. H., and Carlton, P. L., 1968   Retrograde amnesia produced by hippocampal spreading depression. *Science*, **161**, 73–75.

Bailey, M. Y., Garman, M. W., and Cherkin, A., 1969   Incubation of learning: Absence in one-trial avoidance conditioning in the chick. Part A. *Commun. Behav. Biol.*, **3**, 295–297.

Banker, G., Hunt, E. B., and Pagano, R., 1969   Evidence supporting the memory disruption hypothesis of electroconvulsive shock action. *Physiol. Behav.*, **4**, 895–899.

Barbizet, J., 1963   Defect of memorizing of hippocampal-mammillary origin: A review. *J. Neurol. Neurosurg. Psychiat.*, **26**, 127–135.

Barbizet, J., 1970   *Human memory and its pathology.* San Francisco: W. H. Freeman.

Barcik, J. D., 1969   Hippocampal afterdischarges and memory disruption. *Proc. 77th Ann. Conv. Amer. Psychol. Assoc.*, **4**, 185–186.

Barondes, S., 1968   Effect of inhibitors of cerebral protein synthesis on "long-term" memory in mice. In D. H. Efron et al. (eds.), *Psychopharmacology: A review of progress, 1957–1967*, PHS Publ. 1836, pp. 905–908. Washington, D.C.: U.S. Government Printing Office.

Barondes, S. H., and Cohen, H. D., 1966   Puromycin effect on successive phases of memory storage. *Science*, **151**, 594–595.

Barondes, S. H., and Cohen, H. D., 1967   Delayed and sustained effect of acetoxycycloheximide on memory in mice. *Proc. Nat. Acad. Sci.*, **58**, 157–164.

Barondes, S., and Cohen, H. D., 1968*a*   Memory impairment after subcutaneous injection of acetoxycycloheximide. *Science*, **160**, 556–557.

Barondes, S., and Cohen, H. D., 1968*b*   Arousal and the conversion of "short-term" to "long-term" memory. *Proc. Nat. Acad. Sci.*, **61**, 923–929.

Barondes, S. H., and Jarvik, M. E., 1964   The influence of actinomycin-D on brain RNA synthesis and on memory. *J. Neurochem.*, **11**, 187–195.

Beitel, R. E., and Porter, P. B., 1968.   Deficits in short- and long-term retention and impairments in learning induced by severe hypothermia in mice. *J. Comp. Physiol. Psychol.*, **66**, 53–59.

Benevento, L. A., and Kandel, G. L., 1967   Influence of strychnine on classically conditioned defensive reflexes in the cat. *J. Comp. Physiol. Psychol.*, **63**, 117–120.

Beresford, W. A., 1965   A discussion on retrograde changes in nerve fibers. *Progr. Brain Res.*, **14**, 33–56.

Bivens, L. W., and Ray, O. S., 1966   Effects of electroconvulsive shock and strychnine sulphate on memory consolidation. *Proc. Fifth Internat. Cong. College Internat. Neuropsychopharmacol.*, **1966**, 1030–1034.

Bloch, V., 1970   Facts and hypotheses concerning memory consolidation. *Brain Res.*, **24**, 561–575.

Bloch, V., Denti, A., and Schmaltz, G., 1966   Effets de la stimulation réticulaire sur la phase de consolidation de la trace amnésique. *J. Physiol.*, **58**, 469–470.

Bloch, V., Deweer, B., and Hennevin, E., 1970   Suppression de l'amnésie rétrograde et consolidation d'un apprentissage à essai unique par stimulation réticulaire. *Physiol. Behav.*, **5**, 1235–1241.

Blodgett, H. C., 1929   The effect of introduction of reward upon the maze performance of rats. *Univ. Calif. Publ. Psychol.*, **4**, 113–134.

Bohdanecka, M., Bohdanecký, Z., and Jarvik, M. E., 1967   Amnesic effects of small bilateral brain puncture in the mouse. *Science*, **157**, 334–336.

Bohdanecký, Z., Kopp, R., and Jarvik, M. E., 1968   Comparison of ECS and flurothyl-induced retrograde amnesia in mice. *Psychopharmacologia* (Berlin) **12**, 91–95.

Booth, D. A., 1967   Vertebrate brain ribonucleic acids and memory retention. *Psychol. Bull.*, **68**, 149–177.

Bovet, D., McGaugh, J. L., and Oliverio, A., 1966   Effects of post trial administration of drugs on avoidance learning of mice. *Life Sci.*, **5**, 1309–1315.

Brady, J. V., 1951   The effect of electroconvulsive shock on a conditioned emotional response: The permanence of the effect. *J. Comp. Physiol. Psychol.*, **44**, 507–511.

Brady, J. V., 1952   The effect of electroconvulsive shock on a conditioned emotional response: The significance of the interval between the emotion conditioning and the electroconvulsive shock. *J. Comp. Physiol. Psychol.*, **45**, 9–13.

Breen, R. A., and McGaugh, J. L., 1961   Facilitation of maze learning with posttrial injections of picrotoxin. *J. Comp. Physiol. Psychol.*, **54**, 498–501.

Brunner, R. L., Rossi, R. R., Stutz, R. M., and Roth, T. G., 1970   Memory loss following posttrial electrical stimulation of the hippocampus. *Psychon. Sci.*, **18**, 159–160.

Buchwald, N. A., Heuser, G., Wyers, E. J., and Lauprecht, C. W., 1962   Integration of visual impulses and the "caudate loop." *Exp. Neurol.*, **5**, 1–20.

Buchwald, N. A., Rakic, L., Wyers, E. J., Hull, C., and Heuser, G., 1961a   The "caudate-spindle." IV. A behavioral index of caudate-induced inhibition. *Electroencephalog. Clin. Neurophysiol.*, **13**, 531–537.

Buchwald, N. A., Wyers, E. J., Carlin, J., and Farley, R. E., 1961b   Effects of caudate stimulation on visual discrimination. *Exp. Neurol.*, **4**, 23–36.

Buchwald, N. A., Wyers, E. J., Okuma, T., and Heuser, G., 1961c   The "caudate-spindle." I. Electrophysiological properties. *Electroencephalog. Clin. Neurophysiol.*, **13**, 509–518.

Bureš, J., and Burešová, O., 1960a   The use of Leao's spreading depression in the study of interhemispheric transfer of memory traces. *J. Comp. Physiol. Psychol.*, **53**, 558–563.

Bureš, J., and Burešová, O., 1960b   The use of Leao's spreading cortical depression in research on conditioned reflexes. *Electroenceph. Clin. Neurophysiol.*, suppl. **13**, 359–376.

Bureš, J., and Burešová, O., 1963   Cortical spreading depression as a memory disturbing factor. *J. Comp. Physiol. Psychol.*, **56**, 268–272.

Bureš, J., and Burešová, O., 1970   The reunified split brain. In R. E. Whalen et al. (eds.), *The neural control of behavior*. New York: Academic Press.

Burešová, O., and Bureš, A., 1969   The effect of prolonged cortical spreading depression on learning and memory in rats. *J. Neurobiol.* **2**, 135–146.

Burnham, W. H., 1903   Retroactive amnesia: Illustrative cases and a tentative explanation. *Amer. J. Psychol.*, **14**, 382–396.

Burns, B. D., 1954   The production of afterbursts in isolated unanesthetized cerebral cortex. *J. Physiol.* (London), **125**, 427–446.

Burns, B. D., 1958   *The mammalian cerebral cortex*. London: Arnold.

Burns, N. M., and Mogenson, G. J., 1958   Effects of cortical stimulation on habit acquisition. *Canad. J. Psychol.*, **12**, 77–82.

Calhoun, W. H., 1966 Effect of level of external stimulation on rate of learning and interaction of this effect with strychnine treatment in mice. *Psychol. Rep.*, **18**, 715–722.

Carew, T. J., 1970 Retrograde amnesia: A behavioral and electrophysiological analysis. Doctoral dissertation, University of California, Riverside.

Carlini, G. R. S., and Carlini, E. A., 1965 Effects of strychnine and cannabis sativa (marijuana) on the nucleic acid content in brain of the rat. *Med. Pharmacol. Exp.*, **12**, 21–26.

Carlson, K. R., 1967 Cortical spreading depression and subcortical memory storage. *J. Comp. Physiol. Psychol.*, **64**, 422–430.

Carman, J. B., Cowan, W. M., and Powell, T. P. S., 1963 The organization of corticostriate connexions in the rabbit. *Brain*, **86**, 525–561.

Cerletti, U., and Bini, L., 1938 Electric shock treatment. *Boll. Accad. Med. Roma*, **64**, 36.

Chamberlin, T. J., Rothchild, G. H., and Gerard, R. W., 1963 Drugs affecting RNA and learning. *Proc. Nat. Acad. Sci.*, **49**, 918–925.

Cherkin, A., 1966*a* Memory consolidation: Probit analysis of retrograde-amnesia data. *Psychon. Sci.*, **4**, 169–170.

Cherkin, A., 1966*b* Toward a quantitative view of the engram. *Proc. Nat. Acad. Sci.*, **55**, 88–91.

Cherkin, A., 1968 Retrograde amnesia: Role of temperature, dose and duration of amnesic agent. *Psychon. Sci.*, **13**, 255–256.

Cherkin, A., 1969 Kinetics of memory consolidation: Role of amnesic treatment parameters. *Proc. Nat. Acad. Sci.*, **63**, 1094–1101.

Cherkin, A., 1970*a* Retrograde amnesia: Impaired memory consolidation or impaired memory retrieval. *Commun. Behav. Biol.*, **5**, 183–190.

Cherkin, A., 1970*b* Eye to eye transfer of an early response modification in chicks. *Nature*, **227**, 1153.

Cherkin, A., 1971 Biphasic time course of performance after one-trial avoidance training in the chick. *Commun. Behav. Biol.*, **5**, 379–381.

Cherkin, A., and Lee-Teng, E., 1965 Interruption by halothane of memory consolidation in chicks. *Fed. Proc.*, **24**, 328 (abstract).

Chevalier, J. A., 1965 Permanence of amnesia after a single posttrial electroconvulsive seizure. *J. Comp. Physiol. Psychol.*, **59**, 125–127.

Cholewiak, R. W., Hammond, R., Seigler, I. C., and Papsdorf, J. D., 1968 The effects of strychnine sulphate on the classically conditioned nictating membrane response of the rabbit. *J. Comp. Physiol. Psychol.*, **66**, 77–81.

Chorover, S. L., and DeLuca, A. M., 1969 Transient change in electrocorticographic reaction to ECS in the rat following footshock. *J. Comp. Physiol. Psychol.*, **69**, 141–149.

Chorover, S. L., and Schiller, P. H., 1965 Short-term retrograde amnesia in rats. *J. Comp. Physiol. Psychol.*, **59**, 73–78.

Chorover, S. L., and Schiller, P. H., 1966 Reexamination of prolonged retrograde amnesia in one-trial learning. *J. Comp. Physiol. Psychol.*, **61**, 34–41.

Cohen, H. D., and Barondes, S. H., 1966 Further studies of learning and memory after intracerebral actinomycin-D. *J. Neurochem.*, **13**, 207–211.

Cohen, H. D., and Barondes, S. H., 1967 Puromycin effect on memory may be due to occult seizures. *Science*, **157**, 333–334.

Cohen, H. D., and Barondes, S. H., 1968a Acetoxycycloheximide effect on learning and memory of a light-dark discrimination. *Nature*, **218**, 271.

Cohen, H. D., and Barondes, S. H., 1968b Cycloheximide impairs memory of an appetitive task. *Commun. Behav. Biol.*, **1**, 337–339.

Cohen, H. D., Ervin, F., and Barondes, S. H., 1966 Puromycin and cycloheximide: Different effects on hippocampal electrical activity. *Science*, **154**, 1557–1558.

Coker, D. L., and Abbott, D. W., 1967 The effect of strychnine sulfate on maze-learning as a function of task difficulty. *Psychon. Sci.*, **9**, 607.

Coons, E. E., and Miller, N. E., 1960 Conflict vs. consolidation of memory traces to explain "retrograde amnesia" produced by ECS. *J. Comp. Physiol. Psychol.*, **53**, 524–531.

Cooper, R. M., and Koppenaal, R. S., 1964 Suppression and recovery of a one-trial avoidance response after a single ECS. *Psychon. Sci.*, **1**, 303–304.

Corning, W. C., and John, E. R., 1961 Effect of ribonuclease on retention of a conditioned response in regenerated planarians. *Science*, **134**, 1363–1364.

Cotman, C., Banker, G., Zornetzer, S., and McGaugh, J. L., 1971 Electroshock effects on brain protein synthesis: Relation to brain seizures and retrograde amnesia. *Science*, **173**, 454–456.

Davis, R. E., 1968 Environmental control of memory fixation in goldfish. *J. Comp. Physiol. Psychol.*, **65**, 72–78.

Davis, R. E., and Agranoff, B. W., 1965 Effect of electroconvulsive shock and of puromycin on memory in goldfish. *Fed. Proc.*, **24**, 329.

Davis, R. E., and Agranoff, B. W., 1966 Stages of memory formation in goldfish: Evidence for an environmental trigger. *Proc. Nat. Acad. Sci.*, **55**, 555–559.

Davis, R. E., and Klinger, P. D., 1969 Environmental control of amnesic effects of various agents in goldfish. *Physiol. Behav.*, **4**, 269–271.

Davis, R. E., Bright, P. J., and Agranoff, B. W., 1965 Effect of ECS and puromycin on memory in fish. *J. Comp. Physiol. Psychol.*, **60**, 162–166.

Dawson, R. G., 1971 Retrograde amnesia and conditioned emotional response: A further evaluation. *Psychol. Bull.*, **75**, 278–285.

Dawson, R. G. Unpublished findings.

Dawson, R. G., and McGaugh, J. L., 1969a Electroconvulsive shock effects on a reactivated memory trace: Further examination. *Science*, **166**, 525–527.

Dawson, R. G., and McGaugh, J. L., 1969b Electroconvulsive shock–produced retrograde amnesia: Analysis of the familiarization effect. Part A. *Commun. Behav. Biol.*, **4**, 91–95.

Dawson, R. G., and McGaugh, J. L., 1970 Familiarization and retrograde amnesia: A re-evaluation re-evaluated. Part A. *Commun. Behav. Biol.* **4**, 257–259.

Dawson, R. G., and McGaugh, J. L., 1971 Drug facilitation of learning and memory. In J. A. Deutsch (ed.), *Biology of memory.* New York: Academic Press, in press.

Dawson, R. G., and Pryor, G. T., 1965 Onset vs. recovery in the aversive effects of electroconvulsive shock. *Psychon. Sci.*, **3**, 273–274.

De Groot, J., 1959 *The rat forebrain in stereotaxic coordinates.* Amersterdam: N. V. Noord-Hollandische Uitgevers Maatschappij.

BIBLIOGRAPHY

Denti, A., 1965 Facilitation of conditioning by reticular stimulation in the fixation phase of memory. Doctoral dissertation, University of Paris.

Denti, A., McGaugh, J. L., Landfield, P., and Shinkman, P., 1970 Facilitation of learning with posttrial stimulation of the reticular formation. *Physiol. Behav.*, **5**, 659–662.

De Toledo, L., and Black, A. H., 1966 Heart rate: Changes during conditioned suppression in rats. *Science*, **152**, 1404–1406.

Deutsch, J. A., 1969 The physiological basis of memory. *Ann. Rev. Psychol.*, **20**, 85–104.

Deweer, B., 1970 La période de consolidation amnésique: Quelques données apportées par l'expérimentation sur l'animal. *L'Année psychol.*, **70**, 195–221.

Deweer, B., 1970 Accélération de l'extinction d'un conditionnement par stimulation réticulaire chez le rat. *J. Physiol.*, **62**, 270.

Dingman, W., and Sporn, M. B., 1961 The incorporation of 8-azaguanine into rat brain RNA and its effect on maze-learning by the rat: An inquiry into the biochemical bases of memory. *J. Psych. Res.*, **1**, 1–11.

Dorfman, L. F., and Jarvik, M. E., 1968*a* Comparative effects of transcorneal and transpinnate ECS in mice. *Physiol. Behav.*, **3**, 815–818.

Dorfman, L. F., and Jarvik, M. E., 1968*b* A parametric study of electroshock-induced retrograde amnesia in mice. *Neuropsychologia*, **6**, 373–380.

Doty, B. A., and Doty, L. A., 1966 Facilitative effects of amphetamine on avoidance conditioning in relation to age and problem difficulty. *Psychopharmacologia* (Berlin), **9**, 234–241.

Douglas, R. J., 1967 The hippocampus and behavior. *Psychol. Bull.*, **67**, 416–442.

Drachman, D. A., and Arbit, J., 1966 Memory and the hippocampal complex. *Arch. Neurol.*, **15**, 52–61.

Duncan, C. P., 1949 The retroactive effect of electroshock on learning. *J. Comp. Physiol. Psychol.*, **42**, 32–44.

Dusser de Barenne, J. C., and McCulloch, W. S., 1941 Suppression of motor response obtained from area 4 by stimulation of area 4s. *J. Neurophysiol.*, **4**, 311–323.

Edwards, A. L., 1960 *Experimental design in psychological research* (rev. ed.). New York: Rinehart.

Erickson, C. K., and Patel, J. B., 1969 Facilitation of avoidance learning by posttrial hippocampal electrical stimulation. *J. Comp. Physiol. Psychol.*, **68**, 400–406.

Essman, W. B., 1966 Effect of trycyanoaminopropene on the amnesic effect of ECS. *Psychopharmacologia*, **9**, 426–433.

Essman, W. B., and Alpern, H. P., 1964 Single trial conditioning: Methodology and results in mice. *Psychol. Rev.*, **14**, 731–740.

Essman, W. B., and Hamburgh, M., 1962 Retrograde effect of audiogenic seizure upon the retention of a learned response. *Exp. Neurol.*, **6**, 245–251.

Essman, W. B., and Jarvik, M. E., 1961 Impairment of retention for a conditioned response by ether anesthesia in mice. *Psychopharmacologia* (Berlin), **2**, 172–176.

Fifkova, E., and Syka, J., 1964 Relationships between cortical and striatal spreading depression in rat. *Exp. Neurol.*, **9**, 355–366.

Finan, J. L., 1942 Delayed response with redelay reinforcement in monkeys after removal of the frontal lobes. *Amer. J. Psychol.*, **55**, 202–214.

Fishbein, W., 1970   Interference with conversion of memory from short-term to long-term storage by partial sleep deprivation. *Commun. Behav. Biol.*, **5**, 171–175.

Fishbein, W.   Disruptive effects of rapid eye movement sleep deprivation on long-term memory. Unpublished findings.

Fishbein, W., McGaugh, J. L., and Swarz, J. R., 1971   Retrograde amnesia: ECS effects after termination of rapid eye movement sleep deprivation. *Science*, **172**, 80–82.

Fishbein, W., McGaugh, J. L., and Tusa, R. J.   The effects of rapid eye movement sleep deprivation during the retention interval on long-term memory. *Psychophysiology*, in press (abstract).

Fishbein, W., Swarz, J. R., and McGaugh, J. L.   The effects of electroconvulsive shock during recovery from rapid eye movement sleep deprivation on long-term memory. *Psychophysiology*, in press.

Fitzgerald, R. D., and Teyler, T. J., 1970   Trace and delayed heart-rate conditioning in rats as a function of US intensity. *J. Comp. Physiol. Psychol.*, **70**, 242–253.

Flescher, G., 1941   I. L'amnesia retrograda dopo l'elettroshock: Contributo allo studio della patogenesi delle amnesie in genere. *Schweiz. Arch. Neurol. Psychiat.*, **48**, 1–28.

Flexner, J. B., and Flexner, L. B., 1967   Restoration of expression of memory lost after treatment with puromycin. *Proc. Nat. Acad. Sci.*, **57**, 1651–1654.

Flexner, L. B., and Flexner, J. B., 1968   Intracerebral saline: Effect on memory of trained mice treated with puromycin. *Science*, **159**, 330–331.

Flexner, J. B., and Flexner, L. B., 1970   Adrenalectomy and the suppression of memory by puromycin. *Proc. Nat. Acad. Sci.*, **66**, 48–52.

Flexner, J. B., Flexner, L. B., and Stellar, E., 1963   Memory in mice as affected by intracerebral puromycin. *Science*, **141**, 57–59.

Flexner, J. B., Flexner, L. B., Stellar, E., de la Haba, G., and Roberts, R. B., 1962   Inhibitition of protein synthesis in brain and learning and memory following puromycin. *J. Neurochem.*, **9**, 595–605.

Flexner, J. B., Flexner, L. B., Stellar, E., de la Haba, G., and Roberts, R. B., 1965   Loss of memory as related to inhibition of cerebral protein synthesis. *J. Neurochem.*, **12**, 535–541.

Flynn, J. P., MacLean, P. D., and Kim, C., 1961   Effects of hippocampal after-discharges on conditioned responses. In D. E. Sheer (ed.), *Electrical stimulation of the brain.* Austin, Tex.: University of Texas Press.

Fox, S. S., and O'Brien, J. H., 1962   Inhibition and facilitation of afferent information by the caudate nucleus. *Science*, **137**, 423–425.

Franchina, J. J., and Grandolfo, P., 1970   Stimulus change and the effects of strychnine on response witholding. *Proc. Eastern Psychol. Assoc., Atlantic City, N.J.*

Franchina, J. J., and Moore, M. H., 1968   Strychnine and the inhibition of previous performances. *Science*, **160**, 903–904.

Freckleton, W. C., Jr., and Wahlsten, D., 1968   Carbon dioxide-induced amnesia in the cockroach. *Psychon. Sci.*, **12**, 179–180.

French, J. D., Gernandt, B. E., and Livingston, R. B., 1956   Regional differences in seizure susceptibility in monkey cortex. *AMA Arch. Neurol. Psychiat.*, **75**, 260–274.

Friedman, M. H., 1953   Electroconvulsive shock as a traumatic (fear-producing) experience in the albino rat. *J. Abnorm. Soc. Psychol.*, **48**, 555–562.

Galosy, R. A., and Thompson, R. W., 1971   A further investigation of familiarization effects on ECS-produced retrograde amnesia. *Psychon. Sci.*, **22**, 147–148.

Garg, M., and Holland, H. C., 1968   Consolidation and maze learning: The effects of posttrial injections of a stimulant drug (Picrotoxin). *Psychopharmacologia*, **12**, 96–103.

Gastaut, H., and Fischer-Williams, M., 1959   The physiopathology of epileptic seizures. In J. Field (ed.), *Handbook of physiology*, vol. I. Washington, D.C.: American Physiological Society.

Geller, A., and Jarvik, M. E., 1968*a*   Electroconvulsive shock induced amnesia and recovery. *Psychon. Sci.*, **10**, 15–16.

Geller, A., and Jarvik, M. E., 1968*b*   The time relations of ECS-induced amnesia. *Psychon. Sci.*, **12**, 169–170.

Gerard, R. W., 1949   Physiology and psychiatry. *Amer. J. Psychiat.*, **106**, 161–173.

Gerard, R. W., 1955   Biological roots of psychiatry. *Science*, **122**, 225–230.

Gerbrandt, L. K., 1965   Neural systems of response release and control. *Psychol. Bull.*, **64**, 113–123.

Gerbrandt, L. K., and Thomson, C. W., 1964   Competing response and amnesic effects of electroconvulsive shock under extinction and incentive shifts. *J. Comp. Physiol. Psychol.*, **58**, 208–211.

Giurgea, C., and Mouravieff-LeSuisse, F.   Pharmacological studies on an elementary model of learning: The fixation of an experience at spinal level. I. Pharmacological reactivity of the spinal cord fixation time. *Arch. Int. Pharmacodyn.*, in press.

Glassman, E., 1967   *Molecular approaches to psychobiology*. Belmont, Calif.: Dickenson.

Glassman, E., 1969   The biochemistry of learning: An evaluation of the role of RNA and protein. *Ann. Rev. Biochem.*, **38**, 605–646.

Glees, P., Cole, J., Whitty, C. W. M., and Cairns, H. W. B., 1950   The effects of lesions in the cingular gyrus and adjacent areas in monkeys. *J. Neurol. Neurosurg. Psychiat.*, **13**, 178–190.

Glickman, S. E., 1958   Deficits in avoidance learning produced by stimulation of the ascending reticular formation. *Canad. J. Psychol.*, **12**, 97–102.

Glickman, S. E., 1961   Perseverative neural processes and consolidation of the memory trace. *Psychol. Bull.*, **58**, 218–233.

Goddard, G. V., 1964   Amygdaloid stimulation and learning in the rat. *J. Comp. Physiol. Psychol.*, **58**, 23–30.

Gold, P. E., Farrell, W., and King, R. A.   Retrograde amnesia after localized brain shock in passive avoidance learning. *Physiol. Behav.*, in press.

Gold, P. E., and King, R. A., 1971   Proactive effects of footshock-ECS pairing: Failures to obtain the effect. Unpublished findings.

Goodman, L. S., and Gillman, A. (eds.), 1965   *The pharmacological basis of therapeutics.* New York: MacMillan.

Gorski, J., Aizawa, Y., and Mueller, G. C., 1961 Effect of puromycin *in vivo* on the synthesis of protein, RNA and phospholipids in rat tissues. *Arch. Biochem. Biophys.*, **95**, 508–511.

Green, J. D., 1958 A simple micro-electrode for recording from the central nervous system. *Nature*, **182**, 962.

Greenough, W. T., and Schwitzgebel, R. L., 1966 Effect of a single ECS on extinction of a bar-press. *Psychol. Rep.*, **19**, 1227–1230.

Greenough, W. T., Schwitzgebel, R. L., and Fulcher, J. K., 1968 Permanence of ECS-produced amnesia as a function of test conditions. *J. Comp. Physiol. Psychol.*, **66**, 554–556.

Grossman, S. P., 1969 Facilitation of learning following intracranial injections of pentylenetetrazol. *Physiol. Behav.*, **4**, 625–628.

Gurowitz, E. M., 1969 *The molecular basis of memory*. Englewood Cliffs, N.J.: Prentice-Hall.

Gutekunst, R., and Youniss, J., 1963 Interruption of imprinting following anesthesia. *Percept. Motor Skills*, **16**, 348.

Guzman, C. F., Alkaraz, V. M., and Fernandez, C. A., 1958 Rapid procedure to localize electrodes in experimental neurophysiology. *Bol. Inst. estud. med. biol. Mex.*, **16**, 29–31.

Hall, M. E., 1969 Effects of posttrial amphetamine and strychnine on learning as a function of task difficulty. *Commun. Behav. Biol.*, **4**, 171–175.

Hartelius, H., 1952 Cerebral changes following electrically induced convulsions. *Acta Psychiat. Neurol. Scand.*, suppl. **77**, 7–128.

Hayes, K. J., 1948 Cognitive and emotional effects of electroconvulsive shock in rats. *J. Comp. Physiol. Psychol.*, **41**, 40–61.

Hebb, D. O., 1949 *The organization of behavior*. New York: Wiley.

Hebb, D. O., 1958 *A textbook of psychology*. Philadelphia: Saunders.

Heinze, W. J., 1970 Quantitative genetic analysis of learning and induced retrograde amnesia in the rodent *rattus norvedicus*. Doctoral dissertation, University of California, Berkeley.

Heriot, J. T., and Coleman, P. D., 1962 The effect of electroconvulsive shock on retention of a modified "one-trial" conditioned avoidance. *J. Comp. Physiol. Psychol.*, **55**, 1082–1084.

Herz, M. J., 1969 Interference with one-trial appetitive and aversive learning by ether and ECS. *J. Neurobiol.*, **1**, 111–122.

Herz, M. J., and Peeke, H. V. S., 1967 Permanence of retrograde amnesia produced by electroconvulsive shock. *Science*, **156**, 1396–1397.

Herz, M. J., and Peeke, H. V. S., 1968 ECS-produced retrograde amnesia: Permanence vs. recovery over repeated testing. *Physiol. Behav.*, **3**, 517–521.

Herz, M. J., and Peeke, H. V. S. Impairment of extinction with caudate nucleus stimulation. *Brain Res.*, in press.

Herz, M. J., Peeke, H. V. S., and Wyers, E. J., 1966 Amnesia effects of ether and electroconvulsive shock in mice. *Psychon. Sci.*, **4**, 375–376.

Herz, M. J., Spooner, C. E., and Cherkin, A., 1970 Effects of the amnesic agent flurothyl on EEG and multiple-unit activity in the chick. *Exp. Neurol.*, **27**, 227–237.

Heuser, G., Buchwald, N. A., and Wyers, E. J., 1961 The "caudate-spindle."
II. Facilitatory and inhibitory caudate-cortical pathways. *Electroencephalog.
Clin. Neurophysiol.*, **13**, 519–523.

Hilgard, E. R., and Marquis, D. G., 1940 *Conditioning and learning*. New York:
Appleton-Century-Crofts.

Hine, B., and Paolino, R. M., 1970 Retrograde amnesia: Production of skeletal
but not cardiac response gradients by electroconvulsive shock. *Science*,
169, 1224–1226.

Hirano, T., 1965 Effects of functional disturbances of the limbic system on the
memory consolidation. *Jap. Psychol. Res.*, **7**, 171–182.

Hirano, T., 1966 Effects of hippocampal electrical stimulation on memory consolidation. *Psychologia*, **9**, 63–75.

Horner, J. L., Longo, N., and Bitterman, M. E., 1961 A shuttle box for fish and
a control circuit of general applicability. *Amer. J. Psychol.*, **74**, 114–120.

Hudson, B. B., 1950 One-trial learning in the domestic rat. *Genet. Psychol.
Monogr.*, **41**, 99–143.

Hudspeth, W. J., 1964 Strychnine: Its facilitating effect on the solution of a
simple oddity problem by the rat. *Science*, **145**, 1331–1333.

Hudspeth, W. J., 1966 Doctoral dissertation, Claremont University Center,
Claremont, Calif.

Hudspeth, W. J., 1967 Unpublished observations, University of California,
Los Angeles.

Hudspeth, W. J., and Gerbrandt, L. K., 1965 Electroconvulsive shock: Conflict,
competition, consolidation and neuroanatomical functions. *Psychol. Bull.*,
63, 377–383.

Hudspeth, W. J., McGaugh, J. L., and Thomson, C. W., 1964 Aversive and
amnesic effects of electroconvulsive shock. *J. Comp. Physiol. Psychol.*, **57**,
61–64.

Hudspeth, W. J., and Weening, D. L., 1968 Unpublished observations, University
of Waterloo, Waterloo, Ontario.

Hudspeth, W. J., and Wilsoncroft, W. E., 1969 Retrograde amnesia: Time dependent effects of rhinencephalic lesions. *J. Neurobiol.*, **1**, 221–232.

Hughes, R. A., 1969 Retrograde amnesia in rats produced by hippocampal injections of potassium chloride: Gradient of effect and recovery. *J. Comp.
Physiol. Psychol.*, **68**, 637–644.

Hughes, R. A., Barrett, R. J., and Ray, O. S., 1970a Retrograde amnesia in rats
increases as a function of ECS-test interval and ECS intensity. *Physiol.
Behav.*, **5**, 27–30.

Hughes, R. A., Barrett, R. J., and Ray, O. S., 1970b Training to test interval as
a determinant of a temporally graded ECS-produced response decrement in
rats. *J. Comp. Physiol. Psychol.*, **71**, 318–324.

Hunt, E., and Duncan, N., 1969 Interactive effects of electroconvulsive shock
and strychnine on memory. *Univer. Wash. Tech. Rep.* 68-1-27, pp. 1–28.

Hunt, E., and Duncan, N. Reduction of ECS produced retrograde amnesia by
post-trial introduction of strychnine. *Physiol. Behav.*, in press.

Hunt, E., and Krivanek, J., 1966 The effects of pentylenetetrazol and methyl-
phenoxypropane on discrimination learning. *Psychopharmacologia* (Berlin),
9, 1–16.

Hunt, H. F., 1965 Electroconvulsive shock and learning. *Trans. N.Y. Acad. Sci.*,
27, 923–945.

Hunt, H. F., Jernberg, P., and Lawlor, W. G., 1953   The effect of electroconvulsive shock on a conditioned emotional response: The effect of electroconvulsive shock under ether anesthesia. *J. Comp. Physiol. Psychol.*, **46**, 64–68.

Hyden, H., and Egyhazi, E., 1962   Nuclear RNA changes of nerve cells during a learning experiment with rats. *Proc. Nat. Acad. Sci.*, **48**, 1366–1373.

Hyden, H., Egyhazi, E., John, E. R., and Bartlett, F., 1969   RNA base ratio change in planaria during conditioning. *J. Neurochem.*, **16**, 813–821.

Irwin, S., and Banuazizi, A., 1966   Pentylenetetrazol enhances memory function. *Science*, **152**, 100–102.

Jacobs, B. L., and Sorenson, C. A., 1969   Memory disruption in mice by brief posttrial immersion in hot or cold water. *J. Comp. Physiol. Psychol.*, **68**, 239–244.

Jacobsen, C. F., 1931   A study of cerebral function in learning the frontal lobes. *J. Compar. Neurol.*, **52**, 271–340.

Jamieson, J. L., and Albert, D. J., 1970   Amnesia from ECS: The effect of pairing ECS and footshock. *Psychon. Sci.*, **18**, 14–15.

Jarvik, M. E., 1964   The influence of drugs upon memory. In Steinberg et al. (eds.), *Ciba Foundation symposium on animal behavior and drug action*, pp. 44–61. London: Churchill.

Jarvik, M. E., 1968   Consolidation of memory. In D. H. Efron et al. (eds.), *Psychopharmacology: A review of progress, 1957–1967*, PHS Publ. 1836, pp. 885–889. Washington, D.C.: U.S. Government Printing Office.

Jarvik, M. E., and Essman, W. B., 1960   A simple one-trial learning situation for mice. *Psychol. Rep.*, **6**, 290.

Jarvik, M. E., and Kopp, R., 1967a   An improved one-trial passive avoidance learning situation. *Psychol. Rep.*, **21**, 221–224.

Jarvik, M. E., and Kopp, R., 1967b   Transcorneal electroconvulsive shock and retrograde amnesia in mice. *J. Comp. Physiol. Psychol.*, **64**, 431–433.

John, E. R., 1967   *Mechanisms of memory*. New York: Academic Press.

Kalinowsky, L. B., and Hoch, P. H., 1946   *Shock treatments and other somatic procedures in psychiatry*. New York: Grune and Stratton.

Kelemen, K., and Bovet, D., 1961   Effect of drugs upon the defensive behavior of rats. *Acta Physiol. Acad. Sci. Hung.*, **19**, 143–154.

Kesner, R. P., and Doty, R. W., 1968   Amnesia produced in cats by local seizure activity initiated from the amygdala. *Exp. Neurol.*, **21**, 58–68.

Kesner, R. P., Gibson, W. E., and LeClair, M. J., 1970   ECS as a punishing stimulus: Dependency on route of administration. *Physiol. Behav.*, **5**, 683–686.

Kimble, D. P., 1968   Hippocampus and internal inhibition. *Psychol. Bull.*, **70**, 285–295.

King, R. A., 1965   Consolidation of the neural trace in memory: Investigation with one-trial avoidance conditioning and ECS. *J. Comp. Physiol. Psychol.*, **59**, 283–284.

King, R. A., 1967   Consolidation of the neural trace in memory: ECS-produced retrograde amnesia is not an artifact of conditioning. *Psychon. Sci.*, **9**, 409–410.

King, R. A., and Glasser, R. L., 1970   Duration of electroconvulsive shock-induced retrograde amnesia in rats. *Physiol. Behav.*, **5**, 335–339.

BIBLIOGRAPHY

Kohlenberg, R., and Trabasso, T., 1968 Recovery of a conditioned emotional response after one or two electroconvulsive shocks. *J. Comp. Physiol. Psychol.*, **65**, 270–273.

Kopp, R., Bohdanecký, Z., and Jarvik, M. E., 1966 Long temporal gradient of retrograde amnesia for a well-discriminated stimulus. *Science*, **153**, 1547–1549.

Koppenaal, R. J., Jagoda, E., and Cruce, J. A. F., 1967 Recovery from ECS-produced amnesia following a reminder. *Psychon. Sci.*, **9**, 293–294.

Krech, D., Rosenzweig, M. R., and Bennett, E. L., 1960 Effects of environmental complexity and training on brain chemistry. *J. Comp. Physiol. Psychol.*, **53**, 509–519.

Krivanek, J., 1968 The effects of pentylenetetrazol on avoidance learning: A study in biological integration. Doctoral dissertation, University of California, Irvine.

Krivanek, J., and Hunt, E. B., 1967 The effects of posttrial injections of pentylenetetrazol, strychnine, and mephenesin on discrimination learning. *Psychopharmacologia*, **10**, 189–195.

Krivanek, J., and McGaugh, J. L., 1968 Effects of pentylenetetrazol on memory storage in mice. *Psychopharmacologia* (Berlin), **12**, 303–321.

Krivanek, J., and McGaugh, J. L., 1969 Facilitating effects of pre- and posttrial amphetamine administration on discrimination learning in mice. *Agents and Actions*, **1**, 36–42.

Kupfermann, I., 1966 Is the retrograde amnesia that follows cortical spreading depression due to subcortical spread? *J. Comp. Physiol. Psychol.*, **61**, 466–467.

Landfield, P. W., McGaugh, J. L., and Tusa, R. Relationship of hippocampus and EEG to memory storage in rats. Unpublished findings.

Lashley, K. S., 1917 The effects of strychnine and caffeine upon the rate of learning. *Psychobiology*, **1**, 141–170.

Lashley, K. S., 1929 *Brain mechanisms and intelligence: A quantitative study of injuries to the brain.* Chicago: University of Chicago Press.

Leão, A. A. P., 1944 Spreading depression of activity in the cerebral cortex. *J. Neurophysiol.*, **7**, 359–390.

Leão, A. A. P., 1947 Further observations on the spreading depression of activity in the cerebral cortex. *J. Neurophysiol.*, **10**, 409–414.

LeBoeuf, B. J., and Peeke, H. V. S., 1969 The effect of strychnine administration during development on adult maze learning in the rat. *Psychopharmacologia*, **16**, 49–53.

LeConte, P., and Bloch, V., 1971 Déficit de la rétention d'un conditionnement après privation de sommeil paradoxal chez le rat. *Compt. Rend. Acad. Sci. Paris*, **271**, 226–229.

Lee-Teng, E., 1967 Retrograde amnesia in relation to current intensity and seizure pattern in chicks. *Proc. 75th Ann. Conv. Amer. Psychol. Assoc.*, **2**, 87–88.

Lee-Teng, E., 1969 Retrograde amnesia in relation to subconvulsive and convulsive currents in chicks. *J. Comp. Physiol. Psychol.*, **67**, 135–139.

Lee-Teng, E., and Giaquinto, S., 1969 Electrocorticograms following threshold transcranial electroshock for retrograde amnesia in chicks. *Exp. Neurol.*, **23**, 485–490.

Lee-Teng, E., and Sherman, S. M., 1966 Memory consolidation of one-trial learning in chicks. *Proc. Nat. Acad. Sci.*, **56**, 926–931.

Leonard, D. J., and Zavala, A., 1964 Electroconvulsive shock, retroactive amnesia, and the single-shock method. *Science*, **146**, 1073–1074.

Leukel, F., 1957 A comparison of the effects of ECS and anesthesia on acquisition of the maze habit. *J. Comp. Physiol. Psychol.*, **50**, 300–306.

Leukel, F., and Quinton, E., 1964 CO_2 effects on acquisition and extinction of avoidance behavior. *J. Comp. Physiol. Psychol.*, **57**, 267–270.

Levinthal, C. F., and Papsdorf, J. D., 1970 Experimental variables in the effects of postsession injections of strychnine sulphate on a classically conditioned response. *Psychopharmacologia*, **17**, 100–104.

Lewis, D. J., 1969 Sources of experimental amnesia. *Psychol. Rev.*, **76**, 461–472.

Lewis, D. J., and Adams, H. E., 1963 Retrograde amnesia from conditioned competing responses. *Science*, **141**, 516–517.

Lewis, D. J., and Maher, B. A., 1965 Neural consolidation and electroconvulsive shock. *Psychol. Rev.*, **72**, 225–239.

Lewis, D. J., Miller, R. R., and Misanin, J. R., 1968a Control of retrograde amnesia. *J. Comp. Physiol. Psychol.*, **66**, 48–52.

Lewis, D. J., Miller, R. R., and Misanin, J. R., 1969 Selective amnesia in rats produced by electroconvulsive shock. *J. Comp. Physiol. Psychol.*, **69**, 136–140.

Lewis, D. J., Misanin, J. R., and Miller, R. R., 1968b Recovery of memory following amnesia. *Nature*, **220**, 704–705.

Lidsky, A., and Slotnick, B. N., 1970 Electrical stimulation of hippocampus and electroconvulsive shock produce similar amnestic effects in mice. *Neuropsychologia*, **8**, 363–369.

Lindquist, E. F., 1956 *Design and analysis of experiments in psychology and education*. Boston: Houghton Mifflin.

Livingston, R. B., 1967 In G. C. Quarton et al. (eds.), *The neurosciences: A study program*, p. 514. New York: Rockefeller University Press.

Longo, V. F., Silvestrini, B., and Bovet, D., 1959 An investigation of convulsant properties of the 5-7-diphenyl-1-3-diazadamantan-6-ol (1757 I.S.) *J. Pharmacol. Exp. Therapeutics*, **126**, 41–49.

Lorente de No, R., 1938 Analysis of the activity of the chains of internuncial neurons. *J. Neurophysiol.*, **1**, 207–244.

Louttit, R. T., 1965 Central nervous system stimulants and maze learning in rats. *Psychol. Rec.*, **15**, 97–101.

Luttges, M. W., and McGaugh, J. L., 1967 Permanence of retrograde amnesia produced by electroconvulsive shock. *Science*, **156**, 408–410.

Luttges, M. W., and McGaugh, J. L., 1970 Facilitating effects of megimide on a visual discrimination task. *Agents and Actions*, **1**, 234–239.

Madow, L., 1956 Brain changes in electroshock therapy. *Amer. J. Psychiat.*, **113**, 237–247.

Madsen, M. C., and Luttges, M. W., 1963   Effect of electroconvulsive shock (ECS) on extinction of an approach response. *Psychol. Rep.*, **13**, 225–226.

Madsen, M. C., and McGaugh, J. L., 1961   The effect of ECS on one-trial avoidance learning. *J. Comp. Physiol. Psychol.*, **54**, 522–523.

Magnus, J. G., Kanner, M., and Hochman, H.   Unpublished findings.

Mahut, H., 1962   Effects of subcortical electrical stimulation of learning in the rat. *J. Comp. Physiol. Psychol.*, **55**, 472–477.

Mahut, H., 1964   Effects of subcortical electrical stimulation on discrimination learning in cats. *J. Comp. Physiol. Psychol.*, **58**, 390–395.

Malmo, R. B., 1942   Interference factors in delayed response in monkeys after removal of frontal lobes. *J. Neurophysiol.*, **5**, 295–308.

Mayer-Gross, W., 1943   Retrograde amnesia. *Lancet*, **2**, 603–605.

McCleary, R. A., 1961   Response specificity in the behavioral effects of limbic system lesions in the cat. *J. Comp. Physiol. Psychol.*, **54**, 605–613.

McDougall, W., 1901   Experimentelle Beitrage zur Lehre vom Gedachtniss, by G. E. Müller and A. Pilzecker. *Mind*, **10**, 388–394.

McGaugh, J. L., 1961   Facilitative and disruptive effects of strychnine sulphate on maze learning. *Psychol. Rep.*, **8**, 99–104.

McGaugh, J. L., 1965   Facilitation and impairment of memory storage processes. In D. P. Kimble (ed.), *The anatomy of memory*, pp. 240–291. Palo Alto, Calif.: Science and Behavior Books.

McGaugh, J. L., 1966   Time-dependent processes in memory storage. *Science*, **153**, 1351–1358.

McGaugh, J. L., 1968a   Drug facilitation of memory and learning. In D. H. Efron et al. (eds.), *Psychopharmacology: A review of progress, 1957–1967.* PHS Publ. 1836, pp. 891–904. Washington, D.C.: U.S. Government Printing Office.

McGaugh, J. L., 1968b   Electroconvulsive shock. In *International encyclopedia of the social sciences*, pp. 21–25. New York: Crowell Collier and MacMillan.

McGaugh, J. L., 1968c   A multi-trace view of memory storage processes. In Bovet et al. (eds.), *Attuali orientamenti della ricerca sull' apprendimento e la memoria*, pp. 13–24. Accad. Naz. Lincei.

McGaugh, J. L., 1970   Memory storage processes. In K. H. Pribram and D. H. Broadbent (eds.), *Biology of memory*, New York: Academic Press.

McGaugh, J. L., and Alpern, H. P., 1966   Effects of electroshock on memory: Amnesia without convulsions. *Science*, **152**, 665–666.

McGaugh, J. L., Alpern, H. P., and Luttges, M. W.   Further analysis of retrograde amnesia as a function of the footshock-electroconvulsive shock interval. Unpublished findings.

McGaugh, J. L., and Dawson, R. G., 1971   Modification of memory storage processes. *Behav. Sci.*, **16**, 45–63.

McGaugh, J. L., Dawson, R. G., Coleman, R., and Rawie, J.   Amnesia without convulsions: A test of the CER incubation hypothesis. *Commun. Behav. Biol.*, in press.

McGaugh, J. L., and Landfield, P. W., 1970   Delayed development of amnesia following electroconvulsive shock. *Physiol. Behav.*, **5**, 751–755.

McGaugh, J. L., and Landfield, P. W.   Evidence of a temporary short-term memory in mice following ECS. Unpublished findings.

McGaugh, J. L., Landfield, P. W., and Dawson, R. G. Delayed development of amnesia following electroconvulsive shock: A further examination. Unpublished findings.

McGaugh, J. L., and Longacre, B., 1969 Effect of electroconvulsive shock on performance of a well-learned avoidance response: Contribution of the convulsion. Part A. *Commun. Behav. Biol.*, **4**, 177–181.

McGaugh, J. L., and Krivanek, J., 1970 Strychnine effects on discrimination learning in mice: Effects of dose and time of administration. *Physiol. Behav.*, **5**, 1437–1442.

McGaugh, J. L., and Madsen, M. C., 1964 Amnesic and punishing effects of electroconvulsive shock. *Science*, **144**, 182–183.

McGaugh, J. L., and Petrinovich, L. F., 1959 The effect of strychnine sulphate on maze-learning. *Amer. J. Psychol.*, **72**, 99–102.

McGaugh, J. L., and Petrinovich, L. F., 1965 Effects of drugs on learning and memory. *Internat. Rev. Neurobiol.*, **8**, 139–196.

McGaugh, J. L., and Petrinovich, L. F., 1966 Neural consolidation and electroconvulsive shock reexamined. *Psychol. Rev.*, **73**, 382–387.

McGaugh, J. L., and Thomson, C. W., 1962 Facilitation of simultaneous discrimination learning with strychnine sulphate. *Psychopharmacologia*, **3**, 166–172.

McGaugh, J. L., Thomson, C. W., Westbrook, W. H., and Hudspeth, W. J., 1962*a* A further study of learning facilitation with strychnine sulphate. *Psychopharmacologia* (Berlin), **3**, 352–360.

McGaugh, J. L., Westbrook, W., and Burt, G., 1961 Strain differences in the facilitative effects of 5-7-diphenyl-1-3-diazadamantan-6-ol (1757 I.S.) on maze learning. *J. Comp. Physiol. Psychol.*, **54**, 502–505.

McGaugh, J. L., Westbrook, W. H., and Thomson, C. W., 1962*b* Facilitation of maze learning with posttrial injections of 5-7-diphenyl-1-3-diazadamantan-6-ol (1757 I.S.). *J. Comp. Physiol. Psychol.*, **55**, 710–713.

McGaugh, J. L., and Zornetzer, S., 1970 Amnesia and brain seizure activity in mice: Effects of diethyl ether anesthesia prior to electroshock stimulation. *Commun. Behav. Biol.*, **5**, 243–248.

McIntyre, D. C., 1970 Differential amnesic effect of cortical vs. amygdaloid elicited convulsions in rats. *Physiol. Behav.*, **5**, 747–753.

Meier, G. W., and Huff, F. W., 1962 Altered adult behavior following chronic drug administration during infancy and prepuberty. *J. Comp. Physiol. Psychol.*, **55**, 469–471.

Mendoza, J. E., and Adams, H. E., 1969 Does electroconvulsive shock produce retrograde amnesia? *Physiol. Behav.*, **4**, 307–309.

Meyer, A., Beck, E., and McClardy, T., 1947 Prefrontal leukotomy: A neuroanatomical report. *Brain*, **70**, 18–49.

Miller, A. J., 1968 Variations in retrograde amnesia with parameters or electroconvulsive shock and time of testing. *J. Comp. Physiol. Psychol.*, **66**, 40–47.

Miller, R. R., and Misanin, J. R., 1969 Critique of electroconvulsive shock-induced retrograde amnesia: Analysis of the familiarization effect. *Commun. Behav. Biol.*, **4**, 255–256.

Miller, R. R., and Spear, N. E., 1969 Memory and the extensor phase of convulsions induced by electroconvulsive shock. *Psychon. Sci.*, **15**, 164–166.

Milner, B., 1966 Amnesia following operation on the temporal lobes. In C. W. M. Whitty and O. L. Zangwill (eds.), *Amnesia*, pp. 109–133. London: Butterworths.

Milner, B., and Penfield, W., 1955 The effect of hippocampal lesions on recent memory. *Trans. Amer. Neurol. Assoc.*, **80**, 42–48.

Misanin, J. R., Miller, R. R., and Lewis, D. J., 1968 Retrograde amnesia produced by electroconvulsive shock after reactivation of a consolidated memory trace. *Science*, **160**, 554–555.

Morris, A., Favelukes, S., Arlinghaus, R., and Schweet, R., 1962 Mechanism of puromycin inhibition of hemoglobin synthesis. *Biochem. Biophys. Res. Commun.*, **7**, 326–330.

Müller, G. E., and Pilzecker, A., 1900 Experimentelle Beitrage zur Lehre vom Gedachtniss. *Z. Psychol.*, **1**, 1–288.

Nakajima, S., 1968 Interference with relearning in the rat after hippocampal injection of actinomycin D. *J. Comp. Physiol. Psychol.*, **3**, 618–622.

Nasello, A. G., and Izquierdo, I., 1969 Effect of learning and of drugs on the ribonucleic acid concentration of brain structures of the rat. *Exp. Neurol.*, **23**, 521–528.

Nathans, D., 1964 Puromycin inhibition of protein synthesis: Incorporation of puromycin into peptide chains. *Proc. Nat. Acad. Sci.*, **51**, 585–592.

Nielson, H. C., 1968 Evidence that electroconvulsive shock alters memory retrieval rather than memory consolidation. *Exp. Neurol.*, **20**, 3–20.

Nielson, H. C., Justeson, D. R., and Porter, P. D., 1968 Effects of anticonvulsant drugs upon patterns of seizure discharge and brain thresholds: Some implications for memory mechanisms. *Psychol. Rep.*, **23**, 843–850.

Nieschulz, O., 1967 Experimentelle retrograde Amnesien bei Mäusen: *Arzneimittel-Forsch.*, **17**, 1151–1155.

Nissen, H. W., Riesen, A. H., and Nowlis, V., 1938 Delayed response and discrimination learning by chimpanzees. *J. Comp. Physiol. Psychol.*, **26**, 361–386.

Oliverio, A., 1968 Effects of nicotine and strychnine on transfer of avoidance learning in the mouse. *Life Sci.*, **7**, 1163–1167.

Orbach, H., and Fischer, G. J., 1959 Bilateral resection of frontal granular cortex. *AMA Arch. Neurol.* **1**, 78–86.

Orkin, L., Bergman, P. S., and Nathmanson, M., 1956 Effect of atropine, scopolamine, and meperidine on man. *Anesthesiology*, **17**, 30–37.

Otis, L. S., and Cerf, J. A., 1958 The effect of heat narcosis on the retention of a conditioned avoidance response in goldfish. *Amer. Psychol.*, **13**, 419 (abstract).

Ottosson, J. O., 1960 Experimental studies of memory impairment after electroconvulsive therapy. *Acta Psychiat. Neurol. Scand.*, suppl. **145**, 103–131.

Pagano, R. R., Bush, D. F., Martin, G., and Hunt, E. B., 1969 Duration of retrograde amnesia as a function of electroconvulsive shock intensity. *Physiol. Behav.*, **4**, 19–21.

Palfai, T., and Chillag, D. Time-dependent memory deficits produced by pentylene-tetrazol (Metrazol): The effect of reinforcement magnitude. *Physiol. Behav.*, in press.

Paolino, R. M., and Kovachevick, L.   Unpublished findings.

Paolino, R. M., and Levy, H. M., 1971   Amnesia produced by spreading depression and ECS: Evidence for time-dependent memory trace localization. *Science*, **172**, 746–749.

Paolino, R. M., Quartermain, D., and Levy, H. M., 1969   Effect of electroconvulsive shock duration on the gradient of retrograde amnesia. *Physiol. Behav.*, **4**, 147–149.

Paolino, R. M., Quartermain, D., and Miller, N. E., 1966   Different temporal gradients of retrograde amnesia produced by carbon dioxide anesthesia and electroconvulsive shock. *J. Comp. Physiol. Psychol.*, **62**, 270–274.

Papsdorf, J. D., Eichenbaum, H. B., and Brooks, G. W.   Uric acid: Facilitation of classical conditioning in the rabbit. Unpublished findings.

Paré, W., 1961   The effect of caffeine and seconal on a visual discrimination task. *J. Comp. Physiol. Psychol.*, **54**, 506–509.

Patel, J. B., 1968   Facilitation of avoidance learning by hippocampal electrical stimulation. Masters' thesis, University of Kansas, Lawrence.

Pearlman, C. A., Jr., 1966   Similar retrograde amnesic effects of ether and spreading cortical depression. *J. Comp. Physiol. Psychol.*, **61**, 306–308.

Pearlman, C. A., Jr., Sharpless, S. K., and Jarvik, M. E., 1959   Effects of ether, pentobarbital, and pentylenetetrazol upon one-trial learning of an avoidance response. *Fed. Proc.*, **18**, 432 (abstract).

Pearlman, C. A., Jr., Sharpless, S. K., and Jarvik, M. E., 1961   Retrograde amnesia produced by anesthetic and convulsant agents. *J. Comp. Physiol. Psychol.*, **54**, 109–112.

Peeke, H. V. S., and Herz, M. J., 1971   Caudate nucleus stimulation retroactively impairs complex maze learning in the rat. *Science*, **173**, 80–82.

Peeke, H. V. S., LeBoeuf, B., and Herz, M. J., 1971   Effects of strychnine administration during development on adult maze learning in the rat. II: Drug administration from day 51 to 70. *Psychopharmacologia*. **19**, 262–265.

Peeke, H. V. S., McCoy, F., and Herz, M. J., 1969   Drive consummatory response effects on memory consolidation for appetitive learning in mice. Part A. *Commun. Behav. Biol.*, **4**, 49–53.

Pennington, D. F., 1957   The effect of brain damage on retention following ECS. Doctoral dissertation, Louisiana State University, Baton Rouge.

Petrinovich, L. F., 1963   Facilitation of successive discrimination learning by strychnine sulphate. *Psychopharmacologia* (Berlin), **4**, 103–113.

Petrinovich, L. F., 1967   Drug facilitation of learning: Strain differences. *Psychopharmacologia* (Berlin), **10**, 375–378.

Petrinovich, L., Bradford, D., and McGaugh, J. L., 1965   Drug facilitation of memory in rats. *Psychon. Sci.*, **2**, 191–192.

Pevzner, L. Z., 1966   Nucleic acid changes during behavioral events. In J. Gaito (ed.), *Macromolecules and behavior*, pp. 43–70. New York: Appleton-Century-Crofts.

Pinel, J. P. J., 1969   A short gradient of ECS-produced amnesia in a one-trial appetitive learning situation. *J. Comp. Physiol. Psychol.*, **68**, 650–655.

Pinel, J. P. J., and Cooper, R. M., 1966   The relationship between incubation and ECS gradient effects. *Psychon. Sci.*, **6**, 125–126.

Pribram, K., and Broadbent, D. E. (eds.), 1970   *Biology of memory.* New York: Academic Press.

Prien, R. F., Wayner, M. J., Jr., and Kahan, S., 1963   Lack of facilitation in maze learning by picrotoxin and strychnine sulphate. *Amer. J. Physiol.*, **204**, 448–492.

Quartermain, D., and McEwen, B.S.   Temporal characteristics of amnesia induced by protein synthesis inhibition: Determination by shock level. *Nature*, in press.

Quartermain, D., McEwen, B. S., and Azmitia, E. C., Jr., 1970   Amnesia produced by electroconvulsive shock or cycloheximide: Conditions for recovery. *Science*, **169**, 683–686.

Quartermain, D., Paolino, R. M., and Miller, N. E., 1965   A brief temporal gradient of retrograde amnesia independent of situational change. *Science*, **149**, 1116–1118.

Quinton, E. E., 1966   Retrograde amnesia induced by carbon dioxide inhalation. *Psychon. Sci.*, **5**, 17–18.

Ransmeier, R. E., and Gerard, R. W., 1954   Effects of temperature, convulsion and metabolic factors on rodent memory and EEG. *Amer. J. Physiol.*, **179**, 663–664.

Ray, O. S., and Barrett, R. J., 1969a   Disruptive effects of electroconvulsive shock as a function of current level and mode of delivery. *J. Comp. Physiol. Psychol.*, **67**, 110–116.

Ray, O. S., and Barrett, R. J., 1969b   Step-through latencies in mice as a function of ECS-test interval. *Physiol. Behav.*, **4**, 583–586

Ray, O. S., and Bivens, L. W., 1968   Reinforcement magnitude as a determinant of performance decrement after electroconvulsive shock. *Science*, **160**, 330–332.

Ray, O. S., and Emley, G., 1964   Time factors in interhemispheric transfer of learning. *Science*, **144**, 76–78.

Riccio, D. C., Gaebelin, C., and Cohen, P., 1968a   Some behavioral aspects of retrograde amnesia produced by hypothermia. *Physiol. Behav.*, **3**, 973–976.

Riccio, D. C., Hodges, L. A., and Randall, P. R., 1968b   Retrograde amnesia produced by hypothermia in rats. *J. Comp. Physiol. Psychol.*, **3**, 618–622.

Riccio, D. C., and Stikes, E. R., 1969   Persistent but modifiable retrograde amnesia produced by hypothermia. *Physiol. Behav.*, **4**, 649–652.

Richter, C. P., and Hines, M., 1938   Increased spontaneous activity produced in monkeys by brain lesions. *Brain*, **61**, 1–16.

Riddell, W. I., 1969   Effect of electroconvulsive shock: Permanent or temporary retrograde amnesia. *J. Comp. Physiol. Psychol.*, **67**, 140–144.

Riege, W. H., 1969   Disruption of radiation-induced aversion to saccharin by electroconvulsive shock. *Physiol. Behav.*, **4**, 157–161.

Roberts, R. B., Flexner, J. B., and Flexner, L. B., 1970   Some evidence for the involvement of adrenergic sites in the memory trace. *Proc. Nat. Acad. Sci.*, **66**, 310–313.

Robustelli, F., and Jarvik, M. E., 1968   Retrograde amnesia from detention. *Physiol. Behav.*, **3**, 543–547.

Rose, J. E., and Woolsey, C. N., 1948   Structure and relations of limbic cortex and anterior thalamic nuclei in rabbit and cat. *J. Comp. Neurol.*, **89**, 279–348.

Rosenbaum, M., Cohen, H. D., and Barondes, S. H., 1968   Effect of intracerebral saline on amnesia produced by inhibition of cerebral protein synthesis. *Commun. Behav. Biol.*, **2**, 47–50.

Rosenzweig, M. R., Bennett, E. L., and Krech, D., 1964   Cerebral effects of environmental complexity and training among adult rats. *J. Comp. Physiol. Psychol.*, **57**, 438–439.

Rosenzweig, M. R., and Leiman, A. L., 1968   Brain functions. *Ann. Rev. Psychol.* **19**, 55–98.

Rosvold, H. E., and Delgado, J. M. R., 1956   The effect on delayed-alternation test performance of stimulating or destroying electrical structures within the frontal lobes of the monkey's brain. *J. Comp. Physiol. Psychol.*, **49**, 365–372.

Russell, I. S., and Ochs, S., 1963   Localization of a memory trace in one cortical hemisphere and transfer to the other hemisphere. *Brain*, **86**, 37–54.

Russell, W. R., 1959   *Brain: Memory and learning.* London: Oxford University Press.

Russell, W. R., and Nathan, P. W., 1946   Traumatic amnesia. *Brain*, **69**, 280–300.

Russell, R. W., Pierce, J. F., Rohrer, W. M., and Townsend, J. C., 1948   A new apparatus for the controlled administration of electroconvulsive shock. *J. Psychol.*, **26**, 71–82.

Schaeffer, B. H., 1968   Strychnine and maze behavior: Limited effects of varied concentrations and injection times. *J. Comp. Physiol. Psychol.*, **66**, 188–192.

Schneider, A. M., 1967   Control of memory by spreading cortical depression: A case for stimulus control. *Psychol. Rev.*, **74**, 201–215.

Schneider, A. M., Kapp, B., Aron, C., and Jarvik, M. E., 1969   Retroactive effects of transcorneal and transpinnate ECS on step-through latencies of mice and rats. *J. Comp. Physiol. Psychol.*, **69**, 506–509.

Schneider, A. M., and Sherman, W., 1968   Amnesia: A function of the temporal relation of footshock to electroconvulsive shock. *Science*, **159**, 219–221.

Schiller, P. H., and Chorover, S. L., 1967   Short-term amnesic effects of electroconvulsive shock in a one-trial maze learning paradigm. *Neuropsychologia*, **5**, 155–163.

Schwartzbaum, J. S., Kellicutt, M. H., Spieth, T. M. and Thompson, J. B., 1964   Effects of septal lesions in rats on response inhibition associated with food-reinforced behavior. *J. Comp. Physiol. Psychol.*, **58**, 217–224.

Scoville, W. B., and Milner, B., 1957   *J. Neurol. Neurosurg. Psychiat.*, **20**, 11.

Shandro, N. E., and Schaeffer, B. H., 1969   Environment and strychnine: Effects on maze behavior. *Proc. Western Psychol. Assoc., Vancouver, B.C.*

Sharpless, S. K., 1959   The effect of intravenous epinephrine and norepinephrine on a conditioned response in the cat. *Psychopharmacologia*, **1**, 140–149.

Sheer, D. E., 1970   Electrophysiological correlates of memory consolidation. In G. Ungar (ed.), *Molecular mechanisms in memory and learning,* pp. 177–211. New York: Plenum Press.

Siegal, A., and Flynn, J. P., 1968   Differential effects of electrical stimulation and lesions of the hippocampus and adjacent regions upon attack behavior in cats. *Brain Res.*, **7**, 252–267.

Siegal, P. S., 1943   The effect of electroshock convulsions on the acquisition of a simple running response in the rat. *J. Comp. Physiol. Psychol.*, **36**, 61–65.

Siegal, P. S., McGinnies, E. M., and Box, J. C., 1949   Runway performance of rats subjected to electroconvulsive shock following nembutal anesthesia. *J. Comp. Physiol. Psychol.*, **42**, 417–422.

Siegel, S., 1956   *Nonparametric statistics for the behavioral sciences.* New York: McGraw-Hill.

Spevack, A. A., and Suboski, M. D., 1969   Retrograde effects of electroconvulsive shock on learned responses. *Psychol. Bull.*, **72**, 66–76.

Stainbrook, E. J., and Lowenbach, H., 1942   The reorientation and maze behavior of the rat after noise-fright and electroshock convulsions. *J. Comp. Physiol. Psychol.*, **34**, 293–299.

Stamm, J. S., 1961   Electrical stimulation of frontal cortex in monkeys during learning of an alternation task. *J. Neurophysiol.*, **24**, 414–426.

Stein, D. G., and Chorover, S. L., 1968   Effects of posttrial stimulation of hippocampus and caudate nucleus on maze learning in the rat. *Physiol. Behav.*, **3**, 787–791.

Stein, D. G., and Kimble, D. P., 1966   Effects of hippocampal lesions and posttrial strychnine administration on maze behavior in the rat. *J. Comp. Physiol. Psychol.*, **62**, 243–249.

Stephens, G., and McGaugh, J. L., 1968   Retrograde amnesia effects of periodicity and degree of training. Part A. *Commun. Behav. Biol.*, **1**, 267–275.

Stephens, G., McGaugh, J. L., and Alpern, H. P., 1967   Periodicity and memory in mice. *Psychon. Sci.*, **8**, 201–202.

Stepien, L. S., Cordeau, J. P., and Rasmussen, T., 1960   The effect of temporal lobe and hippocampal lesions on auditory and visual recent memory in monkeys. *Brain*, **83**, 470–489.

Stone, C. P., and Walker, A. H., 1949   Note on modification of effects of electroconvulsive shocks on maternal behavior by ether anesthesia. *J. Comp. Physiol. Psychol.*, **42**, 429–432.

Stratton, L. O., and Petrinovich, L. F., 1963   Posttrial injections of an anticholinesterase drug on maze learning in two strains of rats. *Psychopharmacologia*, **5**, 47–54.

Summerfield, A., and Steinberg, H., 1959   Using drugs to alter memory experimentally in man. In P. B. Bradley et al. (eds.), *Neuro-psychopharmacology*, pp. 481–483. Amsterdam: Elsevier.

Swanson, R.   Unpublished findings.

Swanson, R., McGaugh, J. L., and Cotman, C., 1969   Acetoxycycloheximide effects on one-trial inhibitory avoidance learning. *Commun. Behav. Biol.*, **4**, 239–245.

Symposium, 1964   Antimetabolites affecting protein or nucleic acid synthesis, *48th Ann. Meeting Fed. Amer. Soc. Exp. Biol.*, *Fed. Proc.*, **23**, 940–989.

Taber, R. I., and Banuazizi, A., 1966 CO_2-induced retrograde amnesia in a one-trial learning situation. *Psychopharmacologia* (Berlin), **9**, 382–391.

Talwar, G. P., Goel, B. K., Chopra, S. P., and D'Monte, B., 1966   Brain RNA: Some information on its nature and metabolism as revealed by studies during experimentally induced convulsions and in response to sensory stimulation. In J. Gaito, (ed.), *Macromolecules and behavior*, pp. 71–88. New York: Appleton-Century-Crofts.

Tenen, S. S., 1965a Retrograde amnesia from electroconvulsive shock in a one-trial appetitive learning task. *Science*, **148**, 1248–1250.

Tenen, S. S., 1965b Retrograde amnesia. *Science*, **149**, 1521.

Thiessen, D. D., Schlesinger, K., and Calhoun, W. H., 1961 Better learning: Neural enhancement or reduced interference? *Psychol. Rep.*, **9**, 493–496.

Thomas, G. J., and Slotnick, B. M., 1962 Effects of lesions in the cingulum on maze learning and avoidance conditioning in the rat. *J. Comp. Physiol. Psychol.*, **55**, 1085–1091.

Thompson, C. E., and Neely, J. E., 1970 Dissociated learning in rats produced by electroconvulsive shock. *Physiol. Behav.*, **5**, 783–786.

Thompson, R., 1957a The comparative effects of ECS and anoxia on memory. *J. Comp. Physiol. Psychol.*, **50**, 397–400.

Thompson, R., 1957b The effect of ECS on retention in young and adult rats. *J. Comp. Physiol. Psychol.*, **50**, 644–646.

Thompson, R., 1958a The effects of degree of learning and problem difficulty on perseveration. *J. Exp. Psychol.*, **55**, 496–500.

Thompson, R., 1958b The effect of intracranial stimulation on memory in cats. *J. Comp. Physiol. Psychol.*, **51**, 421–426.

Thompson, R., and Bryant, J. H., 1955 Memory as affected by activity of the relevant receptor. *Psychol. Rep.*, **1**, 393–400.

Thompson, R., and Dean, W., 1955 A further study of the retroactive effect of ECS. *J. Comp. Physiol. Psychol.*, **48**, 488–491.

Thompson, R., Haravey, F., Pennington, D. F., Smith, J., Jr., Ganon, D., and Stockwell, F., 1958 An analysis of the differential effects of ECS on memory in young and adult rats. *Canad. J. Psychol.*, **12**, 83–96.

Thompson, R., and Langer, S. K., 1963 Deficits in position reversal learning following lesions of the limbic system. *J. Comp. Physiol. Psychol.*, **56**, 987–995.

Thompson, R., and Pennington, D. F., 1957 Memory decrement produced by ECS as a function of distribution in original learning. *J. Comp. Physiol. Psychol.*, **50**, 401–404.

Thompson, R., and Pryer, R. S., 1956 The effect of anoxia on the retention of a discrimination habit. *J. Comp. Physiol. Psychol.*, **49**, 297–300.

Tolman, E. C., and Honzik, C. H., 1930 Introduction and removal of reward and maze performance in rats. *Univ. Calif. Publ. Psychol.*, **4**, 257–275.

Tryon, R. C., 1940 Genetic differences in maze-learning ability in rats. *Yearbook Nat. Soc. Stud. Educ.*, **39**, 111–119.

Vanderwolf, C. H., 1964 Improved shuttle-box performance following electroconvulsive shock. *J. Comp. Physiol. Psychol.*, **56**, 983–986.

Van Harreveld, A., and Schade, J. P., 1959 Chloride movements in cerebral cortex after circulatory arrest and during spreading depression. *J. Cell. Comp. Physiol.*, **54**, 65–84.

Vardaris, R. M., and Gehres, L. D., 1970 Brain seizure patterns and ESB-induced amnesia for passive avoidance. *Physiol. Behav.*, **5**, 1271–1275.

BIBLIOGRAPHY

Verzeano, M., Laufer, M., Spear, P., and McDonald, S., 1970 The activity of neuronal networks in the thalamus of the monkey. In K. Pribram and D. E. Broadbent (eds.), *Biology of memory*, pp. 239–271. New York: Academic Press.

Verzeano, J., and Negishi, K., 1960 Neuronal activity in cortical and thalamic networks: A study with multiple electrodes. *J. Gen. Physiol.*, **43** (6, pt. 2), 177–195.

Webster, K. E., 1961 Cortico-striate interrelations in the albino rat. *J. Anat.*, **95**, 532–543.

Weiskrantz, L., 1964 In D. P. Kimble (ed.), *Second Princeton conference on learning, remembering and forgetting*. Palo Alto, Calif.: Science and Behavior Books.

Weiskrantz, L., 1966 Experimental studies of amnesia. In C. W. M. Whitty and O. L. Zangwill (eds.), *Amnesia*, pp. 1–35. London: Butterworths.

Weissman, A., 1963 Effect of electroconvulsive shock intensity and seizure pattern on retrograde amnesia in rats. *J. Comp. Physiol. Psychol.*, **56**, 806–810.

Weissman, A., 1964 Retrograde amnesic effect of supramaximal electroconvulsive shock on one-trial acquisition in rats: A replication. *J. Comp. Physiol. Psychol.*, **57**, 248–250.

Weissman, A., 1965 Effect of anticonvulsant drugs on electroconvulsive shock-induced retrograde amnesia. *Arch. Internat. Pharmacodyn.*, **154**, 122–130.

Weissman, A., 1967 Drugs and retrograde amnesia. *Internat. Rev. Neurobiol.*, **10**, 167–198.

Westbrook, W. H., and McGaugh, J. L., 1964 Drug facilitation of latent learning. *Psychopharmacologia* (Berlin), **5**, 440–446.

Whishaw, I. Q., and Cooper, R. M., 1970 Strychnine and suppression of exploration. *Physiol. Behav.*, **5**, 647–649.

Whitty, C. W. M., and Lewin, W., 1960 A Korsakoff synchrome in the post-cingulectomy confusional state. *Brain*, **83**, 648–653.

Worchel, P., and Gentry, G., 1950 Electroconvulsive shock and memory: The effect of shocks administered in rapid succession. *Comp. Psychol. Monogr.*, **20**, 95–119.

Worchel, P., and Narciso, J. C., 1950 The nature of the memory decrement following electroconvulsive shock. *J. Comp. Physiol. Psychol.*, **43**, 325–328.

Wyers, E. J., and Deadwyler, S. A., 1971 Duration and nature of retrograde amnesia produced by stimulation of caudate nucleus. *Physiol. Behav.*, **6**, 97–103.

Wyers, E. J., Peeke, H. V. S., Williston, J. S., and Herz, M. J., 1968 Retroactive impairment of passive avoidance learning by stimulation of the caudate nucleus. *Exp. Neurol.*, **22**, 350–366.

Yarmolinsky, M. B., and de la Haba, G. L., 1959 Inhibition by puromycin of amino acid incorporation into protein. *Proc. Nat. Acad. Sci.*, **45**, 325–328.

Zeigler, H. P., 1957 Electrical stimulation of the brain and the psycho-physiology of learning and motivation. *Psychol. Bull.*, **54**, 363–382.

Zeiner, A. R., Nathan, M. A., and Smith, O. A., 1969 Conditioned emotional responding (CER) mediated by interference. *Physiol. Behav.*, **4**, 645–648.

Zemp, J. W., Wilson, J. E., Schlesinger, K., Boggan, W. O., and Glassman, E., 1966 Brain function and macromolecules. I. Incorporation of uridine into RNA of mouse brain during short-term training experience. *Proc. Nat. Acad. Sci.*, **55**, 1423–1431.

Zerbolio, D. J., Jr., 1967   Within-strain facilitation and disruption of avoidance learning by picrotoxin. *Psychon. Sci.*, **9**, 411–412.

Zerbolio, D. J., Jr., 1969   The proactive effect of electroconvulsive shock on memory storage: With and without convulsions. *Commun. Behav. Biol.*, **4**, 23–27.

Zerbolio, D. J., 1971   Retrograde amnesia: The first posttrial hour. *Commun. Behav. Biol.*, **6**, 25–29.

Zinkin, S., and Miller, A. J., 1967   Recovery of memory after amnesia induced by electroconvulsive shock. *Science*, **155**, 102–104.

Zornetzer, S., and McGaugh, J. L., 1969   Effects of electroconvulsive shock upon inhibitory avoidance: The persistence and stability of amnesia. Part A. *Commun. Behav. Biol.*, **3**, 173–180.

Zornetzer, S., and McGaugh, J. L., 1970   Effects of frontal brain electroshock stimulation on EEG activity and memory in rats: Relationship to ECS-produced retrograde amnesia. *J. Neurobiol.* **1**, 379–394.

Zornetzer, S., and McGaugh, J. L.   Retrograde amnesia and brain seizures in mice. *Physiol. Behav.*, in press.

Zubin, J., and Barrera, S. E., 1941   Effect of electric convulsive therapy on memory. *Proc. Soc. Exp. Biol. Med.*, **48**, 596–597 (abstract).